Cyber Security:
Law and Practice

Cyber Security:
Law and Practice

Dean Armstrong QC
2 Bedford Row Chambers

Dan Hyde
Penningtons Manches LLP

Sam Thomas
2 Bedford Row Chambers

LexisNexis®

Published by LexisNexis

LexisNexis
Regus
Terrace Floor
Castlemead
Lower Castle Street
Bristol BS1 3AG

British Library Cataloguing-in-Publication Data

A catalogue record for this book is available from the British Library.

ISBN 9 78178 473345 2

Typeset by Letterpart Limited, Caterham on the Hill, Surrey CR3 5XL

Printed in Great Britain by CPI Group (UK) Ltd, Croydon, CR0 4YY

Dedicated to my son, Freddie.
My special thanks to my parents, Merle and Paul, and to Paula, Oliver
and Anna for their unstinting help, encouragement and support in all
that I do.
Dean Armstrong QC

Dedicated to Emily Greenwood, Lesley Rockley and Roger Thomas,
thank you for all your support.
Sam Thomas

Dedicated to my parents, Terence and Shirley Hyde,
for their inestimable support and faith in this and everything.
Dan Hyde

PREFACE

This work seeks to cover a wide spectrum of legal issues, both civil and criminal, that can conveniently be termed 'cyber security law'. We define 'cyber' to mean using, involving or relating to computers and the online environment. Cyber law, in the context of this book, refers to those laws that govern the use and control of information within this cyber arena. Accordingly a 'cyber-attack' denotes the misappropriation or misuse of this information as well as any crime perpetrated by use of a computer or other electronic storage device. A cyber-attack can take a multitude of forms, be launched by a diverse range of perpetrators against a range of victims for innumerable purposes; we have sought to ensure this work addresses all those possibilities and is equally relevant to online trade mark infringement or employee misuse of confidential data as it is to disruption of service attacks or other such system or equipment attacks. While striving to provide comprehensive coverage we accept this book does not cover every element of cyber-related law. In particular, certain well-referenced areas within intellectual property are deliberately excluded as being outside the scope of this work.

The law faces huge challenges to keep up with the rapid development of technology, which provides opportunities for the misuse of information for commercial gain or other objectives.

Legislation in this area must strike a balance between enabling interception, monitoring and proper surveillance of communications by intelligence and investigative agencies on the one hand and maintaining user security and confidentiality on the other. A conflict often arises where the rights to privacy and freedom of expression are set against the desire to access all areas so as to effectively police cyber communications and data use. End-to-end encryption used in applications such as WhatsApp, iMessage or BBM are an example where security may be viewed as welcome confidentiality by the user but as dark corners of inaccessibility by the state.

The worldwide dimension adds a further complexity. There can be serious problems in bringing civil suits where there is little prospect of obtaining or enforcing judgments, or where countries have neither the means nor the political will to effectively investigate and prosecute criminal offences. The Serious Crime Act 2015 recognised this and introduced amendments to the Computer Misuse Act 1990 to address the issues by extending the United Kingdom territorial reach and ability to prosecute where there is a significant link to the United Kingdom. This may be no more than a sticking plaster given the situations where it will be impractical or impossible to prosecute and international perspective is even more difficult where a state, as has frequently been alleged, is itself either perpetrating or aiding the behaviour. We have sought to tackle this and other issues, both legal and practical, that may arise in a cyber security context. We acknowledge the novel and developing nature of law in this area made that objective a challenge.

Our aim was to produce a comprehensive reference work that provides both a narrative and practical guidance on the many aspects of cyber security law. Cyber laws cover a vast range of areas and such is the volume of material that each chapter in this book could be a book in itself. With that in mind we have been selective in the hope that the book's content is sufficiently focused as to enable an understanding of the law as it applies to cyber security. We hope we have achieved our objective. The law is stated as at 1 February 2017.

The authors would like to thank Anita Noerr for her research and Christopher Saad for his help with Chapter 10.

Dean Armstrong QC and Sam Thomas, 2 Bedford Row Chambers
Dan Hyde, Pennington Manches LLP

1 February 2017

CONTENTS

TABLE OF CASES

References are to paragraph numbers.

TABLE OF STATUTES

References are to paragraph numbers.

TABLE OF STATUTORY INSTRUMENTS

References are to paragraph numbers.

TABLE OF EUROPEAN MATERIALS

References are to paragraph numbers.

Part 1

THE LEGAL FRAMEWORK

CHAPTER 1

CYBER CRIME

CONTENTS   *Para*

THE OFFENCES

> 'The twenty-first century has already witnessed remarkable technological breakthroughs and has been considered to be a revolutionary period of history – a "second machine age".[1] This revolution has been driven by the development of digital technology and is taking place on a global scale – affecting everyone – at a pace that is historically unprecedented.'[2] [3]

1.01 Digital technology has changed our lives, work and society. It has brought with it huge opportunities but also significant risks.[4] Half of crimes are now online.[5] Offences involving the use of, or access to, computers can be found in a large number of statutes. While the numbers reported within the press relate to instances of harassment or cyberstalking, online offences are increasingly likely to be committed by professionals or those in a position of employment. When employees commit online offences, organisations, or data controllers within those organisations, may be liable.

---

[1]   See Erik Brynjolffson and Andrew McAfee, *The Second Machine Age: Work, Progress and Prosperity in a Time of Brilliant Technologies* (New York: W W Norton & Company, 2014).

[2]   Deloitte, 'London Futures: Agiletown: the relentless march of technology and London's response' (November 2014): http:// www2.deloitte.com/uk/en/pages/growth/articles/agiletown-the-relentless-march-of-technology-and-londons-response.html (last accessed 13 February 2017).

[3]   House of Lords Select Committee on Digital Skills, Report of Session 2014–15: Make or Break: The UK's Digital Future; Ordered to be printed 4 February 2015 and published 17 February 2015 (HL Paper 111), p 9. Nb footnotes 1 and 2 above taken from original source material.

[4]   Ibid, p 6.

[5]   *Independent*, 25 June 2014.

1.02 This chapter identifies the major statutory provisions which create online criminal offences and, where appropriate, provides advice to organisations that might encounter these offences.

OFFENCES UNDER THE COMPUTER MISUSE ACT 1990

1.03 The Computer Misuse Act 1990 (CMA 1990) was enacted principally in response to the threat of unauthorised access to computers or what is commonly known as hacking offences.[6] During its passage through Parliament the CMA 1990 received criticism for being hastily introduced and poorly conceived.[7] When in force it was little used. This was attributed to perceived difficulties in securing convictions, partly blamed on the police for not prioritising CMA 1990 offences, and because of the problems of securing evidence, especially given the international aspect to many CMA 1990 offences.[8] Prosecutors have instead used alternative remedies such as the Fraud Act 2006 to deal with identity theft and banking fraud, and the Communications Act 2003[9] for telephone hacking. The CMA 1990 was retained for computer hacking offences.

1.04 The CMA 1990 has been amended by the Police and Justice Act 2006 and the Serious Crime Act 2007 to create five offences:

- unauthorised access to a computer (s 1);
- unauthorised access with intent to commit another offence (s 2);

---

[6] In particular *R v Gold & Schifreen* [1988] AC 1063, [1988] 2 WLR 984, which concerned the hacking of British Telecommunication's Prestel Computer Network (PCN) to access the interactive view data service. The appellants accessed the PCN using legitimate usernames and passwords but without the knowledge of the authorised user. They were convicted of an offence contrary to the Forgery and Counterfeiting Act 1981 on the basis that the input of a username and password into the log-on screen, which was not their own, constituted the creation of a false instrument. The Court of Appeal quashed the conviction, and made it expressly clear that the Forgery and Counterfeiting Act 1981 was not appropriate to address this form of conduct (see [1987] QB 1116, per Lord Lane CJ, at 1124). The House of Lords, upholding the decision of the Court of Appeal to quash the conviction, held that the Forgery and Counterfeiting Act 1981 required the false information to be stored on the instrument for some appreciable time (see [1988] AC 1063, per Lord Brandon of Oakbrook, at 1073).

[7] Hansard, HC Deb 09 February 1990 vol 166 cc1134–84, per Mr Harry Cohen (Leyton), at 1163: 'The Bill is ill defined. We have heard already that it does not define what a computer is. It is lopsided and does not tackle the most important aspects of computer misuse, its implications have not been well thought out. For example, it contains unnecessary criminalisation, and in years to come will affect areas which the sponsor does not envisage'.

[8] Revision of the Computer Misuse Act Report of an Inquiry by the All Party Internet Group June 2004, at [71]: '... it is also obvious that the police do not have the resources to tackle even a small fraction of the DoS attacks that take place every day, and where these attacks take place across jurisdictional boundaries there may be significant barriers to their investigations. We observe that there may be negative value in creating an offence where everyone knows that, absent links with more serious criminal activity, the chances of investigation and prosecution are essentially nil'. At [107]: 'It is clear from the evidence presented to us that a root cause of the discontent with the CMA 1990 is that the police are failing to meet expectations in the investigation of computer crime'.

[9] Formerly the Telecommunications Act 1984.

- doing an act or acts with intent to impair the workings of a computer (s 3);
- making, supplying or obtaining articles for use in offences under s 1, 3 or 3ZA (s 3A); and
- unauthorised acts causing, or creating risk of, serious damage (s 3ZA).

1.05 The interpretation section of the CMA 1990 applies equally to all three offences:

17 Interpretation

(1) The following provisions of this section apply for the interpretation of this Act.

(2) A person secures access to any program or data held in a computer if by causing a computer to perform any function he –

(a) alters or erases the program or data;
(b) copies or moves it to any storage medium other than that in which it is held or to a different location in the storage medium in which it is held;
(c) uses it; or
(d) has it output from the computer in which it is held (whether by having it displayed or in any other manner);

and references to access to a program or data (and to an intent to secure such access or to enable such access to be secured) shall be read accordingly.

(3) For the purposes of subsection (2)(c) above a person uses a program if the function he causes the computer to perform –

(a) causes the program to be executed; or
(b) is itself a function of the programme.

(4) For the purposes of subsection (2)(d) above –

(a) a program is output if the instructions of which it consists are output; and
(b) the form in which any such instructions or any other data is output (and in particular whether or not it represents a form in which, in the case of instructions, they are capable of being executed or, in the case of data, it is capable of being processed by a computer) is immaterial.

(5) Access of any kind by any person to any program or data held in a computer is unauthorised if –

(a) he is not himself entitled to control access of the kind in question to the program or data; and
(b) he does not have consent to access by him of the kind in question to the program or data from any person who is so entitled;

but this subsection is subject to section 10.

(6) References to any program or data held in a computer include references to any program or data held in any removable storage medium which is for the time being in the computer; and a computer is to be regarded as containing any program or data held in any such medium.

(7) ...

(8) An act done in relation to a computer is unauthorised if the person doing the act (or causing it to be done) –

(a)   is not himself a person who has responsibility for the computer and is entitled to determine whether the act may be done; and
(b)   does not have consent to the act from any such person.

In this subsection 'act' includes a series of acts.

(9) References to the home country concerned shall be read in accordance with section 4(6) above.

(10) References to a program include references to part of a program.

Unauthorised access to a computer (s 1)

1.06   The CMA 1990 was amended by the Police and Justice Act 2006 (PJA 2006), s 35:[10]

1 Unauthorised access to computer material

(1) A person is guilty of an offence if –

(a)   he causes a computer to perform any function with intent to secure access to any program or data held in any computer;
(b)   the access he intends to secure is unauthorised; and
(c)   he knows at the time when he causes the computer to perform the function that that is the case.

(2) The intent a person has to have to commit an offence under this section need not be directed at –

(a)   any particular program or data;
(b)   a program or data of any particular kind; or
(c)   a program or data held in any particular computer.

(3) A person guilty of an offence under this section shall be liable –

(a)   on summary conviction in England and Wales, to imprisonment for a term not exceeding 12 months or to a fine not exceeding the statutory maximum or to both;

---

10   As from 1 October 2008: see SI 2008/2503, subject to transitional provisions specified in PJA 2006, s 38(1) and (2).

(b) [Scotland.]

(c) on conviction on indictment, to imprisonment for a term not exceeding two years or to a fine or to both.

1.07 Where an offence was committed prior to 1 October 2008, the maximum sentence under subs (3) was for 6 months. The maximum sentence was increased to 12 months following the implementation of the Criminal Justice Act 2003 (CJA 2003), s 154(1), which was brought into force by PJA 2006, s 38(6).

1.08 An offence under s 1 is a specified serious offence within Sch 1 to the Serious Crime Act 2007 (SCA 2007).

1.09 The words of s 1(1)(a) should be interpreted to give their plain and ordinary meaning, and an offence under the section need not involve the use of one computer to secure access to another. The section is also contravened where a person causes a computer to perform a function with intent to gain unauthorised access to any program or data held in the same computer:[11]

> 'To read those words in that way, in our judgment, would be to give them a meaning quite different from their plain and natural meaning. It is a trite observation, when considering the construction of statutes, that one does not imply or introduce words which are not there when the plain and natural meaning is clear. In our judgment there are no grounds whatsoever for implying, or importing the word "other" between "any" and "computer", or excepting the computer which is actually used by the offender from the phrase "any computer" at the end of the subsection (1)(a).'

1.10 The offence is committed when there is interference with data and/or someone else's computer without permission over that specific data or computer.

1.11 It is unclear whether an offence is committed under s 1 by a person who is authorised to secure access to computer material, but does so for unauthorised purposes. In *DPP v Bignell*,[12] police officers, through the medium of an innocent computer operator, extracted details of cars from the Police National Computer. It was held that the officers were not committing the s 1 offence in such circumstances.

1.12 The decision in *DPP v Bignell* was overruled in part by the House of Lords in *Bow Street Metropolitan Stipendiary Magistrate ex p United States (No 2)*.[13] This was an extradition case in which the US Government was seeking the deportation of the appellant for conspiracy to secure unauthorised access to a company's computer system with intent to commit theft and forgery (the s 2 offence). The appellant had been provided with credit card account

---

[11] *Attorney-General's Reference (No 1 of 1991)* [1993] QB 94, CA, per Lord Taylor CJ, at 99F–100A.

[12] [1998] 1 Cr App R 1.

[13] [2000] 2 AC 216.

details by an employee that did not have authority to access those specific files. The Divisional Court, following the *ratio* in *DPP v Bignell*, held that the appellant could not be guilty of the offence because the employee had been entitled to access the computer.

1.13 The House of Lords (Lord Steyn, Lord Hutton, Lord Saville, Lord Hobhouse of Woodborough, Lord Millett) held that 'entitlement to control' as defined within s 17(5) of the CMA 1990, did not relate to control of the computer rather the ability to authorise individuals to access specific data. Authority to access a particular piece of data was not authorisation to access other similar data in the absence of permission:[14]

> 'Authority to view data may not extend to authority to copy or alter that data. The refinement of the concept of access requires a refinement of the concept of authorisation. The authorisation must be authority to secure access of the kind in question. As part of this refinement, the subsection lays down two cumulative requirements of lack of authority. The first is the requirement that the relevant person be not the person entitled to control the relevant kind of access. The word "control" in this context clearly means authorise and forbid. If the relevant person is so entitled, then it would be unrealistic to treat his access as being unauthorised. The second is that the relevant person does not have the consent to secure the relevant kind of access from a person entitled to control, i.e. authorise, that access.'

1.14 An individual can be authorised in respect of a specific area of data; however, unless there is specific authorisation in relation to the actions with that date the individual may still be committing the offence:[15]

> 'It also makes clear that the authority must relate not simply to the data or program but also to the actual kind of access secured … It does not introduce any concept that authority to access one piece of data should be treated as authority to access other pieces of data "of the same kind" notwithstanding that the relevant person did not in fact have authority to access that piece of data.'

1.15 The House of Lords disapproved of the reasoning in *DPP v Bignell* rather than the result. Authorisation relates to the actual kind of access secured, and it is a fact as to whether an individual is so authorised.

1.16 It is most likely that an offence contrary to s 1 will be deployed in the more straightforward cases of identity theft; use of someone's personal information; and/or passwords without authority. These 'hacking offences' are likely to be prosecuted under this amended section rather than resorting to offences under the Fraud Act 2006.

---

[14] *Bow Street Metropolitan Stipendiary Magistrate ex p United States (No 2)*, per Lord Hobhouse, at 224.
[15] See *Bow Street Metropolitan Stipendiary Magistrate ex p United States (No 2)*, at 224.

1.17 There is no offence under CMA 1990, s 1 if a person is authorised to access particular computer data but does so for unauthorised purposes. However, they may have committed an offence contrary to s 3.

1.18 If, as a matter a fact, a person is authorised to access a computer or data but subsequently obtains unauthorised access to a computer or data, with the requisite intent, they are committing the s 1 offence. This is of huge potential significance to those working in organisations because they are now liable if, for example, they provide information to someone outside the organisation who sends a hacking tool in to the computer remotely.

1.19 There may be exceptional circumstances where employees who undertake hacking offences will not be prosecuted because their actions were in the public interest.[16] There is no public interest defence for offences contained within the CMA 1990. If the Crown Prosecution Service, or other enforcement agency, decides to prosecute the assertion of public interest will not assist.

Unauthorised access with intent to commit further offences (s 2)

1.20 Section 2 relates to unauthorised access with intent to commit or facilitate the commission of further offences. The 'further' offence or offences envisaged by the section must in themselves carry a sentence of 5 years' imprisonment or more. As an example, the offence of theft is punishable in this way, making it most likely that this section will be used for the unauthorised access to a computer to steal material such as designs for new products; those matters where copyright is pending; and banking details.

2 Unauthorised access with intent to commit or facilitate commission of further offences

(1) A person is guilty of an offence under this section if he commits an offence under section 1 above ('the unauthorised access offence') with intent –

(a) to commit an offence to which this section applies; or
(b) to facilitate the commission of such an offence (whether by himself or by any other person);

and the offence he intends to commit or facilitate is referred to below in this section as the further offence.

---

[16] See [2013] EntLR 257, at 259 where the Director of Public Prosecution declined to prosecute a Sky News journalist who admitted to hacking into the email account of an individual accused of conspiring with her husband to fraudulently obtain life assurance payments as a result of him faking his own death. The journalist accepted that he had committed an offence contrary to s 1 of the Computer Misuse Act 1990 but provided the emails to the police immediately. In this case, the emails were hacked in circumstances where there was a real prospect that the relevant evidence would go unnoticed by the police. Further, the journalist secured approval from the Sky News Deputy Head of News and Managing Editor before accessing the accounts in question.

(2) This section applies to offences –

(a)   for which the sentence is fixed by law; or
(b)   for which a person who has attained the age of twenty-one years (eighteen in relation to England and Wales) and has no previous convictions may be sentenced to imprisonment for a term of five years (or, in England and Wales, might be so sentenced but for the restrictions imposed by section 33 of the Magistrates' Courts Act 1980).

(3) It is immaterial for the purposes of this section whether the further offence is to be committed on the same occasion as the unauthorised access offence or on any future occasion.

(4) A person may be guilty of an offence under this section even though the facts are such that the commission of the further offence is impossible.

(5) A person guilty of an offence under this section shall be liable –

(a)   on summary conviction in England and Wales, to imprisonment for a term not exceeding 12 months or to a fine not exceeding the statutory maximum or to both;
(b)   on summary conviction in Scotland, to imprisonment for a term not exceeding 12 months or to a fine not exceeding the statutory maximum or to both;
(c)   on conviction on indictment, to imprisonment for a term not exceeding five years or to a fine or to both.

1.21   The reference to '12 months' in subs (5) should be read as '6 months' in relation to any offence committed before the commencement of the CJA 2003, s 154(1): see the PJA 2006, s 38(6).

Unauthorised acts with intent to impair the operation of a computer (s 3)

3 Unauthorised acts with intent to impair, or with recklessness as to impairing, operation of computer, etc

(1) A person is guilty of an offence if –

(a)   he does any unauthorised act in relation to a computer;
(b)   at the time when he does the act he knows that it is unauthorised; and
(c)   either subsection (2) or subsection (3) below applies.

(2) This subsection applies if the person intends by doing the act –

(a)   to impair the operation of any computer;
(b)   to prevent or hinder access to any program or data held in any computer;
(c)   to impair the operation of any such program or the reliability of any such data; or

(d) to enable any of the things mentioned in paragraphs (a) to (c) above to be done.

(3) This subsection applies if the person is reckless as to whether the act will do any of the things mentioned in paragraphs (a) to (d) of subsection (2) above.

(4) The intention referred to in subsection (2) above, or the recklessness referred to in subsection (3) above, need not relate to –

(a) any particular computer;
(b) any particular program or data; or
(c) a program or data of any particular kind.

(5) In this section –

(a) a reference to doing an act includes a reference to causing an act to be done;
(b) 'act' includes a series of acts;
(c) a reference to impairing, preventing or hindering something includes a reference to doing so temporarily.

(6) A person guilty of an offence under this section shall be liable –

(a) on summary conviction in England and Wales, to imprisonment for a term not exceeding 12 months or to a fine not exceeding the statutory maximum or to both;
(b) on summary conviction in Scotland, to imprisonment for a term not exceeding 12 months or to a fine not exceeding the statutory maximum or to both;
(c) on conviction on indictment, to imprisonment for a term not exceeding ten years or to a fine or to both.

1.22 This section was amended by the PJA 2006, s 36, and subsequently by the SCA 2007, ss 61(1), (3) and 92 and Sch 14. An offence cannot be committed under the amended s 3 unless every element was committed after the commencement dates of the amendment provisions, specifically 1 October 2008. If any element of the offence was committed before this date the previous, unamended, s 3 applies.[17]

1.23 Like the previous sections within the CMA 1990, any reference to '12 months' is in fact '6 months' prior to the enforcement of the CJA 2003, s 154(1): see the PJA 2006, s 38(6).

1.24 Section 3 relates to unauthorised acts with intent to impair the operation of a computer, for example, inserting a 'Trojan Horse' to steal data. The *mens rea* in this section is significant. First, the person must know that the act is unauthorised. Secondly, he must intend, by doing the act, to impair the operation of the computer or program or data or to prevent or hinder access to any program or data held in a computer, or be reckless as to whether his act

---

[17] See PJA 2006, s 38(3).

will do any of those things. The type of activity to be caught under this section would include sending a virus to another computer either disguised in an email or using a program to send multiple emails such as to effectively not allow the computer to be able to function.

1.25 In *DPP v Lennon*,[18] the High Court (Keene LJ, Jack J) held that for the purposes of the CMA 1990, the owner of a computer able to receive emails would ordinarily be taken to have consented to the sending of emails to his computer. However, such implied consent was not without limits, and the consent did not cover emails that had been sent not for the purpose of communication with the owner but to interrupt his computer system (see *DPP v Lennon*, at [9]).

1.26 If a computer is caused to record information which shows that it came from one person, when it in fact came from someone else, that affects its reliability, and thus the reliability of the data in the computer is impaired within the meaning of s 3(2)(c).

1.27 In *Zezev and Yarimaka v Governor of HM Prison Brixton*[19] the High Court (Lord Woolf CJ, Wright J), held that if a computer was caused to record information which showed that it came from one person, when it in fact came from someone else, that manifestly affected its reliability, and was sufficient to sustain a charge contrary to s 3 of the CMA 1990.

1.28 *Zezev* was also an extradition matter. The extradition proceedings were based, *inter alia*, on a charge that the applicants conspired with each other to cause an unauthorised modification of computer material in the complainant's computer. There was evidence against the first applicant that he would use the computer so as to record the arrival of information which did not come from the purported source. The High Court rejected the argument that this did not affect the reliability of the data:[20]

> 'The question of the meaning of the words "reliability of such data" has in the first place to be considered against the language used by the draftsman in the section itself. If a computer is caused to record information which shows that it came from one person, when it in fact came from someone else, that manifestly affects its reliability. The information is undoubtedly data.'

1.29 The court found that the insertion of information that would *tell a lie about itself* was sufficient to impair the operation of a computer. The court did not decide whether the information had to be false. However, it would be unnecessary for the Crown to prove that the information posted was untrue. The Crown are required only to prove that it derived from someone without consent and that it was purported to come from an authorised source (see *Zezev*, at [15]).

---

[18] [2006] EWHC 1201 (Admin).
[19] [2002] 2 Cr App R 33, DC.
[20] See *Zezev*, per Lord Woolf, at [18].

Making, adapting, supplying or offering to supply an article (s 3A)

3A Making, supplying or obtaining articles for use in offence under section 1, 3 or 3ZA

(1) A person is guilty of an offence if he makes, adapts, supplies or offers to supply any article intending it to be used to commit, or to assist in the commission of, an offence under section 1, 3 or 3ZA.

(2) A person is guilty of an offence if he supplies or offers to supply any article believing that it is likely to be used to commit, or to assist in the commission of, an offence under section 1, 3 or 3ZA.

(3) A person is guilty of an offence if he obtains any article –

(a)   intending to use it to commit, or to assist in the commission of, an offence under section 1, 3 or 3ZA, or
(b)   with a view to its being supplied for use to commit, or to assist in the commission of, an offence under section 1, 3 or 3ZA.

(4) In this section 'article' includes any program or data held in electronic form.

(5) A person guilty of an offence under this section shall be liable –

(a)   on summary conviction in England and Wales, to imprisonment for a term not exceeding 12 months or to a fine not exceeding the statutory maximum or to both;
(b)   [Scotland];
(c)   on conviction on indictment, to imprisonment for a term not exceeding two years or to a fine or to both.

1.30   Reference to an offence contrary to s 3ZA was inserted by the Serious Crime Act 2015 (SCA 2015), ss 41(1) and (3), 42 and 85(1), and Sch 4, para 8, following the enactment of the Serious Crime Act 2015 (Commencement No 1) Regulations 2015.[21] The relevant date is 3 May 2015. An offence is not committed by virtue of the amendment of subs (3) unless every act or other event, proof of which is required for conviction of the offence, takes place after it took effect.[22]

1.31   An offence under s 3A is a specified serious offence within Sch 1 to the Serious Crime Act 2007.

1.32   Section 37 of the PJA 2006 introduced new s 3A to the CMA 1990 to address the making, adapting, supplying, or offering to supply an article intending to be used to commit, or to assist in the commission of an offence. The articles would more colloquially be known as 'hacker tools'.

---

[21]   SI 2015/820.
[22]   See SCA 2015, s 86(5).

1.33 It imposes liability on someone who makes an article, supplies an article which includes any program or data, with the intention of using it to commit an offence under ss 1 or 3; or makes or supplies such an article believing that it is likely to be used to commit an offence under s 3A(1) and (2). Section 3A(3) states that a person commits an offence if he/she obtains any article to facilitate the commission of an offence under ss 1 or 3.

1.34 On 12 August 2013, the European Parliament and European Council adopted Directive 2013/40/EU on attacks against information systems (the Directive) and replacing Council Framework Decision 2005/222/JHA. The SCA 2015 made two amendments to the CMA 1990 to ensure that the UK law is fully compliant with the Directive. The Explanatory Notes to the SCA 2015 provide useful background to the changes:

Section 42: Obtaining articles for purposes relating to computer misuse

134. Article 7 of the Directive requires Member States to criminalise certain activities in relation to the commission of the substantive offences at Articles 3 to 6 of the Directive (those Articles relate to illegal access to information systems, illegal system interference, illegal data interference and illegal interception). It provides as follows:

> 'Tools used for committing offences Member States shall take the necessary measures to ensure that the intentional production, sale, procurement for use, import, distribution or otherwise making available, of one of the following tools, without right and with the intention that it be used to commit any of the offences referred to in Articles 3 to 6, is punishable as a criminal offence, at least for cases which are not minor: (a) a computer programme, designed or adapted primarily for the purpose of committing any of the offences referred to in Articles 3 to 6; (b) a computer password, access code, or similar data by which the whole or any part of an information system is capable of being accessed.'

135. Section 3A of the 1990 Act, in conjunction with ss 1 to 3 of that Act, meets the requirements of Article 7 save in one respect, namely the 'procurement for use' of tools used for committing the Article 3 to 6 offences. Under the existing offence, the prosecution is required to show that the individual obtained the tool with a view to its being supplied for use to commit, or assist in the commission of an offence under ss 1 or 3 of the Act. This section extends subsection (3) of s 3A of the 1990 Act to include an offence of obtaining a tool for use to commit a Computer Misuse Act offence (including one under the new s 3ZA inserted by s 41) regardless of an intention to supply that tool. As amended, that subsection would provide that (additions shown in italics):

> 'A person is guilty of an offence if he obtains any article with a view to article
> – (a) *intending to use it to commit*, or assist in the commission of, an offence under section 1, 3 or 3ZA, or (b) with a view to its being supplied for use to commit, or assist in the commission of, an offence under section 1 or 3.'

1.35 The significance of this amendment is that it removes the requirement for the prosecution to prove that a third party was involved. The amendment made by s 42 removes the involvement, or intended involvement, of a third party, and ensures that the offence covers individuals acting alone.

Unauthorised acts causing or creating the risk of serious damage (s 3ZA)

1.36 From 3 May 2015, the SCA 2015 inserted a new s 3ZA into the CMA 1990:

3ZA Unauthorised acts causing, or creating risk of, serious damage

(1) A person is guilty of an offence if –

(a)   the person does any unauthorised act in relation to a computer;
(b)   at the time of doing the act the person knows that it is unauthorised;
(c)   the act causes, or creates a significant risk of, serious damage of a material kind; and
(d)   the person intends by doing the act to cause serious damage of a material kind or is reckless as to whether such damage is caused.

(2) Damage is of a 'material kind' for the purposes of this section if it is –

(a)   damage to human welfare in any place;
(b)   damage to the environment of any place;
(c)   damage to the economy of any country; or
(d)   damage to the national security of any country.

(3) For the purposes of subsection (2)(a) an act causes damage to human welfare only if it causes –

(a)   loss to human life;
(b)   human illness or injury;
(c)   disruption of a supply of money, food, water, energy or fuel;
(d)   disruption of a system of communication;
(e)   disruption of facilities for transport; or
(f)   disruption of services relating to health.

(4) It is immaterial for the purposes of subsection (2) whether or not an act causing damage –

(a)   does so directly;
(b)   is the only or main cause of the damage.

(5) In this section –

(a)   a reference to doing an act includes a reference to causing an act to be done;
(b)   'act' includes a series of acts;
(c)   a reference to a country includes a reference to a territory, and to any place in, or part or region of, a country or territory.

(6) A person guilty of an offence under this section is (unless subsection (7) applies) liable, on conviction on indictment, to imprisonment for a term not exceeding 14 years, or to a fine, or to both.

(7) Where an offence under this section is committed as a result of an act causing or creating a significant risk of –

(a)   serious damage to human welfare of the kind mentioned in subsection (3)(a) or (3)(b), or
(b)   serious damage to national security,

a person guilty of the offence is liable, on conviction on indictment, to imprisonment for life, or to a fine, or to both.

1.37   The new s 3ZA creates a new offence which provides that a person is guilty of the offence if they do any unauthorised act in relation to a computer, know that the act is unauthorised, and the act causes serious damage of a 'material kind, including damage to human welfare'.

1.38   The offence will carry a maximum sentence of life imprisonment for cyber-attacks which result in loss of life, serious illness or injury, or serious damage to national security, and 14 years' imprisonment for cyber-attacks causing, or creating a significant risk of severe economic or environmental damage or social disruption.

1.39   This is an aggravated form of the s 3 offence where the aggravating feature is that the act must cause 'serious damage of a material kind' or create a significant risk of such damage and, in particular, that the person concerned intends by the doing the act to cause such damage or is reckless as to whether such damage is caused.

1.40   For the purposes of s 3ZA, damage is of a 'material kind' if it is damage to human welfare in any place, damage to the environment of any place, damage to the economy of any country, or damage to the national security of any country.

1.41   Under s 3ZA(3), an act causes damage to human welfare only if it causes loss to human life, human illness or injury, disruption of a supply of money, food, water, energy or fuel, disruption of a system of communication, disruption of facilities for transport, or disruption of services relating to health. The damage may be suffered in any country.

1.42   This offence is indictable only with a maximum of 14 years but where the serious damage or significant risk thereof is to national security or to human welfare causing loss of life or illness or injury the maximum penalty is life imprisonment.

1.43 This section is designed for the most serious cyber-attacks, for example where interference will involve widespread public disruption, ie to essential systems controlling power supply, communications, food or fuel distribution.

1.44 The resulting effect of an attack of this type would involve the risk of loss of life, serious illness or injury, severe social disruption or serious damage to the economy, the environment or national security.

1.45 The *actus reus* of the offence comprises two elements:

(1)   a person must do an unauthorised act to a computer; and

(2)   the unauthorised act must result in serious damage to the economy, the environment, national security or human welfare, or create a significant risk of such damage.

1.46 The *mens rea* comprises a further two distinct elements:

(1)   the defendant must know that the act s/he does is unauthorised; and

(2)   the defendant will have intended to cause harm or have been reckless as to whether such harm was caused.

1.47 The nature of the reckless element is yet to be determined. There is little doubt that the test for recklessness will be the same as that set out in the case of *Cunningham*;[23] however, to what extent will a potential offender require foresight of the risk of the actual harm caused rather than some harm in general? Will an individual have been sufficiently reckless if they envisaged serious damage to the economy but environmental harm was caused? Further, would recklessness to a 'lesser' form of harm be sufficient to sustain an offence that caused 'serious damage' to human welfare or national security? The authorities in relation to acts of homicide would suggest that an intent to a lesser harm would be sufficient, but mere foresight of a risk, ie recklessness, would not be sufficient. Guidance from the Court of Appeal in relation to this specific provision will be required.

Defences

Territorial scope

1.48 The SCA 2015, s 43, amended the territorial scope of the CMA 1990, at ss 4 and 5, by extending the offences to cover 'nationality' as a category with a 'significant link to the domestic jurisdiction'.

---

[23]   See *Cunningham* [1957] 2 QB 396, at 399: in any statutory definition of a crime, malice must be taken not in the old vague sense of wickedness in general but as requiring either (1) an actual intention to do the particular kind of harm that in fact was done; or (2) recklessness as to whether such harm should occur or not (ie, the accused has foreseen that the particular kind of harm might be done and yet has gone on to take the risk of it).

4 Territorial scope of offences under this Act

(1) Except as provided below in this section, it is immaterial for the purposes of any offence under section 1, 3 or 3ZA above –

(a)   whether any act or other event proof of which is required for conviction of the offence occurred in the home country concerned; or
(b)   whether the accused was in the home country concerned at the time of any such act or event.

(2) Subject to subsection (3) below, in the case of such an offence at least one significant link with domestic jurisdiction must exist in the circumstances of the case for the offence to be committed.

(3) There is no need for any such link to exist for the commission of an offence under section 1 above to be established in proof of an allegation to that effect in proceedings for an offence under section 2 above.

(4) Subject to section 8 below, where –

(a)   any such link does in fact exist in the case of an offence under section 1 above; and
(b)   commission of that offence is alleged in proceedings for an offence under section 2 above;

section 2 above shall apply as if anything the accused intended to do or facilitate in any place outside the home country concerned which would be an offence to which section 2 applies if it took place in the home country concerned were the offence in question.

(4A) It is immaterial for the purposes of an offence under section 3A whether the accused was in the home country concerned at the time of any act or other event proof of which is required for conviction of the offence if there is a significant link with domestic jurisdiction in relation to the offence.

(5)–(6) ...

5 Significant links with domestic jurisdiction

(1) The following provisions of this section apply for the interpretation of section 4 above.

(1A) In relation to an offence under section 1, 3, 3ZA or 3A, where the accused was in a country outside the United Kingdom at the time of the act constituting the offence there is a significant link with domestic jurisdiction if –

(a)   the accused was a United Kingdom national at that time; and
(b)   the act constituted an offence under the law of the country in which it occurred.

(1B) In subsection (1A) – 'country' includes territory; 'United Kingdom national' means an individual who is –

(a)   a British citizen, a British overseas territories citizen, a British National (Overseas) or a British Overseas citizen;
(b)   a person who under the British Nationality Act 1981 is a British subject; or
(c)   a British protected person within the meaning of that Act.

(2) In relation to an offence under section 1, either of the following is a significant link with domestic jurisdiction –

(a)   that the accused was in the home country concerned at the time when he did the act which caused the computer to perform the function; or
(b)   that any computer containing any program or data to which the accused by doing that act secured or intended to secure unauthorised access, or enabled or intended to enable unauthorised access to be secured, was in the home country concerned at that time.

(3) In relation to an offence under section 3, either of the following is a significant link with domestic jurisdiction –

(a)   that the accused was in the home country concerned at the time when [he did the unauthorised act (or caused it to be done); or
(b)   that the unauthorised act was done in relation to a computer in the home country concerned.

(3A) In relation to an offence under section 3ZA, any of the following is also a significant link with domestic jurisdiction –

(a)   that the accused was in the home country concerned at the time when he did the unauthorised act (or caused it to be done);
(b)   that the unauthorised act was done in relation to a computer in the home country concerned;
(c)   that the unauthorised act caused, or created a significant risk of, serious damage of a material kind (within the meaning of that section) in the home country concerned.

1.49   The home countries are those contained within the United Kingdom of Great Britain and Northern Ireland.

1.50   The amended extra-territorial scope was required in order to comply with Art 12 of the European Union Directive (2013/40/EU) on attacks against information systems:

1. Member States shall establish their jurisdiction with regard to the offences referred to in Articles 3 to 8 where the offence has been committed:

(a)   in whole or in part within their territory; or
(b)   by one of their nationals, at least in cases where the act is an offence where it was committed.

2. When establishing jurisdiction in accordance with point (a) of paragraph 1, a Member State shall ensure that it has jurisdiction where:

(a)   the offender commits the offence when physically present on its territory, whether or not the offence is against an information system on its territory; or

(b)   the offence is against an information system on its territory, whether or not the offender commits the offence when physically present on its territory...'

1.51   The Explanatory Notes to the SCA 2015 provide useful background to the reasons for this change and the mechanism by which it has been brought about:

> 137. Sections 4 and 5 of the 1990 Act already provide for limited extra-territorial jurisdiction in relation to the offences in sections 1 and 3 of that Act. Under those provisions, it is possible to prosecute a person in this country for an act committed abroad which would constitute an offence under section 1 or 3 provided that there was a 'significant link' to the appropriate jurisdiction in the UK. Subsection (2) amends section 4 of the 1990 Act to apply such extra-territorial jurisdiction to the offence in new section 3ZA inserted by section 41; subsection (5) amends section 5 of the 1990 Act to define what constitutes a 'significant link' in the context of the new offence. A significant link is established if the accused was in the UK at the time of the offence, or if the affected computer or the intended affected computer was in the UK. Accordingly, it would, for example, be possible under the current law to prosecute a French national resident in England and Wales who hacked into a computer system in France or a UK national who hacked into a computer system in the UK whilst temporarily resident in France (but who subsequently returned to the UK). Subsection (3) inserts new subsection (4A) into section 4 of the 1990 Act, the effect of which is to apply extra-territorial jurisdiction to the offence under section 3A of the 1990 Act. Subsection (4) amends section 5 of the 1990 Act to extend the current extra-territorial jurisdiction in order to fully comply with Article 12; the effect of new section 5(1A) and (1B) is to permit prosecutions of a UK national for all offences under the 1990 Act even where the conduct concerned has no other significant link to the UK, provided also that the offence was an offence in the country where it took place.

1.52   For an offence to be committed under ss 1–3 the requirement is that there should be at least one significant link with domestic jurisdiction (see CMA 1990, s 4(2)). However, in relation to the s 2 offence there is no requirement that the underlying offence, for which the individual intends the unauthorised access, be linked to the domestic jurisdiction. Where the domestic link is present in the connected s 1 offence, s 2 comes in to play even if the underlying offence takes place outside the UK with the usual proviso that the conduct would constitute an offence in that country's domestic jurisdiction.

1.53   Section 5(2) engages the significant link test when in respect of s 1. The domestic courts have jurisdiction when the suspect is in the UK when he/she did the act which caused the computer to perform the activity; or the attacked computer to which unauthorised access was gained was in the UK.

1.54   The same considerations apply in relation to s 3 offences.

1.55 Section 4 of the CMA 1990 was amended by the SCA 2015, s 41, to apply extra-territorial jurisdiction to the offence in new s 3ZA. Section 5 was amended to define 'significant link' in relation to ss 1, 3, 3ZA and 3A, and 'country' for the purposes of s 5(1A).

1.56 Section 5(1A) provides a legal basis to prosecute a UK national who commits any offence whilst outside the UK, where the offence has no link to the UK other than the offender's nationality, provided that the offence was also an offence in the country where it took place. With reference to the EU Directive and the SCA 2015 Explanatory Note it is clear that this provision will be widely construed. The purpose of expanding the 'significant link' to include UK nationals was to ensure that the UK met its international commitments. It is highly likely that courts will ensure that alleged wrongdoers cannot escape liability on assertions that the offences were conducted outside of the jurisdiction. This would be in accordance with the apparent Parliamentary intention behind the SCA 2015.

Inchoate offences

1.57 The potential liability for inchoate offences are dealt with in ss 6–8:

6 Territorial scope of inchoate offences related to offences under this Act

(1) On a charge of conspiracy to commit an offence under this Act the following questions are immaterial to the accused's guilt –

(a) the question where any person became a party to the conspiracy; and
(b) the question whether any act, omission or other event occurred in the home country concerned.

(2) On a charge of attempting to commit an offence under [this Act] 5 the following questions are immaterial to the accused's guilt –

(a) the question where the attempt was made; and
(b) the question whether it had an effect in the home country concerned.

7 Territorial scope of inchoate offences related to offences under external law corresponding to offences under sections 1 to 3

(3) The following subsections shall be inserted after section 1(1) of the Criminal Attempts Act 1981 –

'(1A) Subject to section 8 of the Computer Misuse Act 1990 (relevance of external law), if this subsection applies to an act, what the person doing it had in view shall be treated as an offence to which this section applies.

(1B) Subsection (1A) above applies to an act if – (a) it is done in England and Wales; and (b) it would fall within subsection (1) above as more than merely preparatory to the commission of an offence under section 3 of the

Computer Misuse Act 1990 but for the fact that the offence, if completed, would not be an offence triable in England and Wales'.

8 Relevance of external law

(1) A person is guilty of an offence triable by virtue of section 4(4) above only if what he intended to do or facilitate would involve the commission of an offence under the law in force where the whole or any part of it was intended to take place.

(2) ...

(3) A person is guilty of an offence triable by virtue of section 1(1A) of the Criminal Attempts Act 1981 only if what he had in view would involve the commission of an offence under the law in force where the whole or any part of it was intended to take place.

(4) Conduct punishable under the law in force in any place is an offence under that law for the purposes of this section, however it is described in that law.

(5) Subject to subsection (7) below, a condition specified in [subsection (1) or (3)] 3 above shall be taken to be satisfied unless not later than rules of court may provide the defence serve on the prosecution a notice –

(a) stating that, on the facts as alleged with respect to the relevant conduct, the condition is not in their opinion satisfied;
(b) showing their grounds for that opinion; and
(c) requiring the prosecution to show that it is satisfied.

(6) In subsection (5) above 'the relevant conduct' means –

(a) where the condition in subsection (1) above is in question, what the accused intended to do or facilitate;
(b) ...
(c) where the condition in subsection (3) above is in question, what the accused had in view.

(7) The court, if it thinks fit, may permit the defence to require the prosecution to show that the condition is satisfied without the prior service of a notice under subsection (5) above.

(8) If by virtue of subsection (7) above a court of solemn jurisdiction in Scotland permits the defence to require the prosecution to show that the condition is satisfied, it shall be competent for the prosecution for that purpose to examine any witness or to put in evidence any production not included in the lists lodged by it.

(9) In the Crown Court the question whether the condition is satisfied shall be decided by the judge alone.

(10) ...

1.58 Section 6(4) of the CMA 1990 states that the immateriality of the location where the conspiracy was formed, or the attempt made, does not extend to Scotland. The CMA 1990, s 6 does not extend into Scottish law. Conspirators in Scotland who agree to commit an offence, contrary to ss 1–3 of the CMA 1990, or attempt to commit an offence, within the jurisdiction of England and Wales are guilty of that offence.

1.59 Section 8 limits the extra-territorial jurisdiction contained within ss 4(4), 6(2) and 7 to offences that are criminal, in whole or in part, within the relevant foreign jurisdiction. It is the description of the action which is material rather than the description of the offence. Whether an act is illegal within a foreign jurisdiction is a matter of law to be decided in the Crown Court by the judge sitting alone.

Nationality

1.60 British citizenship is deemed to be irrelevant for any offence contained within the CMA 1990 when the proceedings are brought within England and Wales, unless the prosecution are seeking to prove 'significant links with domestic jurisdiction' under s 5 (see CMA 1990, s 9):

9 British citizenship immaterial

(1) Except as provided by section 5(1A), in any proceedings brought in England and Wales in respect of any offence to which this section applies it is immaterial to guilt whether or not the accused was a British citizen at the time of any act, omission or other event proof of which is required for conviction of the offence.

(2) This section applies to the following offences –

(a)   any offence under this Act; and
(c)   any attempt to commit an offence under this Act.

1.61 A suspect is not able to rely on his or her foreign nationality as a defence regardless as to whether a substantive or inchoate offence is charged.

Law enforcement officers

1.62 An 'enforcement officer' being a constable or any other person charged with the duty of investigating offences, is exempt from the offences contained within the CMA 1990, in accordance with s 10(a), when acting in accordance with legislation to facilitate inspection, search or seizure without a person's consent. A police officer cannot be found guilty of an offence contrary to s 1 if he accesses a person's mobile telephone without their consent but in accordance with the relevant provision of the Police and Criminal Evidence Act 1984 or the Regulation of Investigatory Powers Act 2000.[24]

---

[24]   Law enforcement officers can issue a notice under s 49 of the Regulation of Investigatory Powers Act 2000 which compels a person when served with a notice to either hand over an

1.63 The words of s 10 were amended by the SCA 2015. However, the changes did not affect the saving provision, rather they clarified that the exemption applied not only to powers of enforcement officers but also to enactments which authorise inspection, search or seizure. An example would be the legislation relating to the authorisation of intrusive surveillance that permits rather than empowers an enforcement officer.

Serious crime prevention orders

1.64 The SCA 2015, s 47, adds cyber offences into the category of cases for which a serious crime prevention order can be made, by virtue of a new para 11A in Part 1 of Sch 1 to the Serious Crime Act 2007:

11A Computer misuse

An offence under any of the following provisions of the Computer Misuse Act 1990 –

(a)   section 1 (unauthorised access to computer material);

(b)   section 2 (unauthorised access with intent to commit or facilitate commission of further offences);

(c)   section 3 (unauthorised acts with intent to impair, or with recklessness as to impairing, operation of computer etc.);

(d)   section 3ZA (unauthorised acts causing, or creating risk of, serious damage to human welfare etc);

(e)   section 3A (making, supplying or obtaining articles for use in offence under section 1, 3 or 3ZA).

Sentencing

1.65 The seriousness with which the courts view unauthorised obtaining and misuse of information obtained from computers is clearly seen in two recent cases where significant custodial sentences were imposed. In *Mangham*,[25] sentence was reduced on appeal though the custodial sentence remained immediate. In *Martin*[26] the Court of Appeal upheld an immediate custodial sentence.

R v Mangham[27]

1.66 In *Mangham*, the appellant hacked into Facebook's computers between April and May 2011. He was able to infiltrate a Facebook employee's email account and then stole intellectual property which he stored on a portable hard

---

encryption key (password) or render the requested material intelligible. The demand for decryption must be both necessary and proportionate. Anyone who refuses to decrypt material could be imprisoned for a maximum of 5 years' if the investigation relates to national security or child indecency, or up to 2 years' imprisonment in other cases.

25   [2012] EWCA Crim 973.

26   [2013] EWCA Crim 1420.

27   [2012] EWCA Crim 973.

drive. The appellant first accessed Facebook's protected systems including a server known as the 'Puzzle' server. Puzzles are placed within the server by Facebook as a series of tests for prospective employees. The applicant exploited vulnerabilities within the Puzzle server and then infiltrated the private side of the server to download a number of programs which modified their functionality. That enabled a continued breach of security by providing ongoing access. He then used his unfettered access to gain unauthorised entry to the 'Mailman' server, which handles Facebook's internal and external emails. The Mailman server contained email archives, a selection of which the appellant copied. The next step was that he created a program which utilised the compromised electronic identity of a Facebook employee to gain access to the 'Phabricator' server. This allowed the appellant to access the Facebook source code that is the unique software which gives Facebook its functionality. The appellant copied the source code onto a hard drive. Facebook indicated that the direct costs in responding to the incident was approximately \$200,000. This included time to investigate, access and remedy the damage done.

1.67 The Court of Appeal (Hooper LJ, Cranston J, Judge Rook QC) gave guidance on the aggravating and mitigating factors relevant when sentencing these offences.

1.68 A number of aggravating factors would bear on sentencing in these types of case:[28]

(a)   whether the offence was planned and persistent;
(b)   the nature of the damage caused to the system itself;
(c)   motive and benefit with revenge being a serious aggravating factor (see *Lindesay*[29]);
(d)   any financial benefit from the sale of the accessed information;
(e)   value of the intellectual property involved;
(f)   the wider public interest such as:
    (i)   national security;
    (ii)   individual privacy;
    (iii)   public confidence;
    (iv)   commercial confidentiality; and
    (v)   the cost of remediation (although this is not a determining factor).

1.69 In relation to mitigation the psychological profile of the offender deserves close attention. In this case, the appellant suffered from a number of conditions including Asperger's syndrome, personality disorder, social phobia and possibly major depression. The appellant was a man of previous good character and was a young age. The Court of Appeal held that he was not an 'ethical hacker' but accepted that his motive was not financial gain.

---

28   Ibid, at [19].
29   [2002] 1 Cr App R (S) 86 and *Baker* [2011] EWCA Crim 928.

1.70 Regardless the appropriate sentence was 4 months' immediate custody reduced from 6 months' imprisonment as a result of the appellant's guilty plea and personal mitigation:[30]

> '[W]e have concluded that the balance of the aggravating and mitigating factors is such that the more appropriate sentence would have been six months' imprisonment, reduced to four months in the light of the applicant's plea and personal mitigation. In particular, we underline the points which the judge made at the very outset of his sentencing remarks, that the information hacked had not been passed on to anyone and that there was no financial gain involved. The judge was correct, in our view, to identify the damage to Facebook, but it may be that he gave too much emphasis to the potential damage. It will be recalled that Facebook acknowledged that although the applicant's activity resulted in the compromise of sensitive and confidential corporate information all the compromised material was swiftly recovered and Facebook did not suffer any financial loss, apart from the costs of investigation.'

R v Martin[31]

1.71 In *Martin*, the appellant launched a denial of service (DOS) attack on the University of Oxford website shortly before 11.40am on 3 March 2011. DOS attacks involve flooding a website with internet traffic from a single device and internet connection so that the site is not able to respond to legitimate traffic, or responds so slowly as to be rendered effectively unavailable. One of the system administrators at the website discovered that there were a large number of requests from a particular internet provider (IP) address. The requests from this IP address caused the site to be unresponsive. The administrator blocked the address, and normal service was then resumed. However, after the block was put in place, the attack migrated to other sites.

1.72 On 23 March 2011, the appellant sent to that university an email signed SL1NK which said 'You Just Don't fucking learn'. On 2/3 December 2011 he sent it a further email which read:

> 'I have owned you once before (DDOS attack about six to seven months ago?) and I am going to do it again along with Cambridge. I have access to your SQL users and password database, they are encrypted as you obviously know but it won't take long and by the time you have read this message I will have sold the two databases and what is needed to have been done will have been done.'

1.73 The IP address for the sender appeared to be based in the United States. DDOS refers to a 'distributed denial of service attack'. It is similar to a DOS attack, but on a larger scale, using any number of devices and internet connections. It causes greater disruption and is more difficult to detect. SQL means structured query language and can be attacked by a 'structured query language injection attack', which takes advantage of insecure codes on a system

---

[30] See *Mangham*, at [23].
[31] [2013] EWCA Crim 1420.

connected to the internet, to bypass Firewalls and access data not normally available. This was count 1 on the indictment.

1.74 Count 10 concerned conduct initiated a week after count 1. On 10 March 2011, the appellant made an anonymous telephone call to an individual and told him that all of his personal and financial information was available on the internet as a result of a Trojan which had been placed on his computer. The appellant said these details included his loans, credit cards, bank statements, date of birth, address, telephone number, passwords, and his girlfriend's details. The appellant said he felt sorry for him and had changed his internet banking password to stop others from accessing his account. The victim was only able to then access his bank account using the password provided by the appellant.

1.75 The Court of Appeal (Leveson LJ, Sharp J, Spencer J) held that the appellant's actions fell into the highest level of culpability. The offences were carefully planned and intended to cause harm. The harm caused was akin to burglary or identity theft. Such offences had the potential to cause great damage to the community at large and the public, as well as to the individuals more directly affected by them. It was appropriate for sentences for such offences to involve a real element of deterrence, and the case of *Mangham* should not be considered as a benchmark for the sentence in such cases, which were likely to attract sentences measured in years rather than months. The appellant had targeted a number of victims during a time when he was on bail. The impact had been significant to both organisations and individuals. However, there was no motivation for financial benefit. Had such a motivation for profit existed a sentence greater than 2 years' immediate custody would have been appropriate despite of the appellant's youth (see *Martin*, at [43]–[44]).

FRAUD

1.76 Arguably the Fraud Act 2006 (FA 2006) meets many of the lacunas in law that existed prior to the creation of the CMA 1990.[32] The offence of fraud by false representation, contained within ss 1 and 2 of the FA 2006, specifies that a false representation includes one 'in any form to any system or device designed to receive, convey or respond to communications (with or without human intervention)' (see FA 2006, s 2(5)). This definition is sufficiently broad to encompass the use of another's password to access a system without authorisation which could otherwise be charged under s 1 of the CMA 1990.

1.77 Although the offences contrary to s 1 of the CMA 1990 and s 2 of the FA 2006 are potentially interchangeable, it is the preparation offences contained within the FA 2006which provide greater utility to prosecutors. In instances where a potential hacker is creating malware, whether through experimentation

---

[32] The Fraud Act 2006, rather than the Forgery and Counterfeiting Act 1981, would have been suitable to address the offending behaviour in *R v Gold & Schifreen* [1988] AC 1063, [1988] 2 WLR 984.

or for financial gain, without a specific end point in mind, the FA 2006 provides a legal basis for prosecution. The FA 2006 also allows for the criminal prosecution of an individual acting alone who is merely preparing a cyber-attack.

Fraud Act 2006

1.78 The FA 2006, ss 6–8, define offences for the creation and supply of articles for the use in fraud. In accordance with s 8 an 'article' can include 'any program or data held in electronic form'. This definition is sufficiently wide for the prosecution of offences in relation to cyber crime.

6 Possession etc. of articles for use in frauds

(1) A person is guilty of an offence if he has in his possession or under his control any article for use in the course of or in connection with any fraud.

(2) A person guilty of an offence under this section is liable –

(a)   on summary conviction, to imprisonment for a term not exceeding 12 months or to a fine not exceeding the statutory maximum (or to both);
(b)   on conviction on indictment, to imprisonment for a term not exceeding 5 years or to a fine (or to both).

7 Making or supplying articles for use in frauds

(1) A person is guilty of an offence if he makes, adapts, supplies or offers to supply any article –

(a)   knowing that it is designed or adapted for use in the course of or in connection with fraud, or
(b)   intending it to be used to commit, or assist in the commission of, fraud.

(2) A person guilty of an offence under this section is liable –

(a)   on summary conviction, to imprisonment for a term not exceeding 12 months or to a fine not exceeding the statutory maximum (or to both);
(b)   on conviction on indictment, to imprisonment for a term not exceeding 10 years or to a fine (or to both).

1.79 In relation to an offence committed before the commencement of s 154(1) of the CJA 2003, the reference to '12 months' in ss 6(2)(a) and 7(2)(a) is to be read as a reference to '6 months'; see the FA 2006, s 14(2), and Sch 2, para 1.

1.80 The prosecution is merely required to prove that the defendant had the article in his possession or under his control and that it was an article for use in the course of or in connection with any fraud, ie any fraud falling within s 1 of the FA 2006. Parliament cannot have intended that other fraudulent conduct was sufficient, otherwise words such as 'or a related offence', similar to that contained in s 13, would have been used.

1.81 Unlike the offence of going equipped, contrary to s 25 of the Theft Act 1968, there is no requirement that the defendant not be at his place of abode. However, if an article were on a defendant's computer completely unbeknown to him, he would not be guilty of the offence, since possession requires some degree of knowledge. Where the file has been deleted, possession also requires the know-how and the software to retrieve it.

1.82 In *Atkins v DPP*,[33] the Divisional Court (Simon Brown LJ, Blofeld J) held in relation to the possession of indecent images that a defendant cannot be found guilty of possessing an article upon his computer unless he has knowledge of the possession. In *Porter*,[34] the Court of Appeal (Dyson LJ, Grigson J, Walker J) held in a similar case involving indecent images that a person could not be in possession of indecent photographs if he no longer had custody or control of the images. In the case of a deleted computer image, if a person could not retrieve or gain access to the image then he no longer had custody or control of it. Both cases were considered and approved by the Court of Appeal (Lord Judge LCJ, Field J, Maddison J) in *Leonard*:[35]

'The central issue in this case was retrievability. That is a direct consequence of the decision of this court in *Porter*. On the basis of that decision there was, in our judgment, no sufficient evidence that the appellant was capable of retrieving the indecent images so as to be treated in law as in possession of them at the date when they were revealed to the investigator conducting the investigation.'

1.83 There is no reason to think that the *ratios* within these authorities would not apply to a computer file which may constitute an article for the use in fraud.

1.84 It is not necessary to prove that the defendant intended the article to be used in the course of or in connection with any specific fraud. It will be enough to prove a general intention that it be so used, whether by himself or by someone else, then or in the future.

1.85 In *Sakalauskas*,[36] a conviction for possession of an article for use in fraud contrary to s 6(1) was quashed, where the judge had wrongly directed the jury that it should convict if it was sure that a petrol can found in the defendant's possession 6 months after committing offences of fraudulently obtaining petrol had been used for the purposes of fraud. The Court of Appeal (Goldring LJ, Mitting J, Phillips J), applying the *ratio* in *Ellames*[37] in relation to going equipped to steal, held that s 6(1) was intended to prevent the possession of

---

[33] [2000] 1 WLR 1427.
[34] [2006] 1 WLR 2633.
[35] [2012] 2 Cr App R 12, at [21].
[36] [2014] 2 Cr App R 11.
[37] [1974] 1 WLR 1391.

articles intended for present or future use, not those which had been used in the past. However, the court highlighted that it was not necessary for the Crown to prove that it was the intention of the person in whose possession the articles had been found to commit the offences:[38]

> 'In our judgment, the observations of the court in *R v Ellames* in relation to count 25 apply with equal force to an offence charged under section 6. If it were not so, then it is easy to see how an innocent person who knew that an article used by somebody else for the purpose of fraud would commit an offence under section 6 if he knowingly had it in his possession. That cannot have been the intention of Parliament. The intention of Parliament as in the case of section 25 was to prevent the possession of articles that were intended for use then or in the future, not those which had been used in the past.'

1.86 Therefore, the prosecution must prove that the defendant did one of the four specified acts in relation to the article, and that he did so with one of the two specified states of mind, viz knowing that it was designed (not necessarily by him) or adapted for use in the course of or in connection with fraud; or intending it to be used (not necessarily by him or by the person to whom he supplied it) to commit, or assist in the commission of, fraud.

1.87 Proof of knowledge requires proof that the article was in fact designed or adapted for use in the course of or in connection with fraud. In *Montilla*,[39] the House of Lords (Lord Bingham of Cornhill; Lord Steyn; Lord Hope of Craighead; Baroness Hale of Richmond; Lord Carswell) were required to consider the elements to an offence of converting property contrary to the Drug Trafficking Act 1994, s 49(2), and the Criminal Justice Act 1988, s 93C(2). It was held that whether the property in question had its origins in criminal conduct or drug trafficking was an essential part of the *actus reus* of the offences, and; therefore, the prosecution was required to prove this fact or circumstance:[40]

> 'The property that is being dealt with in each case must be shown to have been criminal property ... The fact that these offences have been designed on the assumption that proof that the property being dealt with was in fact criminal property fits into the pattern which was set by the international instruments and which the wording of the subsections themselves, when properly construed in their context, indicates.'

1.88 Accordingly, in order for an offence to be committed under s 7, the prosecution must prove that the article found was made, adapted, supplied or offered for the use in a future fraud. There is no requirement that the fraud be specified:[41]

---

38   See *Sakalauskas*, at [6]–[7].
39   [2004] UKHL 50.
40   See *Montilla*, per Lord Hope of Craighead, at [41].
41   See *Ellames*, at 1397.

'In our view, to establish an offence under section 25 (1) the prosecution must prove that the defendant was in possession of the article, and intended the article to be used in the course of or in connection with some future burglary, theft or cheat. But it is not necessary to prove that he intended it to be used in the course of or in connection with any specific burglary, theft or cheat; it is enough to prove a general intention to use it for some burglary, theft or cheat; we think that this view is supported by the use of the word "any" in section 25 (1). Nor, in our view, is it necessary to prove that the defendant intended to use it himself; it will be enough to prove that he had it with him with the intention that it should be used by someone else.'

1.89 The use of ss 6–8 of the FA 2006, provides a method for prosecuting cyber crime offences that have yet to be completed, or are only in contemplation, such as where a person is found with malware on their own personal computer that is ready to be delivered. The inchoate offences within the CMA 1990 may cover this behaviour if a co-conspirator can be identified, or the act is arguably more than merely preparatory. If not then the option to prosecute under the FA 2006 provides an alternative.

FALSE OR OFFENSIVE SOCIAL MEDIA PROFILES

1.90 Conceivably, the act of setting up a false social networking account or website could fall within the ambit of ss 6–8 of the FA 2006 if there was a financial gain or loss incurred as a consequence.

1.91 Alternatively, a false or offensive profile may amount to an offence under the Public Order Act 1986. In the case of *S v DPP*,[42] the defendant was convicted of causing a person harassment, alarm or distress contrary to s 4A of the Act, for loading onto a website an image of the victim, together with text, that alleged by implication a number of false assertions, including that the victim had been convicted of violence in the past. The fact that the victim had not seen the relevant offending material until it was shown to him by police officers, by which time it was no longer on the website where it had been published, did not break the chain of causation for the purposes of a prosecution under the Public Order Act 1986, s 4A.

1.92 The Divisional Court (Maurice Kay LJ, Walker J) upheld the conviction of the defendant responsible for publishing the material, and held that once the defendant had acted with the requisite intent, and posted the image on the website, he took the chance that the intended harassment, alarm or distress would be caused. Whether it was ultimately triggered by an unknown and unconnected member of the public or by a police officer was immaterial.

---

[42]   [2008] EWHC 438 (Admin).

DATA USE OFFENCES

1.93 The Data Protection Act 1998 (DPA 1998) establishes a framework of rights and obligations which are designed to safeguard individuals' personal data. The DPA balances the right of individuals to respect for the privacy of their personal information against business needs to collect and use personal data. The DPA 1998 covers numerous aspects of data protection and privacy and includes eight data protection principles which provide an overarching set of guidelines for the way in which personal data should be handled (DPA 1998, Sch 1). In relation to the first principle: processing personal data fairly and lawfully, the DPA 1998 also provides conditions which must be applied for processing any personal data (DPA 1998, Sch 2), and processing of sensitive personal data (DPA 1998, Sch 3). Data controllers who fail to meet the principles or conditions within the DPA 1998 are acting unlawfully and could be subject to court sanction.

1.94 Section 10 provides individuals with the right to prevent data processing which is likely to cause damage or distress. The application of this provision is wide reaching and can apply to any data controller. For example, there is authority to suggest that the National Crime Agency is susceptible to challenge under this provision for unlawfully providing data to Interpol in relation to Interpol Red Notices.[43]

1.95 Section 17 places a prohibition on processing data without registration. This prohibition applies to any legal entity that may or will act as a data controller, and is strictly enforced by the Information Commissioners Office (ICO). Individual practitioners, professionals and consultants who do not work within the employ of a company with registration must register themselves or face sanction.

1.96 Section 55 makes it an offence to knowingly or recklessly obtain or disclose personal data. There are four statutory defences to this offence.

1.97 An organisation which intentionally discloses personal data, with the consent of the data controller, cannot be guilty of an offence contrary to s 55 but would likely be subject to enforcement under the DPA 1998, Part V. Anonymisation of personal data can often allow for disclosure without the issue of an enforcement notice.

Data Protection Act 1998

1.98 The DPA 1998 provides a right to challenge the use of personal data by a data controller within s 10. This does not create a criminal offence but the courts have the power to deem data processing as unwarranted if it will cause damage or distress.

---

[43]   See *Mikhael Anatolyevich Trushin v National Crime Agency* [2014] EWHC 3551 (Admin), at [18].

10 Right to prevent processing likely to cause damage or distress

(1) Subject to subsection (2), an individual is entitled at any time by notice in writing to a data controller to require the data controller at the end of such period as is reasonable in the circumstances to cease, or not to begin, processing, or processing for a specified purpose or in a specified manner, any personal data in respect of which he is the data subject, on the ground that, for specified reasons –

(a) the processing of those data or their processing for that purpose or in that manner is causing or is likely to cause substantial damage or substantial distress to him or to another, and
(b) that damage or distress is or would be unwarranted.

(2) Subsection (1) does not apply –

(a) in a case where any of the conditions in paragraphs 1 to 4 of Schedule 2 is met, or
(b) in such other cases as may be prescribed by the Secretary of State by order.

(3) The data controller must within twenty-one days of receiving a notice under subsection (1) ('the data subject notice') give the individual who gave it a written notice –

(a) stating that he has complied or intends to comply with the data subject notice, or
(b) stating his reasons for regarding the data subject notice as to any extent unjustified and the extent (if any) to which he has complied or intends to comply with it.

(4) If a court is satisfied, on the application of any person who has given a notice under subsection (1) which appears to the court to be justified (or to be justified to any extent), that the data controller in question has failed to comply with the notice, the court may order him to take such steps for complying with the notice (or for complying with it to that extent) as the court thinks fit.

(5) The failure by a data subject to exercise the right conferred by subsection (1) or section 11(1) does not affect any other right conferred on him by this Part.

1.99 The provisions within s 10 may at first sight appear complicated. However, at its most basic level s 10 allows a data subject to write a letter ('the data subject notice') to a data controller to request that the data controller stop using their personal information in whatever way that is causing damage or distress. The data controller has 21 days to comply with the request. If the data controller refuses to abide by the data subject notice then the data subject can pursue the matter in the civil courts.

1.100 The damage and distress does not have to be felt by the data subject; however, the damage and distress must be substantial and unwarranted regardless as to the individual afflicted.

1.101   A data controller can refuse to abide by the data subject notice on the basis that the data subject has previously consented to the processing of their data; for the performance of a contract to which the data subject is a party, or for the taking of steps at the request of the data subject with a view to entering into a contract; in order to comply with any legal obligation to which the data controller is subject; or to protect the vital interests of the data subject. The data controller can argue that a request within the data subject notice is unjustified but this contention is potentially subject to legal challenge.

1.102   Conceivably once a data subject has gained locus through s 10, the court hearing the application would be required to act in accordance with the Human Rights Act 1998.[44] Arguments could then potentially be advanced that the data controller had infringed the data subject's rights under the European Convention for the Protection of Human Rights (ECHR) such as the right to a private and family life under Art 8. Data controllers should be alive to the possibility that entirely unjustified requests may gain momentum once before a judge, who has to consider whether the processing of data is a necessary and proportionate infringement of a Convention right.

Failure to register as a data controller

17 Prohibition on processing without registration

(1) Subject to the following provisions of this section, personal data must not be processed unless an entry in respect of the data controller is included in the register maintained by the Commissioner under section 19 (or is treated by notification regulations made by virtue of section 19(3) as being so included).

(2) Except where the processing is assessable processing for the purposes of section 22, subsection (1) does not apply in relation to personal data consisting of information which falls neither within paragraph (a) of the definition of 'data' in section 1(1) nor within paragraph (b) of that definition.

(3) If it appears to the Secretary of State that processing of a particular description is unlikely to prejudice the rights and freedoms of data subjects, notification regulations may provide that, in such cases as may be prescribed, subsection (1) is not to apply in relation to processing of that description.

(4) Subsection (1) does not apply in relation to any processing whose sole purpose is the maintenance of a public register.

1.103   The DPA 1998 requires every data controller (eg organisation, sole trader) who is processing personal information to register with the ICO, unless they are exempt. Failure to do so is a criminal offence under s 21(1).

---

[44]   See s 6 of the Human Rights Act 1998 regarding public authorities acting in a manner which is incompatible with a right under the ECHR.

1.104 The DPA 1998 provides exemptions from notification for:

- organisations that process personal data only for:
  - staff administration (including payroll);
  - advertising, marketing and public relations (in connection with their own business activity); and
  - accounts and records;
- some not-for-profit organisations;
- organisations that process personal data only for maintaining a public register;
- organisations that do not process personal information on computer.

1.105 Section 20 imposes a duty on those registered to notify the ICO of any changes. Failure to notify is a criminal offence contrary to s 21(2). It is a defence for a person charged with an offence under subs (2) to show that he exercised all due diligence to comply with the duty.

Unlawfully obtaining or disclosing personal data

55 Unlawful obtaining etc. of personal data

(1) A person must not knowingly or recklessly, without the consent of the data controller –

(a) obtain or disclose personal data or the information contained in personal data, or
(b) procure the disclosure to another person of the information contained in personal data.

(2) Subsection (1) does not apply to a person who shows –

(a) that the obtaining, disclosing or procuring –
  (i) was necessary for the purpose of preventing or detecting crime, or
  (ii) was required or authorised by or under any enactment, by any rule of law or by the order of a court,
(b) that he acted in the reasonable belief that he had in law the right to obtain or disclose the data or information or, as the case may be, to procure the disclosure of the information to the other person,
(c) that he acted in the reasonable belief that he would have had the consent of the data controller if the data controller had known of the obtaining, disclosing or procuring and the circumstances of it, or
(d) that in the particular circumstances the obtaining, disclosing or procuring was justified as being in the public interest.

(3) A person who contravenes subsection (1) is guilty of an offence.

(4) A person who sells personal data is guilty of an offence if he has obtained the data in contravention of subsection (1).

(5) A person who offers to sell personal data is guilty of an offence if –

(a)   he has obtained the data in contravention of subsection (1), or
(b)   he subsequently obtains the data in contravention of that subsection.

(6) For the purposes of subsection (5), an advertisement indicating that personal data are or may be for sale is an offer to sell the data.

(7) Section 1(2) does not apply for the purposes of this section; and for the purposes of subsections (4) to (6), 'personal data' includes information extracted from personal data.

(8) References in this section to personal data do not include references to personal data which by virtue of section 28 or 33A are exempt from this section.

1.106 The offence is completed by merely obtaining personal data with the requisite *mens rea*. It is the statutory defences, primarily those contained in subs (2)(c), that prevents every employee who accesses information from being guilty of a criminal offence. A reasonable belief, objectively viewed, that an employee was permitted to access the information will be sufficient.

1.107 However, in *Rooney*,[45] the appellant worked in a human resources department and had access to personal information about employees for work-related purposes. It was alleged that she had abused her position by accessing information about an employee who had been formerly engaged to her sister, and by disclosing that information. The appellant's defence was that she had accessed the information about the employee's new address to update the department's records, and that she had not passed the address on to her sister. The appellant accepted that she had told her sister in which town the employee lived. The jury were unable to reach a verdict on eight other counts but convicted the appellant of obtaining personal data, and disclosing that to her sister. The Court of Appeal (Gage LJ, Bean J, Judge Goldsack QC) upheld the conviction.

1.108 The maximum sentence for an offence under this provision is a fine. However, it is not uncommon for criminality which could be captured under the DPA 1998 to be indicted as an alternative count to provide for greater sentencing powers.[46]

Enforcement

1.109 If the Information Commissioner is satisfied that a data controller has contravened or is contravening any of the data protection principles, the Commissioner may serve him with an enforcement notice requiring that he take such steps as specified within the notice (see DPA 1998, s 40). Failure to abide

---

45   [2006] EWCA Crim 1841.
46   See *Attorney-General's Reference No 140 of 2004* [2004] EWCA Crim 3525.

by the notice, or making a false statement in relation to the notice, whether knowingly or recklessly, is a criminal offence (see DPA 1998, s 47).

1.110 Organisations which seek to utilise personal data, whether or not online, should consider anonymisation to effectively mitigate the risk of enforcement. The ICO has published a code: *Anonymisation: Managing data protection* risk, to proactively encourage the anonymisation of personal data.

1.111 The Code explains that 'anonymised data' refers to that which does not identify any individual and is unlikely to allow any individual to be identified through combination with other data ('re-identification'). 'Anonymisation' covers various techniques that can be used to convert personal data into anonymised data that can be disclosed. These processes are encouraged by the ICO.

1.112 The definition under the DPA 1998 means that information which does not relate to and identify an individual is not personal data and therefore is exempt from the provisions within the Act. Once personal data is anonymised data it can be released or disclosed regardless that the data controller has the capacity to undertake re-identification. However, the data controller must be alert to the possibility of re-identification by a third party either through the single data source, because anonymisation was insufficient, or through two or more sources of data used in conjunction.

1.113 The data controller should undertake a three-stage process before releasing data:

(1) Decide whether the data is personal data.
(2) Consider whether to anonymise the data.
(3) Determine whether anonymisation is effective.

1.114 When it is not reasonably likely that an individual can be identified from the data then this is not personal data and can be disclosed. However, the data controller must consider whether other data is available, either to the public, to researchers, or to other organisations that could render this data personal data by identifying the individual concerned. The data controller must consider how and why the data could be linked to other data sets.

1.115 If it is personal data but there is a necessity to disclose then anonymisation should be considered. The following factors should be taken into account:

- the likelihood of re-identification being attempted;
- the likelihood of re-identification being successful;
- the anonymisation techniques which are available to use; and
- the quality of the data after anonymisation and whether this meets the requirements of the organisation using the anonymised data.

1.116 Before the anonymised data is disclosed the data controller must consider whether the anonymisation has been effective. The test to be applied is the 'motivated intruder' test.[47] The motivated intruder is taken to be a person who starts without any prior knowledge but who wishes to identify the individual from whose personal data the anonymised data has been derived. This test is meant to assess whether the motivated intruder would be successful. The approach assumes that the motivated intruder is reasonably competent, has access to resources such as the internet, libraries, and all public documents, and would employ investigative techniques such as making enquiries of people who may have additional knowledge of the identity of the data subject or advertising for anyone with information to come forward. The motivated intruder is not assumed to have any specialist knowledge such as computer hacking skills, or to have access to specialist equipment or to resort to criminality such as burglary, to gain access to data that is kept securely.

1.117 Finding out personal data for nefarious personal reasons or financial gain; the possibility of embarrassing others; revealing newsworthy information about public figures; political or activistic purposes; or curiosity are deemed to make certain data more attractive, and, therefore, at a greater risk. However, 'ordinary', 'innocuous' data without apparent value cannot be released without a thorough assessment of the threat of re-identification. In some cases there may be a high level of risk to individuals should re-identification occur. The Information Commissioner, when assessing whether a breach of the DPA 1998 has occurred, will look at the consequences of the disclosure on the individual.

1.118 The motivated intruder test for risk assessment sets the bar for identification higher than considering whether a relatively inexpert member of the public can achieve re-identification, but lower than considering whether someone with access to a great deal of specialist expertise.

1.119 Finally, the Code advises that an organisation involved in the anonymisation and disclosure of data should have in place an effective and comprehensive governance structure.[48] Organisations which have made a serious effort to comply with the DPA 1998 and the Code are less likely to suffer monetary penalties, under s 55A, or be ordered to pay compensation under s 13.

IMPROPER USE OF NETWORKS

1.120 The Communications Act 2003 (CA 2003), ss 125–127, created three criminal offences. Section 125 and 126 create either way offences related to the dishonest obtaining of electronic communication services. Section 127 creates an almost entirely separate offence relating to sending messages via electronic communication services.

---

[47] Anonymisation: managing data protection risk, at 22.
[48] Ibid, at 39.

Dishonestly obtaining electronic communications services (ss 125–126)

125 Dishonestly obtaining electronic communications services

(1) A person who –

(a)   dishonestly obtains an electronic communications service, and
(b)   does so with intent to avoid payment of a charge applicable to the provision of that service,

is guilty of an offence.

(2) It is not an offence under this section to obtain a service mentioned in s 297(1) of the Copyright, Designs and Patents Act 1988 (c. 48) (dishonestly obtaining a broadcasting [. . .] service provided from a place in the UK).

(3) A person guilty of an offence under this section shall be liable –

(a)   on summary conviction, to imprisonment for a term not exceeding six months or to a fine not exceeding the statutory maximum, or to both;
(b)   on conviction on indictment, to imprisonment for a term not exceeding five years or to a fine, or to both.

126 Possession or supply of apparatus etc. for contravening section 125

(1) A person is guilty of an offence if, with an intention falling within subsection (3), he has in his possession or under his control anything that may be used –

(a)   for obtaining an electronic communications service; or
(b)   in connection with obtaining such a service.

(2) A person is guilty of an offence if –

(a)   he supplies or offers to supply anything which may be used as mentioned in subsection (1); and
(b)   he knows or believes that the intentions in relation to that thing of the person to whom it is supplied or offered fall within subsection (3).

(3) A person's intentions fall within this subsection if he intends –

(a)   to use the thing to obtain an electronic communications service dishonestly;
(b)   to use the thing for a purpose connected with the dishonest obtaining of such a service;
(c)   dishonestly to allow the thing to be used to obtain such a service; or
(d)   to allow the thing to be used for a purpose connected with the dishonest obtaining of such a service.

(4) An intention does not fall within subsection (3) if it relates exclusively to the obtaining of a service mentioned in section 297(1) of the Copyright, Designs and Patents Act 1988 (c. 48).

(5) A person guilty of an offence under this section shall be liable –

(a)   on summary conviction, to imprisonment for a term not exceeding six months or to a fine not exceeding the statutory maximum, or to both; and

(b)   on conviction on indictment, to imprisonment for a term not exceeding five years or to a fine, or to both.

(6) In this section, references, in the case of a thing used for recording data, to the use of that thing include references to the use of data recorded by it.

1.121   Sections 125(2) and 126(4) explicitly exclude the offence of fraudulently receiving programmes, which generally deals with the illegitimate reception of cable and Sky television broadcasts without authorisation or payment.

1.122   The criminal behaviour to which the sections under the CA 2003 apply is the receiving of other electronic services, such as WiFi or broadband internet, dishonestly and without payment.

Improper use of public electronic communications network (s 127)

1.123   Section 127 of the CA 2003 makes it an offence to send, by means of a 'public communications network' a message that is grossly offensive, indecent or obscene, or of a menacing character. It is also an offence to use such a network to send, with an intention to cause 'annoyance, inconvenience or anxiety', a message that the sender knows to be false.

1.124   The term 'public electronic communications network' is defined in s 32 of the CA 2003 and includes the internet.

1.125   The punishments for breach of this Act include imprisonment:

127 Improper use of public electronic communications network

(1) A person is guilty of an offence if he –

(a)   sends by means of a public electronic communications network a message or other matter that is grossly offensive or of an indecent, obscene or menacing character; or

(b)   causes any such message or matter to be so sent.

(2) A person is guilty of an offence if, for the purpose of causing annoyance, inconvenience or needless anxiety to another, he –

(a) sends by means of a public electronic communications network, a message that he knows to be false,

(b) causes such a message to be sent; or

(c) persistently makes use of a public electronic communications network.

(3) A person guilty of an offence under this section shall be liable, on summary conviction, to imprisonment for a term not exceeding six months or to a fine not exceeding level 5 on the standard scale, or to both.

1.126 The statutory limitation period for prosecution within the magistrates' court (see the Magistrates Court Act 1980, s 127) is extended within CA 2003, s 127(5) from 6 months to 3 years. The information must be laid before the end of the period of 6 months beginning with the day on which evidence comes to the knowledge of the prosecutor that the prosecutor considers sufficient to justify proceedings.

Chambers v DPP[49]

1.127 In *Chambers v DPP*,[50] the appellant was registered under his own name on the social networking platform Twitter. He was due to fly on 15 January 2010 from Doncaster Robin Hood Airport to Belfast to meet another Twitter user. On 6 January, having heard that the airport had closed, he posted the message: 'Crap! Robin Hood Airport is closed. You've got a week and a bit to get your shit together otherwise I am blowing the airport sky high!!' The message could be seen by the appellant's Twitter 'followers'. On 11 January, the duty manager responsible for the airport's security saw the appellant's tweet while searching for tweets referring to the airport. His manager considered the tweet a non-credible threat but referred it to airport police in accordance with standard practice. Airport police took no action but referred the matter to South Yorkshire Police, who arrested the appellant on 13 January. In interview, the appellant asserted that the message was a joke. He was convicted in the magistrate's court. On appeal the Crown Court found that the message was menacing and he was convicted contrary to s 127 of the CA 2003.

1.128 The Divisional Court (Lord Judge LCJ, Owen J, Griffith Williams J) heard the matter by way of case stated. The tweet was a message sent by an electronic communications service for the purposes of s 127(1), and accordingly Twitter fell within its ambit. However, the offence could not be proved unless the message was of a 'menacing character'. The submissions on behalf of the appellant that the message had to be credible as an immediate threat were rejected: a message which could not or was unlikely to be implemented could nevertheless create a sense of apprehension in the person receiving it. Nevertheless, unless it did so, it was not correct to describe a message as having a menacing character. Accordingly, if the person receiving the message, or who could reasonably be expected to receive it, would brush it aside as a joke or empty banter, it would be a contradiction to describe it as a message of

---

[49] [2012] EWHC 2157 (Admin).

[50] Ibid.

menacing character. A message which did not create fear or apprehension in those to whom it was communicated, or who might reasonably be expected to see it, fell outside s 127(1)(a), for the simple reason that the message lacked menace:[51]

'Before concluding that a message is criminal on the basis that it represents a menace, its precise terms, and any inferences to be drawn from its precise terms, need to be examined in the context in and the means by which the message was sent. The Crown Court was understandably concerned that this message was sent at a time when, as we all know, there is public concern about acts of terrorism and the continuing threat to the security of the country from possible further terrorist attacks. That is plainly relevant to context, but the offence is not directed to the inconvenience which may be caused by the message. In any event, the more one reflects on it, the clearer it becomes that this message did not represent a terrorist threat, or indeed any other form of threat. It was posted on "Twitter" for widespread reading, a conversation piece for the defendant's followers, drawing attention to himself and his predicament. Much more significantly, although it purports to address "you", meaning those responsible for the airport, it was not sent to anyone at the airport or anyone responsible for airport security, or indeed any form of public security. The grievance addressed by the message is that the airport is closed when the writer wants it to be open. The language and punctuation are inconsistent with the writer intending it to be or to be taken as a serious warning. Moreover, as Mr Armson noted, it is unusual for a threat of a terrorist nature to invite the person making it to ready identified, as this message did. Finally, although we are accustomed to very brief messages by terrorists to indicate that a bomb or explosive device has been put in place and will detonate shortly, it is difficult to image a serious threat in which warning of it is given to a large number of tweet "followers" in ample time for the threat to be reported and extinguished.'

1.129   The court went on to consider the *mens rea* necessary for the offence. It was concluded, *obiter*, that the offence is satisfied if the offender is proved to have intended that the message should be of a menacing character (the most serious form of the offence) or alternatively, if he is proved to have been aware of or to have recognised the risk at the time of sending the message that it may create fear or apprehension in any reasonable member of the public who reads or sees it (see *Chamber v DPP*, at [38]):

'We would merely emphasise that even expressed in these terms, the mental element of the offence is directed exclusively to the state of the mind of the offender, and that if he may have intended the message as a joke, even if a poor joke in bad taste, it is unlikely that the *mens rea* required before conviction for the offence of sending a message of a menacing character will be established.'

1.130   The comments of the Lord Chief Justice in *Chambers v DPP* were incorporated into the DPP's Guidelines on Prosecuting Cases involving Communications sent via Social Media.

---

[51]   See *Chambers v DPP*, at [31].

The Guidelines on Prosecuting Cases involving Communications sent via Social Media

1.131 These guidelines are primarily concerned with offences that may be committed by reason of the nature or content of a communication sent via social media. Where social media is simply used to facilitate some other substantive offence, prosecutors are advised to proceed under the substantive offence in question.

1.132 Offences are divided into four categories:

- Category 1: Communications which may constitute credible threats of violence to the person or damage to property.

- Category 2: Communications which specifically target an individual or individuals and which may constitute harassment or stalking, controlling or coercive behaviour, revenge pornography, an offence under the Sexual Offences Act 2003, blackmail or another offence.

- Category 3: Communications which may amount to a breach of a court order or a statutory prohibition. This can include:
  – offences under the Juries Act 1974;
  – offences under the Contempt of Court Act 1981;
  – an offence under s 5 of the Sexual Offences (Amendment) Act 1992;
  – breaches of court orders or bail.

- Category 4: Communications which do not fall into any of the categories above fall to be considered separately ie those which may be considered grossly offensive, indecent, obscene or false.

1.133 As with the vast majority of prosecutions within England and Wales, prosecutors may only start a prosecution if a case satisfies the test set out in the Code for Crown Prosecutors (the Code). This test has two stages: the first is the requirement of evidential sufficiency and the second involves consideration of the public interest.

1.134 However, following the Lord Chief Justice's comments in *Chambers v DPP*,[52] the DPP's Guideline in relation to offences within Category 1 and 4 imposes a high threshold that must be achieved before the evidential stage in the Code will be met. Furthermore, even if the high evidential threshold is met, in many cases a prosecution is unlikely to be required in the public interest.

---

[52] *Chambers v DPP* [2013] 1 WLR 1833, at [30]: '… a message which cannot or is unlikely to be implemented may nevertheless create a sense of apprehension or fear in the person who receives or reads it. However, unless it does so, it is difficult to see how it can sensibly be described as a message of a menacing character. So, if the person or persons who receive or read it, or may reasonably be expected to receive, or read it, would brush it aside as a silly joke, or a joke in bad taste, or empty bombastic or ridiculous banter, then it would be a contradiction in terms to describe it as a message of a menacing character. In short, a message which does not create fear or apprehension in those to whom it is communicated, or who may reasonably be expected to see it, falls outside this provision, for the very simple reason that the message lacks menace'.

1.135 The Code must be applied within the context of the right of freedom of expression contained within Art 10 of the ECHR. Accordingly, no prosecution should be brought under s 1 of the Malicious Communications Act 1988 or s 127 of the Communications Act 2003 unless it can be shown on its own facts and merits to be both necessary and proportionate.

1.136 A prosecution is unlikely to be both necessary and proportionate where:

(a) the suspect has expressed genuine remorse;

(b) swift and effective action has been taken by the suspect and/or others for example, service providers, to remove the communication in question or otherwise block access to it;

(c) the communication was not intended for a wide audience, nor was that the obvious consequence of sending the communication; particularly where the intended audience did not include the victim or target of the communication in question; or

(d) the content of the communication did not obviously go beyond what could conceivably be tolerable or acceptable in an open and diverse society which upholds and respects freedom of expression.

1.137 The Guidelines in relation to Category 2 offences discuss many of the offences related to cyberstalking (see below). Prosecutors are advised to apply the Code and the guidelines relevant to potential underlying, non-cyber, offences that may be charged, such as those for stalking and harassment; domestic abuse and sexual orientation (see *CPS Guidance on stirring up hatred on grounds of sexual orientation*).

1.138 Those offences contained within Category 3 generally require specific permission from the Attorney General (AG) or the Director's Legal Advisor (DLA). Cases where there has been an offence alleged to have been committed under the Juries Act 1974 require AG consent and any charging decision must be referred to the DLA. Offences under the Contempt of Court Act 1981 or s 5 of the Sexual Offences (Amendment) Act 1992 should be referred to the Attorney General, via the DLA and the Private Office Legal Team where necessary. A failure to obtain the relevant permission could undermine a successful prosecution.

CYBERSTALKING

1.139 There is no legal definition of cyberstalking, nor is there any specific legislation to address the behaviour. Generally, cyberstalking is described as threatening behaviour or unwanted advances directed at another, using forms of online communications. Cyberstalking and online harassment are often combined with other forms of 'traditional' stalking or harassment, such as being followed or receiving unsolicited phone calls or letters. Examples of cyberstalking may include:

- threatening or obscene emails or text messages;
- spamming (where the offender sends the victim multiple junk emails);
- live chat harassment, 'flaming', or 'trolling';
- leaving improper messages on online forums or message boards;
- sending electronic viruses;
- sending unsolicited email;
- cyber identity theft.

1.140 Whether any of these cyber activities amount to an offence will depend on the context and particular circumstances of the action in question. Communications that are grossly offensive, indecent, obscene or false such as communications that contain images or videos of very serious injuries, or of people being raped, or people being subjected to sadistic acts of violence, accompanied by text that suggests that such assaults/ rape/ acts are acceptable or desirable may, depending on the context and circumstances, be considered grossly offensive. These communications can potentially be prosecuted under either the CA 2003, s 127 (see above), or the Malicious Communications Act 1988, s 1.

1.141 There is now also a specific offence, contrary to s 33 of the Criminal Justice and Courts Act 2015 which addresses 'revenge pornography'.

Malicious Communications Act 1988

1.142 The Malicious Communications Act 1988 (MCA 1988), s 1, was amended by the Criminal Justice and Police Act 2001, s 43(1)(a), to include electronic communications. The amendment was designed to catch cyberstalking and bring this within the ambit of s 1. The offence requires proof that the sender of the indecent, offensive, or threatening communication or article, must intend to cause distress or anxiety to the recipient or any other person who the sender believes will see its content.

1 Offence of sending letters etc. with intent to cause distress or anxiety

(1) Any person who sends to another person –

(a) a letter, electronic communication or article of any description which conveys –
   (i) a message which is indecent or grossly offensive;
   (ii) a threat; or
   (iii) information which is false and known or believed to be false by the sender; or
(b) any article or electronic communication which is, in whole or part, of an indecent or grossly offensive nature,

is guilty of an offence if his purpose, or one of his purposes, in sending it is that it should, so far as falling within paragraph (a) or (b) above, cause distress or anxiety to the recipient or to any other person to whom he intends that it or its contents or nature should be communicated.

(2) A person is not guilty of an offence by virtue of subsection (1)(a)(ii) above if he shows –

(a)   that the threat was used to reinforce a demand made by him on reasonable grounds; and
(b)   that he believed, and had reasonable grounds for believing, that the use of the threat was a proper means of reinforcing the demand.

(2A) In this section 'electronic communication' includes –

(a)   any oral or other communication by means of an electronic communications network; and
(b)   any communication (however sent) that is in electronic form.

(3) In this section references to sending include references to delivering or transmitting and to causing to be sent, delivered or transmitted and 'sender' shall be construed accordingly.

(4) A person guilty of an offence under this section is liable –

(a)   on conviction on indictment to imprisonment for a term not exceeding two years or a fine (or both);
(b)   on summary conviction to imprisonment for a term not exceeding 12 months or a fine (or both).

(5) In relation to an offence committed before section 154(1) of the Criminal Justice Act 2003 comes into force, the reference in subsection (4)(b) to 12 months is to be read as a reference to six months.

(6) In relation to an offence committed before section 85 of the Legal Aid Sentencing and Punishment of Offenders Act 2012 comes into force, the reference in subsection (4)(b) to a fine is to be read as a reference to a fine not exceeding the statutory maximum.

1.143   Whether an online comment will fall within the ambit of the MCA 1988 is difficult to establish other than on a case-by-case basis.

1.144   Online 'flaming' incorporates posting either obviously inflammatory or abusive messages known as 'flames'; however, even this has been considered to be within the law when directed towards public figures as part of a democratic debate.[53] A 'troll' (a person who engages in 'trolling') sows discord on the

---

[53]   See *Chambers v DPP* [2013] 1 WLR 1833, per Lord Judge CJ, at [28]: 'The 2003 Act did not create some newly minted interference with the first of President Roosevelt's essential freedoms – freedom of speech and expression. Satirical, or iconoclastic, or rude comment, the expression of unpopular or unfashionable opinion about serious or trivial matters, banter or humour, even

internet by starting arguments or by posting extraneous or off-topic messages in an online community. This too may not constitute an offence. 'Kudos trolling' is done for the purpose of the mutual and consented entertainment of others and oneself, but may not be immune from the law. The posting of a sexist joke, for example, while entertaining to others around the poster can be viewed as grossly offensive by people who identify with those in the joke. 'Flame trolls' will post extraneous inflammatory comments which are intended to harm but may again be acceptable if directed towards a legitimate debate.

1.145 The posting of messages online that are provocative or offensive but are generally within the confines of free speech can be categorised 'cyber-trolling'. The posting of messages online that are grossly offensive or intended to harm or harass is 'cyberstalking' and may constitute a criminal offence. Free speech is not a defence within the MCA 1988, which must be applied to the specific facts of any case.

1.146 In *Connolly v DPP*,[54] the appellant, who was a committed Christian, had sent photographs of aborted foetuses to three pharmacies that sold the morning-after pill. The Crown's case was that the images were indecent or grossly offensive, and that the appellant had sent them with the purpose of causing distress or anxiety to the recipients. The appellant's defence had been that the images were not indecent or grossly offensive and that she had sent them with the intention of making a lawful protest and educating against the use of the morning-after pill. It was her case that the MCA 1988 should not apply to a lawful protest and to find otherwise would be a breach of her human rights, specifically her right to religious freedom (Art 9) and freedom of expression (Art 10).

1.147 The High Court (Dyson LJ, Stanley Burnton J) held that the fact that a communication was political or educational in nature had no bearing on whether it was indecent or grossly offensive. It was possible to interpret s 1 of the MCA 1988 compatibly with Art 10 by giving heightened meaning to the words 'indecent' and 'grossly offensive', or by reading into s 1 of the Act a provision to the effect that it would not apply where to create an offence that would be an unjustifiable breach of Art 10. The Court of Appeal accepted that Art 10(1) was engaged but that the MCA 1988's interference with the appellant's freedom of expression was justified under Art 10(2) for the protection of the rights of others. The pharmacists targeted had the right not to have sent to them material of the kind sent by the appellant. Moreover, the appellant's conviction was necessary in a democratic society: her right to express her views about abortion did not justify the distress and anxiety that she intended to cause those receiving the images, and it was of particular

---

if distasteful to some or painful to those subjected to it should and no doubt will continue at their customary level, quite undiminished by this legislation. Given the submissions by Mr Cooper, we should perhaps add that for those who have the inclination to use "Twitter" for the purpose, Shakespeare can be quoted unbowdlerised, and with Albany, at the end of King Lear, they are free to speak not what they ought to say, but what they feel'.

54   [2008] 1 WLR 276.

significance that the recipients of the images had not been targeted because they were in a position to influence a public debate on abortion:[55]

> 'The most that Mrs Connolly could have hoped to achieve was to persuade those responsible in the pharmacies for their purchasing policies to stop selling the 'morning after pill'. But it was always likely that the photographs would be seen by persons who had no such responsibility and it was by no means certain that they would be seen by the persons who had that responsibility. In any event, even if the three pharmacies were persuaded to stop selling the pill, it is difficult to see what contribution this would make to any public debate about abortion generally and how that would increase the likelihood that abortion would be prohibited.'

1.148 Although the appellant may have been devoutly religious and exercising her Art 9 right to freedom of thought, conscience and religion, freedom of religious expression was of no higher order and was no more worthy of protection than the freedom of secular expression enshrined in Art 10:[56]

> 'I am prepared to assume that, because she is a devout Roman Catholic, Mrs Connolly was exercising her freedom of thought, conscience and religion when she sent the photographs to the three pharmacies. But it seems to me that article 9(2) is as fatal to her appeal as is article 10(2) and for precisely the same reasons.'

1.149 The appellant would have escaped conviction only if the court believed that the images were provided without the intent to cause distress or anxiety to the recipient. An honest motive which illustrates that the communication was intended as a joke would constitute a defence.[57]

Revenge pornography

1.150 Revenge pornography is a broad term, which usually refers to the actions of an ex-partner, who uploads onto the internet, or posts on a social networking site, or shares by text or email, intimate sexual images of the victim, to cause the victim humiliation or embarrassment.

1.151 Specifically, s 33 of the Criminal Justice and Courts Act 2015 creates an offence of disclosing private sexual photographs or films without the consent of an individual who appears in them and with intent to cause that individual distress.

1.152 The offence will cover anyone who re-tweets or forwards without consent, a private sexual photograph or film, if the purpose, or one of the purposes, was to cause distress to the individual depicted in the photograph or film, who had not consented to the disclosure. However, anyone who sends the message only because he or she thought it was funny would not be committing the offence.

---

[55]   See *Connelly v DPP*, at [32].
[56]   See *Connelly v DPP*, at [36].
[57]   See *Chambers v DPP* [2012] EWHC 2157 (Admin).

1.153 Sections 34 and 35 of the Criminal Justice and Courts Act 2015 define 'disclose', 'photograph or film', 'private' and 'sexual':

33 Disclosing private sexual photographs and films with intent to cause distress

(1) It is an offence for a person to disclose a private sexual photograph or film if the disclosure is made-

(a)   without the consent of an individual who appears in the photograph or film, and

(b)   with the intention of causing that individual distress.

(2) But it is not an offence under this section for the person to disclose the photograph or film to the individual mentioned in subsection (1)(a) and (b).

(3) It is a defence for a person charged with an offence under this section to prove that he or she reasonably believed that the disclosure was necessary for the purposes of preventing, detecting or investigating crime.

(4) It is a defence for a person charged with an offence under this section to show that –

(a)   the disclosure was made in the course of, or with a view to, the publication of journalistic material, and

(b)   he or she reasonably believed that, in the particular circumstances, the publication of the journalistic material was, or would be, in the public interest.

(5) It is a defence for a person charged with an offence under this section to show that –

(a)   he or she reasonably believed that the photograph or film had previously been disclosed for reward, whether by the individual mentioned in subsection (1)(a) and (b) or another person, and

(b)   he or she had no reason to believe that the previous disclosure for reward was made without the consent of the individual mentioned in subsection (1)(a) and (b).

(6) A person is taken to have shown the matters mentioned in subsection (4) or (5) if –

(a)   sufficient evidence of the matters is adduced to raise an issue with respect to it, and

(b)   the contrary is not proved beyond reasonable doubt.

(7) For the purposes of subsections (1) to (5) –

(a)   'consent' to a disclosure includes general consent covering the disclosure, as well as consent to the particular disclosure, and

(b)   'publication' of journalistic material means disclosure to the public at large or to a section of the public.

(8) A person charged with an offence under this section is not to be taken to have disclosed a photograph or film with the intention of causing distress merely because that was a natural and probable consequence of the disclosure.

(9) A person guilty of an offence under this section is liable –

(a)   on conviction on indictment, to imprisonment for a term not exceeding 2 years or a fine (or both), and
(b)   on summary conviction, to imprisonment for a term not exceeding 12 months or a fine (or both).

(10) Schedule 8 makes special provision in connection with the operation of this section in relation to persons providing information society services.

(11) In relation to an offence committed before section 154(1) of the Criminal Justice Act 2003 comes into force, the reference in subsection (9)(b) to 12 months is to be read as a reference to 6 months.

(12) In relation to an offence committed before section 85 of the Legal Aid, Sentencing and Punishment of Offenders Act 2012 comes into force, the reference in subsection (9)(b) to a fine is to be read as a reference to a fine not exceeding the statutory maximum.

34 Meaning of 'disclose' and 'photograph or film'

(1) The following apply for the purposes of section 33, this section and section 35.

(2) A person 'discloses' something to a person if, by any means, he or she gives or shows it to the person or makes it available to the person.

(3) Something that is given, shown or made available to a person is disclosed –

(a)   whether or not it is given, shown or made available for reward, and
(b)   whether or not it has previously been given, shown or made available to the person.

(4) 'Photograph or film' means a still or moving image in any form that –

(a)   appears to consist of or include one or more photographed or filmed images, and
(b)   in fact consists of or includes one or more photographed or filmed images.

(5) The reference in subsection (4)(b) to photographed or filmed images includes photographed or filmed images that have been altered in any way.

(6) 'Photographed or filmed image' means a still or moving image that –

(a)   was originally captured by photography or filming, or

(b)   is part of an image originally captured by photography or filming.

(7) 'Filming' means making a recording, on any medium, from which a moving image may be produced by any means.

(8) References to a photograph or film include –

(a)   a negative version of an image described in subsection (4), and
(b)   data stored by any means which is capable of conversion into an image described in subsection (4).

35 Meaning of 'private' and 'sexual'

(1) The following apply for the purposes of section 33.

(2) A photograph or film is 'private' if it shows something that is not of a kind ordinarily seen in public.

(3) A photograph or film is 'sexual' if –

(a)   it shows all or part of an individual's exposed genitals or pubic area,
(b)   it shows something that a reasonable person would consider to be sexual because of its nature, or
(c)   its content, taken as a whole, is such that a reasonable person would consider it to be sexual.

(4) Subsection (5) applies in the case of –

(a)   a photograph or film that consists of or includes a photographed or filmed image that has been altered in any way,
(b)   a photograph or film that combines two or more photographed or filmed images, and
(c)   a photograph or film that combines a photographed or filmed image with something else.

(5) The photograph or film is not private and sexual if –

(a)   it does not consist of or include a photographed or filmed image that is itself private and sexual,
(b)   it is only private or sexual by virtue of the alteration or combination mentioned in subsection (4), or
(c)   it is only by virtue of the alteration or combination mentioned in subsection (4) that the person mentioned in section 33(1)(a) and (b) is shown as part of, or with, whatever makes the photograph or film private and sexual.

1.154 The statutory offence came into force on 13 April 2015 and does not have retrospective effect. Where an act of revenge pornography is carried out prior to this date, consideration should be given to whether the communication in question is grossly offensive, indecent, obscene or false, and may therefore be prosecuted under one of the CA 2003 offences.

CHAPTER 2

CIVIL LIABILITY UNDER THE DATA PROTECTION ACT 1998

LIABILITY FOR PERSONAL DATA

2.01 Nearly all organisations handle personal data in some form or another. A cyber-attack that results in a breach of personal data, either by a third party or from inside the organisation, may give rise to civil liability for the organisation responsible for processing the data. This is governed by the regime established under the Data Protection Act 1998 (DPA 1998).

2.02 This chapter considers in some detail the provisions of the DPA 1998, with particular reference to the potential liability of organisations to third parties which may arise following a data breach. This chapter should be read in conjunction with Chapter 4 (Cyber Property) and Chapter 5 (Employee Liability and Protection).

DATA PROTECTION ACT 1998 – AN OVERVIEW

2.03 The DPA 1998 sought to implement elements of the European Data Protection Directive, including those in relation to governance of electronic communication. It replaced and effectively consolidated the Data Protection Act 1984 and the Access to Personal Files Act 1987.

2.04 The DPA 1998 is concerned with the processing of data, and contains eight principles of 'good information handling' which give individuals rights in relation to how their personal information is treated, and places obligations on those who process personal information.

DEFINITION OF KEY TERMS (S 1)

2.05 Section 1 of the DPA 1998 sets out the basic interpretive provisions. The most important terms are:

'Data' – electronically stored data, as well as data recorded as part of a relevant filing system.

'Personal Data' – any information which can be used to identify a living individual as opposed to other data such as anonymous aggregated information that is not covered by the Act, eg a person's name, address, email address, shareholding, directorships, CCTV image, photograph on a website, etc.

'Data Controller' – any organisation that controls the processing of personal data.

'Data subject' – the individual person who is the subject of any relevant personal data.

'Processing' – any activity that can be carried out concerning personal data, eg obtaining, storing, printing, filing, copying or transferring such data to a third party.

THE DATA PROTECTION PRINCIPLES (S 4)

2.06 Section 4 of the DPA 1998 makes reference to the data protection principles which are set out in Part 1 of Sch 1.

The eight principles are as follows:

(1) Personal data shall be processed fairly and lawfully and, in particular, shall not be processed unless:
    (a) at least one of the conditions in Sch 2 is met, and
    (b) in the case of sensitive personal data, at least one of the conditions in Sch 3 is also met.
(2) Personal data shall be obtained only for one or more specified and lawful purposes, and shall not be further processed in any manner incompatible with that purpose or those purposes.
(3) Personal data shall be adequate, relevant and not excessive in relation to the purpose or purposes for which they are processed.

(4) Personal data shall be accurate and, where necessary, kept up to date.

(5) Personal data processed for any purpose or purposes shall not be kept for longer than is necessary for that purpose or those purposes.

(6) Personal data shall be processed in accordance with the rights of data subjects under this Act.

(7) Appropriate technical and organisational measures shall be taken against unauthorised or unlawful processing of personal data and against accidental loss or destruction of, or damage to, personal data.

(8) Personal data shall not be transferred to a country or territory outside the European Economic Area unless that country or territory ensures an adequate level of protection for the rights and freedoms of data subjects in relation to the processing of personal data.

2.07 The DPA 1998 further provides at Sch 1, Part II, additional guidance as to how the principles shall be interpreted.

The first principle – 'data must be processed fairly and lawfully'

2.08 All data must be processed fairly and lawfully. In practice this means one must have legitimate grounds for collecting and using the personal data, be transparent about the intended use and ensure, so far as possible, that the intended use is adhered to. Where possible this can be disclosed in advance and agreed in contracts, eg in relation to employees, so that there is consent in place. In a workplace situation an employer is open to the allegation that consent was not freely given because of the inequality of an employee's bargaining position and an impact assessment ought to be conducted to ensure data use is fair, lawful, proportionate and not improper. Schedules 2 and 3 of the DPA 1998 contain the conditions for processing, which are more demanding when sensitive information is involved. Sensitive information is defined in s 2 as personal data consisting of information as to:

(a) the racial or ethnic origin of the data subject;

(b) his political opinions;

(c) his religious beliefs or other beliefs of a similar nature;

(d) whether he is a member of a trade union (within the meaning of the Trade Union and Labour Relations (Consolidation) Act 1992);

(e) his physical or mental health or condition;

(f) his sexual life;

(g) the commission or alleged commission by him of any offence;

(h) any proceedings for any offence committed or alleged to have been committed by him, the disposal of such proceedings or the sentence of any court in such proceedings.

It follows that such private information must be subject to stringent processing conditions but all data covered by the DPA 1998 (personal data) must be handled fairly and in a transparent lawful (authorised) manner.

The second principle – 'data must be obtained only for one or more specified purpose'

2.09   Principle 2 is that the personal data must be obtained only for one or more specified purpose and there should not be deviation from that or those specified purpose(s). This can be achieved by serving a 'privacy notice' specifying the purpose at the time the data is obtained from the individual or by a notification to the Information Commissioner. While both methods achieve the goal it is submitted that serving a 'privacy notice' is the better practice in ensuring true transparency as individuals would otherwise have to make enquiry of the Information Commissioner's Office or check the organisation's notification entry.

2.10   It is possible subsequently to deviate from a specified data purpose but this should only be where that use is compatible with the specified purpose. This might mean that it is ancillary or incidental to a specified purpose. Under the DPA 1998, in determining compatibility one should consider the purposes for which the information is intended to be used by any person to whom it is disclosed. This then includes viewing through the recipient's perspective: what will that person or organisation use the information for and how does that use sit with the original purpose as notified to the person from whom it was obtained? Is this fair, lawful and transparent use of that personal information? Would it have been contemplated at the time the data was obtained and the intended use specified? The safest course and best practice is to obtain additional express consent to any use of personal information that is different to a specified use. That may not always be possible but steps should be taken to avoid what may otherwise constitute a breach.

The third principle – 'personal data shall be adequate, relevant and not excessive'

2.11   The third data protection principle stipulates that 'Personal data shall be adequate, relevant and not excessive in relation to the purpose or purposes for which they are processed'. This requirement is termed the 'data minimisation requirement'. The personal data that is obtained and used should be the minimum amount of information required to satisfy the purpose for which it is processed. Where persons in a group share characteristics or otherwise have personal information that is common to all, care should be taken not to obtain more information that exceeds the need. The words 'adequate', 'relevant' and 'not excessive' are to be given their natural meaning in relation to the purpose to which the data is to be put. Again, the principle of fairness underscores the third principle considerations. It will often be fair to obtain further personal data where the data held is not sufficient to meet the intended purpose or where a foreseeable event or contingency needs to be planned for and the additional personal information is required. Conversely it would not be permissible to obtain and retain personal information that exceeded need simply because it might be of some use in the future; their need should be demonstrable and relevant. Particular attention should be paid to sensitive (see above) personal information and whether this is truly de minimis given the importance of ensuring such sensitive information is kept to an absolute minimum so that it is no more than necessary to satisfy the specified purpose. Sensitive personal information is particularly susceptible to a cyber-attack. Targets of this type render organisations more vulnerable in terms of reputational damage and consequently more willing to meet a ransom demand. It follows that personal data and especially sensitive data could be highly embarrassing and compromising where it is lost or stolen; this situation will be exacerbated where the data held was excessive, irrelevant, for an unexpected non-specified purpose or inaccurate.

The fourth principle – 'personal data shall be accurate and, where necessary, kept up to date'

2.12 The fourth data protection principle stipulates that 'Personal data shall be accurate and, where necessary, kept up to date'. This involves ensuring, so far as is reasonably possible, that the personal data obtained is accurate, that the source is accurate and reliable and reviewing it to ensure it continues to be accurate and up to date and, as appropriate, updating the personal information. This can be particularly significant where the data is in the form of an opinion or other expression of something less than hard fact. Recent high profile cyber-attacks have resulted in the hacking and publication of emails that attribute an opinion or affiliation that is newsworthy and embarrassing for the author of the opinion and the organisation that held it. In relation to all personal data, one must consider whether the accuracy of the information will be open to challenge and what that challenge might be. Opinions, especially those that venture into politics, medicine or other contentious areas, are prone to challenge and caution ought to be exercised as to the need for holding or using such information at all. If the accuracy cannot be verified due to the nature of the content, such as an unprovable opinion or assertion, then should the data be held at all: what specified purpose can it properly and fairly be applied to?

The fifth principle – 'personal data shall not be kept for longer than is necessary'

2.13 The de minimis approach is extended by the fifth data protection principle as to the time the personal information is retained. It should be held for no longer than is necessary for purpose and then deleted. It stipulates that 'Personal data processed for any purpose or purposes shall not be kept for longer than is necessary for that purpose or those purposes'. In a corporate cyber-attack scenario, the personal data unlawfully accessed and published could be highly damaging and exposing where it ought not to have been retained in any event; whether initially or at that later point in time when it may have been beyond the parameters of principle five. Good practice will require a regular review as to both accuracy and on-going need for that personal information when viewed against the original notified purpose or purposes and any (if not notified) compatible purpose to which it might properly be applied. Reference should also be made to Schs 2 and 3 to the DPA 1998, which set out a number of reasons for retaining personal information. These include additional considerations arising from other matters such as public office or employment law requirements (see Chapter 4). Regard must also be taken of specific legal and regulatory requirements such as health and safety, accounting and tax, SRA and other professional regulatory rules as to retention and duration of certain types of information. Does one of these apply? If so does it still apply at the date of the review such that continued retention is fair and demonstrable?

The sixth principle – 'personal data shall be processed in accordance with the rights of data subjects under this Act'

2.14 The sixth data protection principle stipulates 'Personal data shall be processed in accordance with the rights of data subjects under this Act'. This principle does not impose an information standard but declares that the personal information will be subject to the rights and challenges afforded to the person outlined in s 7 et seq addressed later in this chapter. Those rights include the right (subject to limitation) to access, block, delete, revise, prevent and, where there is a breach, pursue a claim for compensation, although that would ultimately fall to be determined by a court if the alleged breach was defended.

The seventh principle – appropriate technical and organisational measures to secure personal data

2.15 The seventh data protection principle stipulates the necessary security that must be in place:

> 'Appropriate technical and organisational measures shall be taken against unauthorised or unlawful processing of personal data and against accidental loss or destruction of, or damage to, personal data.'

2.16 This seventh data protection principle sets out the steps to be taken in the event of an attack ('unauthorised or unlawful processing') or non-deliberate accidental loss, destruction or damage. The express reference to 'technical and organisational measures' is significant. The Information Commissioner's Office current guidance is that in complying with this principle one should:

- design and organise your security to fit the nature of the personal data you hold and the harm that may result from a security breach;
- be clear about who in your organisation is responsible for ensuring information security;

- make sure you have the right physical and technical security, backed up by robust policies and procedures and reliable, well-trained staff; and
- be ready to respond to any breach of security swiftly and effectively.

2.17 The technical and organisational security in place should be bespoke, 'to fit the nature of the personal data ... and the harm that may result from a security breach'. This will involve conducting a detailed information risk assessment to ascertain the sort of data held in terms of extent, sensitivity, confidentiality and the potential impact on individuals a breach and unauthorised access might have. The assessment should include the nature and extent of the organisation's premises and computer systems, the number of staff it has, the extent of their access to the personal data; and personal data held or used by a third party on its behalf (as under the DPA 1998 you are also responsible for ensuring that any data processor you employ has appropriate security).

2.18 Consideration must be given to the need for an information security policy. This will not always have to be a formal, written-up policy document; but it is highly advisable and certainly best practice to have a formal policy. That policy document should demonstrate that the process of information risk assessment had been undertaken and a bespoke approach taken on both technical and organisational levels. The ICO guidance is that it include:

- co-ordination between key people in the organisation (for example, the security manager will need to know about commissioning and disposing of any IT equipment);
- access to premises or equipment given to anyone outside the organisation (for example, for computer maintenance) and the additional security considerations this will generate;
- business continuity arrangements that identify how to protect and recover any personal data the organisation holds; and
- periodic checks to ensure that the organisation's security measures remain appropriate and up to date.

2.19 Staff must also be trained to guard against the risk of breach, and that training should be effectively implemented, documented, reviewed and, ideally, tested. Chapter 5 (Employee Liability and Protection) further examines the need for 'cyber terms of use' to be incorporated into staff contracts and precautions and contractual safeguards to be in place at the earliest opportunity.

The eighth principle – data not be transferred outside the EEA unless that country ensures an adequate level of protection for the processing of personal data

2.20 The eighth and last data protection principle stipulates that:

'Personal data shall not be transferred to a country or territory outside the EEA unless that country or territory ensures an adequate level of protection for the rights and freedoms of data subjects in relation to the processing of personal data.'

2.21 The EEA presently comprises Austria, Belgium, Bulgaria, Croatia, Cyprus, Czech Republic, Denmark, Estonia, Finland, France, Germany, Greece, Hungary, Iceland, Ireland, Italy, Latvia, Liechtenstein, Lithuania, Luxembourg, Malta, Netherlands, Norway, Poland, Portugal, Romania, Slovakia, Slovenia, Spain, Sweden, United Kingdom.

2.22 The legal environment post-Brexit and GDPR are considered within Chapter 12. Given the reference to EEA within the DPA 1998, and the shifting position of the UK following the referendum decision to exit the EU, this may be a significant area for continuous evaluation over the next few years. The UK may or may not remain within the EEA.

2.23 This principle should be read in conjunction with the requirement to use information in a fair and lawful manner.

2.24 The principle deals with restrictions on the transfer of personal data outside of the EEA or to a country not signed up to the 'Safe Harbor Scheme' and specifies that the Commission will need to assess whether the proposed transfer will provide an adequate level of protection for the rights of the data subject in connection with the transfer of their personal data.

2.25 Current practical guidance (at the time of going to press) is contained in 'Assessing Adequacy – International transfers of personal data 20150929 V1.1'.

APPLICATION OF THE ACT (S 5)

2.26 Section 5 makes it clear that the DPA 1998 applies only where the data controller is in the United Kingdom and the data processed is in the context of that United Kingdom establishment or where the data controller is not in the United Kingdom or another EEA state that the equipment used is in the United Kingdom for processing data other than for the purpose of transit through the United Kingdom.

5 Application of Act

(1) Except as otherwise provided by or under Section 54, this Act applies to a Data Controller in respect of any data only if

(a) the Data Controller is established in the United Kingdom and the data is processed in the context of that establishment, or
(b) the Data controller is established neither in the United Kingdom nor in any other EEA State that uses equipment in the United Kingdom for processing the data other than for the purpose of transit through the United Kingdom

(2) A Data Controller falling within subsection (1)(b) must nominate for the purposes of this Act a representative established in the United Kingdom

(3) For the purposes of subsections (1) and (2) each of the following is to be treated as established in the United Kingdom

(a) an individual who is ordinarily resident in the United Kingdom
(b) a body incorporated under law of, or of any part of, the United Kingdom
(c) a partnership or other unincorporated association formed under the law of any part of the United Kingdom
(d) any person who does not fall within paragraphs (a), (b) or (c) but maintains in the United Kingdom:
    (i) an office, branch or agency through which he carried on any activity or
    (ii) a regular practice,

and a reference to establishment in any other EEA State has a corresponding meaning.'

2.27 It is important to note that by virtue of s 5(3) jurisdiction extends to an organisation or individual with a United Kingdom footprint or, in the absence of an office, branch or agency, a regular practice. The jurisdiction then is drawn relatively widely. Given the extra-territorial jurisdiction, care should be taken to ensure if the Act will apply to data that is processed outside the United Kingdom.

RIGHT OF ACCESS TO PERSONAL DATA (S 7)

2.28 An individual is entitled to be informed whether his personal data is being processed by a data controller. On submission of a written request (a subject access request) and payment of a prescribed fee (presently £10 but more for educational or medical records or credit files) the data controller must supply the personal data that falls within the scope of the request by the individual, together with a full description of the personal data that was processed, the purpose of that processing and those to whom they are disclosed and the source of the data. This must all be in a manner that is clear and intelligible.

2.29 Section 7 provides individuals with the right to inspect their personal data and to see how that data is being processed and by whom. A s 7 subject access request can place a considerable burden on a data controller who must also inform the data subject of whether the processing involves an automatic decision process and explain the logic involved in the process.

2.30 Whilst s 7 is well intentioned, it is open to abuse both by employers and by employees who have tried to take advantage of the subject access request process. For employees, it is sometimes used for 'fishing' expeditions, especially where an employee believes he may be able to gather information in anticipation of a dispute. It should be noted that under the usual Civil

Procedure Rules (CPR) or Tribunal Rules an employee would ordinarily need to demonstrate that there was sufficient relevance in the documents for their disclosure. Evidently under s 7 there is no such need and an employee may seek to obtain all records and documents via a s 7 data request in return for a moderate fee. For the employer faced with what it believes to be a fishing expedition and an unwanted s 7 request, the case of *Durant v FSA*,[1] may be of some use. In that case the court expressly stated that:

'The purpose of Section 7, in entitling an individual to have access to information in the form of his "personal data" is to enable him to check whether the data controller's processing of it unlawfully infringes his privacy and, if so, to take such steps as the DPA provides to protect it. It is not an automatic to any information, regularly accessible or not, of matters in which he may be named or involved. Nor is it to assist him, for example, to obtain discovery of documents that may assist him in litigation or complaint against third parties.'

2.31 Notwithstanding *Durant*, it may however be difficult for an employer in receipt of a subject access request to avoid compliance where the employee requesting the information will doubtless demand compliance and, as previously stated, there is unfortunately no requirement that the requestor initially demonstrate the relevance of the documents he seeks to be disclosed. Conversely an employer might seek to exploit the s 7 process.

2.32 It is not unusual for employers to request that job applicants obtain a subject access request providing a way of checking their entire criminal history. This can be distinguished from obtaining criminal records under the Disclosure Barring Service (DBS). That said, an employer or anybody that requires an individual to obtain a subject access request may be committing a criminal offence pursuant to s 56 of the DPA 1998. The commission of that offence is not dependent on an individual suffering loss or damage as a result of any enforced subject access request, the mere requirement may be enough to trigger the criminal offence.

2.33 Section 7(2)–(6) set out whether it is reasonable to comply with a data request, and the scope of the data if it is to be supplied.

2.34 Section 7(8) states that the data controller shall comply promptly to any request under s 7 and in any event before the end of the prescribed period which is 40 days beginning with the relevant day, or such other period as may be prescribed (s 7(10)). The relevant day is defined as being either the day on which the data controller receives the request or, if later, the first day on which the data controller has *both* the required fee *and* the information referred to in subs (3) ie any further requested information as to the identity of the requester.

2.35 A relevant person is defined in subs (12) as:

(12) A person is a relevant person for the purposes of subsection (4)(c) if he –

---

[1] [2003] EWCA Civ 1746.

(a)   is the person referred to in paragraph (4)(a) or (4)(b) or paragraph (8)(a) or (8)(b) of section 11;

(b)   is employed by an education authority (within the meaning of paragraph 6 of Schedule 11 pursuant of its function relating to education and information relates to him or he supplied the information in his capacity as such an employee; or

(c)   is the person making the request.

2.36 Section 8 provides further supplementary provisions for compliance with s 7. That section is not reproduced here.

ENFORCED SUBJECT ACCESS REQUEST (S 56)

2.37 Section 56 of the DPA 1998 was the last section to come into force and did so on 10 March 2015. It is now a criminal offence to require a subject access request. This is often termed an enforced subject access request.

56 Prohibition of requirement to ask for production or certain records.

(1) A person must not, in connection with

(a)   the recruitment of another person as an employee
(b)   the continued employment of another person
(c)   any contract for the provision of services to him by another person,

require that other person or a third party to supply him with a relevant record or to produce a relevant record to him.

(2) A person concerned with the provision (for payment or not) of goods, facilities or services to the public or a section of the public must not, as a condition of providing or offering to provide any goods, facilities or services to another person, require that other person or a third party to supply him with a relevant record or to produce a relevant record to him.

(3) Subsections (1) and (2) do not apply to a person who shows –

(a)   that the imposition of the requirement was required or authorised by or under any enactment, by any rule of law or by the order of a court, or
(b)   that in the particular circumstances the imposition of the requirement was justified as being in the public interest.

(4) Having regard to the provisions of Part V of the M1 Police Act 1997 (certificates of criminal records etc.), the imposition of the requirement referred to in subsection (1) or (2) is not to be regarded as being justified as being in the public interest on the ground that it would assist in the prevention or detection of crime.

(5) A person who contravenes subsection (1) or (2) is guilty of an offence.

2.38 Great care should be taken in attempting to rely on the public interest defence at s 56(3)(b) as it is likely to be construed in a very limited fashion. The sanction for breach is criminal in nature. Furthermore, s 56 does not make it an offence to undertake criminal records (DBS) checks on prospective employees. In fact, the section is aimed squarely at preventing enforced subject access requests as a means of forcing an employee to achieve that end.

2.39 The Information Commissioner has indicated that s 56 will be given a wide interpretation and as a result subs (1) will catch anything relating to employment both at recruitment stage and whilst ongoing and subs (2) will apply to all manner of service providers including insurers, housing associations, agents, contractors and volunteers and the offence will also be committed when the request itself is imposed, not when records are disclosed as a result. It seems clear that even if the enforced subject access request produces no result, the offence would still have been committed at the point when the subject was required to obtain the data by a subject access request.

2.40 The Information Commissioner has stated it knows of no current legal requirements and felt that the second exemption, public interest justification, is a high threshold indeed. In effect an employee would have to provide that the needs of the organisation take precedence over the fundamental human right of the individual and whilst they will doubtless be assessed on a factual basis it is difficult to conceive of a factual matrix that would readily justify an enforced subject access request.

RIGHT TO PREVENT PROCESSING LIKELY TO CAUSE DAMAGE OR DISTRESS (S 10)

2.41 In addition to s 7 other important rights arise pursuant to s 10 which enables an individual, by notice in writing, to require the data controller to stop processing data for a specific purpose or in a specified manner where it is likely to cause the individual substantial damage or distress (to either him or to another) and such damage or distress would be unwarranted.

2.42 The use of s 10 is more limited. Service of an objection notice (pursuant to s 10) can only be made by a person objecting to the processing of their own personal data where processing that personal data is causing unwarranted and substantial damage or distress. The objection notice must specifically set out why the processing causes the unwarranted substantial damage or distress.

2.43 A person has no right to object to processing if:

- they have consented to the processing;
- the processing is necessary:
  (a) in relation to a contract that the individual has entered into; or
  (b) because the person requested that something be done in order that they be able to enter into a contract;
- the processing is necessary because of a legal obligation that applies to the person (but not a contractual obligation); or

- the processing is necessary to protect the person's 'vital interests'.

2.44 An objection may be made on behalf of another; however, an individual cannot object to the processing of data belonging to a third party.

2.45 In order to satisfy the grounds set out in s 10 an applicant must demonstrate that the data processing in question is causing or is likely to cause substantial damage or substantial distress to him or to another. 'Substantial damage' would include financial loss or physical harm; and 'substantial distress' would be a level of upset, or emotional or mental pain, that goes beyond annoyance or irritation, strong dislike, or a feeling that the processing is morally abhorrent.

2.46 The time for responding to a s 10 notice is 21 days; the response can include more detail where a mere 'yes' or 'no' would not suffice.

2.47 These are powerful provisions, the use of which should not be underestimated. In *Mikhael Anatolyevich Trushin v National Crime Agency*,[2] the claimant challenged the National Crime Agency (NCA) for use of his personal data in relation to the issue of an Interpol Red Notice. The Administrative Court (Foskett J) confirmed that the NCA was a data controller, for the purposes of the DPA 1998, and refused to strike-out the claim against the defendant that they had processed data contrary to the data protection principles.

2.48 A person may also serve an objection notice under s 11 of the DPA 1998. This is limited to personal data that is processed for the purpose of direct marketing. On receipt of such a notice it might be preferable to suppress rather than delete the person's details. This is for two reasons. First, deletion might fall foul of requirements in place at the time for the minimum retention period for that type of data. Second, suppression involves retaining only that level of information about that person in order that his/her wishes are respected in future. Suppression allows you to ensure that you do not send marketing to people who have asked you not to, and means that you have a record against which you can check any new marketing lists.

2.49 In terms of best practice an organisation might seek to discover and record a person's data preferences at the time data is provided by them. They can be asked to opt in or out of future marketing initiatives or other such foreseeable use of their information.

---

[2]   [2014] EWHC 3551 (Admin).

RIGHTS IN RELATION TO AUTOMATED DECISION MAKING (S 12)

2.50 There are also grounds to object, pursuant to s 12, where a decision is based purely on automated processing of information. Section 12 will not allow an objection to succeed where any human intervention or involvement occurs.

2.51 For s 12 to apply there are two essential prerequisites:

- The decision was made solely by/on the basis of the automated processing of data. It would not meet this requirement if a human made the decision after considering data that was processed by automated means even if that involved no more that exercising discretion.
- The decision in question has to have a significant effect on the person concerned. Significant means more than trivial and may need to be considered in terms of extent and duration. The significant effect would also have to flow from the decision so that there is sufficient nexus and causation.

2.52 In addition, some decisions will be exempt from objection. Similar to the exclusions that apply to s 7, in relation to s 12 an objection will not succeed where:

- a person has consented or it is required by legislation; or
- it was taken or prepared in relation to a contract with that person; and
- it was give the individual something they have asked for; or
- steps have been taken to safeguard the legitimate interests of the person such as allowing them to appeal the decision.

COMPENSATION FOR BREACH (S 13)

2.53 Where there is a breach then a claim for compensation can be made pursuant to s 13 through the courts. It will be a defence to show that there was not a breach as alleged or, if there was a breach, that there is a due diligence defence, namely that one took all reasonable care in the circumstances to avoid the breach. Reasonableness will include reference as to what was reasonably required to comply with the DPA 1998.

13 Compensation for failure to comply with certain requirements

(1) An individual who suffers damage by reason of any contravention by a data controller of any of the requirements of this Act is entitled to compensation from the data controller for that damage.

(2) An individual who suffers distress by reason of any contravention by a data controller of any of the requirements of this Act is entitled to compensation from the data controller for that distress if –

(a) the individual also suffers damage by reason of the contravention, or
(b) the contravention relates to the processing of personal data for the special purposes.

(3) In proceedings brought against a person by virtue of this section it is a defence to prove that he had taken such care as in all the circumstances was reasonably required to comply with the requirement concerned.

2.54 This section will provide a cause of action where any claimant can show (on the civil burden of proof, ie on the balance of probabilities) that there has been a breach of the DPA 1998 and that he has suffered damage as a result. There must be sufficient causation, ie a direct nexus between the breach and the damage suffered.

2.55 In *Halliday v Creation Consumer Finance Ltd*[3] the Court of Appeal said, however, that the claimant Halliday could **not** claim compensation for distress that was not caused by the actual data protection breach itself. Lady Justice Arden stated that in order to claim compensation:[4]

'... it is clear that the Claimant has to be an individual, that he has to have suffered distress, and that the distress has to have been caused by contravention by a data controller of any of the requirements of the Act.

In other words, this is a remedy which is not for distress at large but only for contravention of the data processing requirements. It also has to be distress suffered by the complainant and therefore would not include distress suffered by family members unless it was also suffered by him. When I say that it has to be caused by breach of the requirements of the Act, the distress which I accept Mr Halliday would have felt at the non-compliance of the order is not, at least directly, relevant because that is not distress by reason of the contravention by a data controller of the requirements of this Act. If the sole cause of the distress had been non-compliance with a court order, then that would have lain outside the Act unless it could be shown that it was in substance about the non-compliance with the Data Protection Act.'

2.56 The court said that as a matter of fact there was little evidence that Halliday had suffered distress as a result of the data protection breach:[5]

'There is, in addition, no contemporary evidence of any manifestation of injury to feelings and distress apart from what one would normally expect from frustration at these prolonged and protracted events.'

Creation Consumer Finance Ltd was, therefore, only required to pay £750 in substantial damages and a further £1 in nominal damages by way of compensation.

---

3   [2013] EWCA Civ 333, [2013] 3 CMLR 4, [2013] Info TLR 351.
4   At para [20].
5   See *Halliday v Creation Consumer Finance Ltd* [2013] EWCA Civ 333 at [35].

2.57 On the face of it the section seems only to allow compensation awards where there has been an element of financial loss so that financial loss alone or together with distress would succeed in an award.

2.58 However, in *Vidal-Hall et al v Google*[6] the Court of Appeal confirmed that under s 13 of the DPA 1998, individuals who suffer 'damage' by reason of any contravention, by a data controller, of any of the requirements of the Data Protection Act are entitled to compensation from the data controller for that damage. To date, pecuniary loss had been a prerequisite for 'damage' to be established. However, the court held that the scope of 'damage' under the DPA 1998 should be interpreted as including types of loss such as emotional distress resulting from the misuse of private information, without having to first establish that pecuniary loss had been suffered by a claimant. A claim under s 13 in a cyber context, and in the case of *Vidal-Hall*, are considered further in Chapter 4 (Cyber Property).

2.59 The scope of a s 13 claim appears to be widening and corporate bodies must be prepared to ensure they can defend the civil liability risk that will inevitably follow a data breach. The advent of group litigation orders, which may enable a class action, are a means by which those groups of individuals who may assert a claim for a data breach can bring a combined high value and reputationally destructive claim. Morrisons, a large supermarket chain, was recently subject to a group litigation order such that 5,954 current or former employees were permitted to combine a data breach claim flowing from an inside cyber leak when an employee deliberately disseminated personal data to the press.

2.60 The advent of group litigation orders, and the expansion of non-pecuniary damages being awarded without financial loss, may increase the number and size of claims against corporate defendants.

---

6   [2015] EWCA Civ 311.

CHAPTER 3

CIVIL LIABILITY AND REDRESS

CONTENTS *Para*

3.01 A cyber-attack will often involve some form of commercial fraud as well as criminality (see Chapter 1 (Cyber Crime)). This chapter looks at the various types of civil wrongs that will be relevant in these circumstances, together with the civil liability to third parties following a cyber-attack or data breach.

DECEIT

3.02 In most, if not all, cyber-attacks there will arguably be a false representation or statement by the perpetrator. Unauthorised access would, by implication, falsely represent the position or certainly withhold information or facts with accompanying falsehood (see *Peek v Gurney*[1]) and a statement or representation of fact in a claim for deceit can be implied from words or conduct (*Contex Drouzhba Ltd v Wiseman*[2]).

In *Ludsin Overseas Limited v ECO3 Capital Ltd*,[3] Jackson LJ set out the ingredients for the tort of deceit:

> '... What the cases show is that the tort of deceit contains four ingredients, namely:
>
> i)   The defendant makes a false representation to the claimant.
> ii) The defendant knows that the representation is false, alternatively he is reckless as to whether it is true or false.
> iii) The defendant intends that the claimant should act in reliance on it.

---

[1]   (1873) LR 6 HL 377.
[2]   [2007] EWCA Civ 1201.
[3]   [2013] EWCA Civ 413.

iv) The claimant does act in reliance on the representation and in consequence suffers loss.

Ingredient (i) describes what the defendant does. Ingredients (ii) and (iii) describe the defendant's state of mind. Ingredient (iv) describes what the claimant does.

I do not accept that 'intention to deceive' is a separate or free standing element of the tort of deceit. The phrase 'intention to deceive' is merely another way of describing the mental element of the tort. It is a compendious description of ingredients (ii) and (iii) as set out in the preceding paragraph.

In the present case ... all four ingredients of the tort of deceit were established.'

Provided such a representation of fact is accompanied by ingredients (ii), (iii) and (iv), then deceit is a highly effective pleading. A cyber-attack is likely to involve a perpetrator either knowing or being reckless as to the fact(s), (the entire purpose is to access and obtain data by deceit), thus satisfying (i) and (iii) and proof of dishonesty is likely to be evidenced by the very nature of the action and the stealth with which it is accomplished.

3.03 On the face of it (iv) seems problematic as a corporate or other victim may be entirely oblivious to events but once it has been established that the misrepresentation was made fraudulently then it is presumed that the victim/claimant was induced to act by it. The presumption is rebuttable but that will be a difficult argument for a hacker or other cyber perpetrator and, if the victim/claimant can show he/she thereby suffered financial loss, all requisite elements should be present and the claim should succeed.

3.04 The advantage of a claim based on deceit is that it allows further time to issue the claim, as the clock does not start running until the claimant is or should have been aware of the fraud (s 32 of the Limitation Act 1980). In many cases, there will be sufficient time to bring the claim, which will be of particular significance in those situations where the cause of action is not discovered until some considerable time later. Deceit also excludes defences such as contributory negligence and exclusion or limitation clauses will usually be of no avail. This may be particularly important where the perpetrator/defendant might seek to blame the claimant for defective systems or insufficient data security measures or other negligence. Damages will also be generous as deceit will result in recovery of all loss that flowed from the deceit regardless of whether it was reasonably foreseeable.

BREACH OF TRUST

3.05 Equity imposes special duties upon those who are held to owe a fiduciary duty to another. A person who owes a fiduciary duty to another may not place himself in a situation where he has a personal interest that may conflict with the interests of the person to whom he owes a fiduciary duty.

3.06 Where the attack made by an employee or director, often seeking to prepare the path for their next move or otherwise undermine the current employer/organisation, breach of trust/fiduciary duty may be pleaded as the cause of action.

3.07 In *Bristol and West Building Society v Mothew*,[4] the Court of Appeal identified the key features of the fiduciary relationship:

> 'The distinguishing obligation of a fiduciary is the obligation of loyalty. The principal is entitled to the single-minded loyalty of his fiduciary ... A fiduciary must act in good faith; he must not make a profit out of his trust; he must not place himself in a position where his duty and his interest may conflict.'

3.08 A high proportion of data breach attacks and cyber espionage will be the work of staff or others connected to the company who will, in all likelihood, have a clear and demonstrable fiduciary relationship and thus a duty not to harm. The advantage of a breach of trust claim is that profit need not have resulted nor the victim suffer any loss. Further it will be no defence for a fiduciary to assert he acted in all honesty or that fraud was absent: in placing himself in the incongruous position where duty and interest may be in conflict, he may be outside the special duty he owes his principal.

3.09 In the right circumstances this will greatly assist. An employee or director who uses cyber surveillance or unauthorised access or something less than can be shown to be in conflict with or undermine the organisation may give rise to an actionable breach of trust.

DISHONEST ASSISTANCE

3.10 A claim of dishonest assistance will also be available where the fiduciary relationship is present. Once that exists there would need to be:

- a causative breach;
- assistance of the breach;
- dishonesty.

3.11 This will be a useful cause of action in relation to other parties (the chain) who have assisted the breach; whilst there must be a breach of fiduciary duty that causes loss, the assistance given to any breach need only be more than of minimal importance in procuring or assisting the breach (of fiduciary duty) so that one need not prove that the assistance *itself* was causative of the loss.[5]

3.12 As for dishonesty, there is a combined objective and subjective test which, per Lord Hutton in *Twinsectra Ltd v Yardley*,[6]'requires ... it must be

---

[4] [1998] Ch 1.
[5] *Baden v Société Générale* [1993] 1 WLR 509.
[6] [2002] 2 AC 164.

established that the defendant's conduct was dishonest by the ordinary standards of reasonable and honest people and that he himself realised that by those standards his conduct was dishonest'. In *Barlow Clowes v Eurotrust*[7] the Privy Council established the test of dishonesty. The Privy Council accepted that although a dishonest state of mind was a subjective mental state, if, by ordinary standards, a defendant's mental state would be characterised as dishonest then it was 'irrelevant that the defendant judges by different standards'. Therefore a deliberate cyber breach would generally fall in to the category of requiring a dishonest mind by ordinary standards and it would be of no avail to a perpetrator to argue otherwise.

3.13   If the breach is by an insider or other fiduciary, then care should be taken as to causation since damages will only be available where it can be proven (on the balance of probabilities) that the loss resulted from the breach of fiduciary duty. This burden of proof would be on the claimant to show that the compensation claimed relates to the loss caused by the breach. We contend that in appropriate deliberate (and thus dishonest) cyber breach cases it ought to be straightforward by determining what would have happened but for the cyber breach (which was itself a breach of fiduciary duty). Caution should however be exercised where the loss sought to be recovered might be too remote from the breach and, therefore, will not be recoverable where the loss was attributable to the breach. An upgrade or improved cyber security expense might fall in to this trap if, for example, it could be properly said the victim would have taken those steps regardless of the fiduciary's breach.

CONVERSION

3.14   Conversion is a tort at common law that was codified by s 2(2) of the Torts (Interference with Goods) Act 1977 which states that:

> 'An action lies in conversion for loss or destruction of goods which a bailee has allowed to happen in breach of his duty to his bailor [that is to say, it lies in a case which is not otherwise conversion but would have been detinue before detinue was abolished].'

3.15   Conversion is a useful tool for cyber breaches as it is widely defined and would likely cover unauthorised interference with personal information and other types of cyber property that results from a cyber breach. A conversion occurs when a person interferes with the personal property of another, so as to amount to appropriating the property for himself. This inappropriate interference with personal property is sufficient for the conversion but it must be an intentional interference that is seriously inconsistent with the other person's possession. Any personal goods (save money as currency) can be subject to conversion.

---

[7]   [2006] 1 WLR 1476.

3.16 Damages are generally measured by the value of the goods (and thus the loss) at the time of conversion; so usually market value at the prevailing time will be the award. In addition, if the claimant incurs financial loss as a direct consequence of the conversion he may recover this as special damages in addition to the market value of the goods. A workman deprived of his tools additionally recovered loss of wages in *Bodley v Reynolds*.[8] The advantage of conversion as a cause of action is that dishonesty is not a prerequisite, only that the interference was intentional. Further remedies include delivery up of the goods and payment of consequential damages. If it is shown to the court's satisfaction that an order for delivery and payment of any consequential damages has not been complied with, the court may revoke the order (or the relevant part of it) and make an order for payment of damages by reference to the value of the goods (s 3(4)(a) and (b)).

3.17 Once the period of limitation has expired, the claimant's title to the goods is extinguished (s 3, Limitation Act 1980). Where there are successive conversions in respect of the same goods, whether by the same person or not, the cause of action is extinguished after 6 years from the first conversion. However, if the action is based on fraud, or if the right of action is concealed by fraud, the period of limitation (normally 6 years under the Act) does not begin to run until the claimant discovers or ought to have discovered the fraud (s 32).

3.18 Where the interference might fall short of being intentional, so that it might be intentional if taken at its highest level, but at its least it is negligent and direct, then trespass may provide a remedy.

TRESPASS

3.19 Trespass is the intentional or negligent interference with any personal goods. The interference must be direct and it would not include accidental interference where negligence was not present. For present purposes moving personal data or cyber property, transferring, deleting or causing injury to them would all fall within its ambit.

3.20 One word of warning: trespass and conversion are not available where the claimant was not in possession of the personal goods or did not have an immediate right to be in possession of them.

CONSPIRACY

3.21 The economic tort of conspiracy requires there to be two or more perpetrators who are legal persons who conspire '... to do an unlawful act, or to do a lawful act by unlawful means'.[9] This can include not only a natural person but also a corporate body. A company is capable of a conspiracy with its

---

[8] (1846) 8 QB 779.
[9] *Mulcahy v R* (1868) LR 3 HL 306.

own directors,[10] thus if a company is behind a cyber-attack then if the director/directors can be shown to have colluded the need to have at least two perpetrators will be met. Conspiracy requires an agreement or combination between the perpetrators to take steps that actually result in damage being caused to another legal person. There are two variants of this tort: unlawful means conspiracy and lawful means conspiracy, both of which are examined in turn below.

'Unlawful means conspiracy'

3.22 An unlawful means conspiracy requires the use of unlawful means to further the agreement or combination coupled with an intent to cause damage. Unlawful includes not only criminal acts but also any civil wrong[11] so that, in the context of a cyber-attack or data breach, there should be little difficulty in establishing an unlawful means conspiracy where harm actually resulted. In terms of *mens rea* the bar is set low; an intention to cause injury is sufficient. It need not be the overriding, predominant or only reason where unlawful means were employed and harm resulted. A civil breach would also be highly likely in the event of a cyber-attack and we submit that this variant will be an effective cause of action where the other pre-requisites are present.

'Lawful means conspiracy'

3.23 A lawful means conspiracy where unlawful means are absent but where it can be demonstrated that the perpetrators only or predominant purpose was to cause damage to the other legal person. We submit that in the context of a deliberate cyber-attack or other non-accidental breach the *mens rea* should be an easy element to satisfy for this variant which is capable of turning an act that might be lawful if taken by one legal person alone in to an actionable conspiracy if two or more take part.

3.24 Once liability is established then damages are 'at large' and not assessed on a narrow, loss calculation basis which makes conspiracy an attractive option.

3.25 In addition, where unlawful means are used there is no requirement that those means must be independently actionable at the suit of the claimant.[12] The use of those means has the effect of lowering the requisite intent that need be demonstrated. The position was put succinctly by Lord Bridge in *Lonrho Plc v Fayed*:[13]

> 'Where conspirators act with the predominant purpose of injuring the Plaintiff and in fact inflict damage on him, but do nothing which would have been actionable if done by an individual acting alone, it is in the fact of their concerted action for

---

[10]   See *Prudential Assurance Co Limited v Newman Industries Limited (No2)* [1982] Ch 204 CA.
[11]   See *Total Network SL v HMRC* [2008] UKHL 19.
[12]   See *Total Network SL v HMRC* [2008] UKHL 19 at **3.22** above.
[13]   [1992] 1 AC 448 at p 465.

that illegitimate purpose that the law, however anomalous it may now seem, finds a sufficient ground to condemn their action as illegal and tortious. But when conspirators intentionally injure the Plaintiff and use unlawful means to do so, it is no defence for them to show that their primary purpose was to further or protect their own interests; it is sufficient to make their action tortious that the means used were unlawful.'

3.26 The tort of conspiracy will readily lend itself to those types of cyber situations where at least two or more parties combine and actual damage is occasioned.

3.27 The tort of conspiracy differs from criminal conspiracy; for the latter it is the agreement itself that is central to the offence, actual harm need not result and the agreement would need to involve the commission of a criminal offence. A deliberate cyber-attack or data breach may thus constitute a criminal conspiracy as well as an actionable civil conspiracy.[14]

LIABILITY TO THIRD PARTIES

Directors' duties

3.28 A director who fails to prevent a cyber-attack or other data breach through inadequate cyber security measures or to mitigate the impact and consequential loss might be in breach of his duty to the company.

3.29 Section 172 of the CA 2006 provides that a director must act in the way he considers, in good faith, would be most likely to promote the success of the company for the benefit of its members as a whole, and in doing so have regard (amongst other matters) to:

(a) the likely consequences of any decision in the long term;

(b) the interests of the company's employees;

(c) the need to foster the company's business relationships with suppliers, customers and others;

(d) the impact of the company's operations on the community and the environment;

(e) the desirability of the company maintaining a reputation for high standards of business conduct; and

(f) the need to act fairly as between members of the company.

3.30 Section 172 may well render a director liable where he has failed to properly consider, address or implement sufficient cyber security systems and measures, or those fit for purpose as expected by the DPA (see Chapter 2) such that he has not promoted the success of the company 'for the benefit of its members as a whole' as required by s 172. It is not simply applying adequate

---

[14] See Chapter 1 for a full examination of cyber crime.

cyber security to meet the expected risks but also the need to have a data breach response plan that takes proper account of disclosure and transparency. A director may be liable on a number of levels including breaches of his duties, disclosure obligations and corporate governance.

3.31 In addition s 174 requires reasonable care, skill and diligence:

174 Duty to exercise reasonable care, skill and diligence

(1) A director of a company must exercise reasonable care, skill and diligence.

(2) This means the care, skill and diligence that would be exercised by a reasonably diligent person with –

(a) the general knowledge, skill and experience that may reasonably be expected of a person carrying out the functions carried out by the director in relation to the company, and
(b) the general knowledge, skill and experience that the director has.

3.32 The director responsible for cyber security must exercise reasonable care and skill in meeting their duty. This standard of care, skill and diligence is not fixed, and will vary depending upon the sensitivity or value of the data, trade secrets or other digital property at risk

3.33 The UK Corporate Governance Code may provide a useful starting point when considering whether directors have an appropriate skillset, and requisite knowledge to properly discharge their duties in relation to cyber security.

3.34 The Prospectus Rules provide further support where any UK listed company seeks to raise equity or debt on capital markets the prospectus must cite all risks that are pertinent to those involved in the exercise and the industry within which the company operates. We submit that this must expressly include the cyber risks that apply to the particular company and all the comprehensive specific detail as to the risk of a cyber-attack and the assets that might be exposed.

3.35 This is given a statutory footing (for UK listed companies) by s 414 of the Companies Act 2006 which requires an annual report to include, at s 414C(2):

(2) The strategic report must contain –

(a) a fair review of the company's business, and
(b) a description of the principal risks and uncertainties facing the company.

3.36 The principal risks and uncertainties would doubtless include cyber risk; it is presently hard to envisage any UK listed business that would not have any cyber reliance such that it was at some risk of cyber-attack or data breach. In the event of an attack a UK listed company would also then have to decide whether it was, pursuant to Disclosure and Transparency Rules, obliged to disclose the information, given the possible impact on share price, and that this cyber-attack might constitute inside information as the information is not generally available (not in the public domain), directly/indirectly affects the company, is sufficiently precise and would likely have a 'significant impact' on share value. Whether it is potentially 'significant' will require careful and minuted assessment. The decision (to disclose) will depend on the prevailing circumstances and the type of attack within the context of that particular business/industry.

Consumer rights

3.37　The Consumer Rights Act 2015 expressly created a new category of consumer protection for digital content. The Act has adopted the definition of 'digital content' used in the Consumer Rights Directive (2011/83/EU) to mean 'data which are produced and supplied in digital form'.

3.38　Examples of data produced in digital form include software, games, apps, ringtones, e-books, online journals and digital media such as music, film and television. Digital content may be supplied in tangible form (for example on a disk), or in intangible form such as downloaded, streamed, or accessed on the web.

3.39　The standards applicable to digital content are that it should be:

- of a satisfactory quality;
- fit for a particular purpose;
- in compliance with description;

3.40　Section 34 provides that every contract for the supply of digital content is to be treated as including a term that the quality of the digital content is satisfactory.

3.41　Section 35 provides that digital content be fit for a particular purpose where before the contract is made the consumer makes known to the trader (expressly or by implication) any particular purpose for which the consumer is contracting for the digital content.

3.42　Section 36 provides that every contract to supply digital content is to be treated as including a term that the digital content will match any description of it given by the trader to the consumer.

3.43　A business/trader will also remain responsible for any damage caused to a device or to other digital content by digital content it supplies, whether for payment or free of charge, where it has failed to exercise reasonable care and skill. In such cases the consumer may require the trader to either repair the damage or compensate the consumer for the damage.

3.44 Remedies to the consumer include the right to enforce contract terms about digital content, the right to repair or replacement and the right to refund or reduction.

CHAPTER 4

CYBER PROPERTY

INTRODUCTION

4.01 Manufacturing and electronics company Siemens believes that it can save $140million per year in energy costs, and decrease carbon emission by approximately 10,000 million tons per year.[1] These savings will not be generated through the invention of a new technological process but rather by the analysis and application of 'big data'. Big data is common parlance for an extremely large data set that may be analysed computationally to reveal patterns, trends, and associations. For Siemens the easiest return on investment that could be obtained from big data is to monitor the thermostats throughout its 300,000 buildings around the globe in order to regulate temperatures and save on energy costs.

4.02 However, big data is not restricted to the examination of technical processes. In fact big data is now more commonly used to determine patterns, trends, and associations relating to human behaviour and interactions. In an online context, where data is generated through everything, from shopping, communications, applications, to social media, the value created is vast. It is this value generated from the use of big data which we consider to be 'cyber property'.

4.03 In the context of this work cyber property should not be confused with intellectual property (IP). IP is information over which an individual or entity can assert a proprietary right, whether through copyright, trade mark or patent.

---

[1] Shacklett, Mary, *A perfect illustration of how the big data value chain works*, Tech Republic, 6 January 2017, http://www.techrepublic.com/article/a-perfect-illustration-of-how-the-big-data-value-chain-works/ (last accessed 10 January 2017).

Although this form of protection exists in a cyber context, and is dealt with at length in Chapter 6 (Commercial Espionage), the proprietary right attaches to information initially generated in a real world environment. Cyber property is different. Data relating to an internet user's browsing history has great value to a potential advertiser but does not fall within the sphere of IP. This information cannot be considered to be an artistic work, a sign capable of being represented graphically, or an industrial application to be registered as a patent. However, the access and use of this data generates profit for some of the biggest companies in the world, whether search engines or online retailers.

4.04 On the micro level, each constituent element of a big data set belongs to an individual. A person has provided the information, and companies should be aware that this data may fall within a person's private and family life. It belongs to the user and cannot be bought or sold without proper consideration of the law. Even if a company has no intention to profit from an individual's personal data, the Data Protection Act 1998 (DPA 1998) requires that a data controller, in other words an entity, processes data fairly (see Chapter 2 Civil Liability under the Data Protection Act). This chapter considers the potential litigation the holder of personal information could face from an individual who has suffered damage or distress by the use of their private information in an online context.

MISUSE OF PRIVATE INFORMATION

4.05 The House of Lords (Lord Bingham of Cornhill, Lord Hoffmann, Lord Hope of Craighead, Lord Hutton, Lord Scott of Foscote) in *Wainwright v Home Office*[2] affirmed that there was not a common law tort of invasion of privacy. However, the courts have had to grapple with how to afford appropriate protection to 'privacy rights' under Art 8 of the European Convention of Human Rights and Fundamental Freedoms (ECHR). The gap was bridged by developing and adapting the law of confidentiality to protect one aspect of invasion of privacy, specifically the misuse of private information. This addressed the tension between the requirement to give appropriate effect to the right to respect for private and family life set out in Art 8 of the ECHR and the common law's perpetual need for legal certainty.

4.06 In *A v B plc*,[3] Lord Woolf CJ, giving the judgment of the court, said, at [4], that Arts 8 and 10 of the ECHR provided new parameters within which the courts would decide actions for breach of confidence, and that the court could act in a way that was compatible with Convention rights, as it was required to do under s 6 of the DPA 1998, by 'absorbing the rights which Arts 8 and 10 protect into the long-established action for breach of confidence'.

4.07 There are now two separate and distinct causes of action: an action for breach of confidence; and one for misuse of private information. The tort of

---

2   [2004] 2 AC 406.
3   [2003] QB 195.

misuse of private information was properly established by the House of Lords in the case of *Campbell v MGN Ltd*,[4] with the speech of Lord Nicholls of Birkenhead seen as highly influential in this process of development.[5]

4.08 In *Campbell*, the claimant was the famous model, Naomi Campbell. The defendant newspaper published articles which disclosed her drug addiction, disclosed the fact that she was receiving therapy through a named self-help group, gave details of group meetings she attended and showed photographs of her in the street as she was leaving a group meeting. She sought damages against the newspaper for breach of confidentiality. The Court of Appeal allowed the newspaper's appeal, but Miss Campbell then succeeded in the House of Lords. Though the House was divided three to two (Lord Hope of Craighead, Baroness Hale of Richmond and Lord Carswell were in the majority, and Lord Nicholls and Lord Hoffmann were in the minority) the difference of opinion related to a narrow point arising on the facts of the case. In the statements of general principle as to the way in which the law should strike the balance between the right to privacy and the right to freedom of expression the court was unanimous.[6]

4.09 Now actions for breach of confidence and actions for misuse of private information rest on different legal foundations. They protect different interests: secret or confidential information on the one hand and privacy on the other. The focus of the actions therefore is also different. Lord Hoffmann described the 'shift in the centre of gravity' when the action for breach of confidence was used as a remedy for the unjustified publication of personal information. In those circumstances, he said, the focus was not on the duty of good faith applicable to confidential personal information and trade secrets alike, but the protection of human autonomy and dignity – the right to control the dissemination of information about one's private life and the right to the esteem and respect of other people.[7]

4.10 Commercial organisations working within a cyber context should be aware of both causes of action. Litigation in relation to breach of confidence is a vital tool to prevent commercial espionage (see Chapter 6) or the dissemination of information obtained by current or former employees (see Chapter 5). Alternatively an awareness of the law in relation to misuse of private information may be necessary to protect against claims made by customers, clients or users of a company's online environment. Lord Nicholls, in *OBG Ltd v Allan; Douglas v Hello! Ltd (No 3); Mainstream Properties Ltd v Young*,[8] highlighted the differences between these causes of action and illustrated the potential uses to be made by a claimant):[9]

---

[4] [2004] 2 AC 457.
[5] See *Campbell*, at [11]–[22].
[6] See *Campbell*, per Lord Hoffmann, at [36].
[7] See *Campbell*, at [51].
[8] [2007] UKHR 21, [2008] AC 1.
[9] See *Douglas v Hello!*, at [255].

'As the law has developed breach of confidence, or misuse of confidential information, now covers two distinct causes of action, protecting two different interests: privacy, and secret ("confidential") information. It is important to keep these two distinct. In some instances information may qualify for protection both on grounds of privacy and confidentiality. In other instances information may be in the public domain, and not qualify for protection as confidential, and yet qualify for protection on the grounds of privacy. Privacy can be invaded by further publication of information or photographs already disclosed to the public. Conversely, and obviously, a trade secret may be protected as confidential information even though no question of personal privacy is involved.'

Misuse of private information in a cyber context

4.11   The case of *Vidal-Hall and others v Google Inc*[10] illustrates the potential misuse of private information within a cyber context. The case concerned the operation of the 'Safari workaround'. Google had secretly tracked private information about the claimants' internet usage, via the use of 'cookies', a small string of text saved on the user's device, without their knowledge or consent and given the information to third parties. This was contrary to Google's publicly stated position that such activity would not be performed without users' consent. The browser-generated information (BGI) was obtained through the claimants' use of the Apple Safari browser, and allowed the defendant to recognise the browser sending the BGI. The BGI was then aggregated and used by the defendant as part of its commercial offering to advertisers via its 'doubleclick' advertising service. This meant advertisers could select advertisements targeted or tailored to the claimants' interests, as deduced from the collected BGI, which could be and were displayed on the screens of the claimants' computer devices. This revealed private information about the claimants, which was or might have been seen by third parties.

4.12   The claimants' brought an action under misuse of private information, and on the basis that they had suffered damaged through the process of their personal data (see DPA 1998, s 13 below). The Court of Appeal (Lord Dyson MR, McFarlane LJ, Sharp LJ) was required to decide preliminary issues, rather than deciding substantive issues of fact; however, the court held that there was a serious issue of law to be tried, and that the judge was entitled to conclude that it was 'clearly arguable' that there was a claim for misuse of private information and one under the DPA 1998:[11]

'On the face of it, these claims raise serious issues which merit a trial. They concern what is alleged to have been the secret and blanket tracking and collation of information, often of an extremely private nature, as specified in the confidential schedules, about and associated with the claimants' internet use, and the subsequent use of that information for about nine months. The case relates to the anxiety and distress this intrusion on autonomy has caused.'

---

10   [2015] EWCA Civ 311, [2015] 3 WLR 40.
11   See *Vidal-Hall*, at [137].

4.13 Companies with an online presence must be aware of the potential litigation which may arise if this information is used without appropriate consent. What is reasonable will be dependent upon the circumstances of the company and the nature of the information collected. Furthermore, what constitutes appropriate consent now, for example a tick-box where a user could opt-out of providing consent, may not be acceptable under the General Data Protection Regulation, which will soon be introduced (see Chapter 12 (Legal Environment post-Brexit)). Advice should be sought if there is any concern.

Jurisdiction

4.14 An action in misuse of private information can be pursued against an individual or company outside of the jurisdiction with the permission of the court, in accordance with the Civil Procedure Rules (CPR), r 6.36 and Practice Direction 6B supplementing CPR, Pt 6. In order to obtain permission, the claimants must establish that:

(i) there is a serious issue to be tried on the merits of the claims (ie, that the claim raises a substantial issue of fact or law or both);

(ii) there is a good arguable case that the claims falls within one of the jurisdictional gateways set out in Practice Direction 6B;

(iii) in all the circumstances England and Wales is clearly or distinctly the appropriate forum for the trial of the dispute; and

(iv) in all the circumstances the court ought to exercise its discretion to permit service of the proceedings out of the jurisdiction.[12]

4.15 The permissibility of service outside of the jurisdiction was confirmed by the Court of Appeal in *Vidal-Hall*, at [51]:

'... we have concluded in agreement with the judge that misuse of private information should now be recognised as a tort for the purposes of service out the jurisdiction.'

DATA PROTECTION ACT 1998

4.16 The DPA 1998 was intended to implement Directive 95/46/EC (Personal Data Directive) on the protection of individuals with regard to the processing of personal data and on the free movement of such data. The DPA 1998, s 13 provides a cause of action for an individual who has suffered damage by reason of a data controller's contravention of the DPA 1998 in relation to that individual's personal data. The relevant sections are set out below:

1. Basic interpretative provisions.

(1) In this Act, unless the context otherwise requires –

---

[12] See *Altimo Holdings and Investment Ltd v Kyrgyz Mobil Tel Ltd)* [2012] 1 WLR 1804.

'personal data' means data which relate to a living individual who can be identified –

(a)   from those data, or

(b)   from those data and other information which is in the possession of, or is likely to come into the possession of, the data controller,

3. The special purposes

In this Act 'the special purposes' means any one or more of the following –

(a)   the purposes of journalism,

(b)   artistic purposes, and

(c)   literary purposes.

13. Compensation for failure to comply with certain requirements

(1)   An individual who suffers damage by reason of any contravention by a data controller of any of the requirements of this Act is entitled to compensation from the data controller for that damage.

(2)   An individual who suffers distress by reason of any contravention by a data controller of any of the requirements of this Act is entitled to compensation from the data controller for that distress if –

(a)   the individual also suffers damage by reason of the contravention, or

(b)   the contravention relates to the processing of personal data for the special purposes.

(3)   In proceedings brought against a person by virtue of this section it is a defence to prove that he had taken such care as in all the circumstances was reasonably required to comply with the requirement concerned.'

4.17   The Personal Data Directive as a whole is aimed at safeguarding privacy rights in the context of data management. This is repeatedly emphasised in the recitals (see Recital 2, 7, 10 and 11) and within the *'Objective of the Directive'*:

Object of the Directive

Article 1

In accordance with this Directive, member states shall protect the fundamental rights and freedoms of natural persons, and in particular their right to privacy with respect to the processing of personal data.

Article 23

(1)   Member states shall provide that any person who has suffered damage as a result of an unlawful processing operation or of any act incompatible with the national provisions adopted pursuant to this Directive is entitled to receive compensation from the controller for the damage suffered.

4.18   In a cyber context the protection of privacy should not be restricted to the consideration of personal data as identification by name, which is plainly incorrect when one considers the definition of personal data in the DPA 1998, s 1. Computerised files registering personal data usually assign a unique identifier to the person's registered, and web traffic surveillance tools make it easy to identify the behaviour of a machine and, behind the machine, that of its user. An individual's personality can, therefore, be pieced together in order to attribute certain decisions to that user, without ever seeking to discover the name and address of the individual. It is possible to categorise this person on the basis of socio-economic, psychological, philosophical or other criteria and attribute certain decisions to the user. In other words, 'the possibility of identifying an individual no longer necessarily means the ability to find out his or her name'.[13] Identification for the purposes of data protection is about data that 'individuates'[14] the individual, in the sense that they are singled out and distinguished from all others.

4.19　Greater guidance on specific identifies can be found from The Working Party on the Protection of Individuals with regard to the Processing of Personal Data, set up under Art 29 of the Personal Data Directive:[15]

> 'The Working Party has considered IP addresses as data relating to an identifiable person. It has stated that "Internet access providers and managers of local area networks can, using reasonable means, identify internet users to whom they have attributed IP addresses as they normally systematically 'log' in a file the date, time, duration and dynamic IP address given to the internet user". The same can be said about Internet Service Providers that keep a logbook on the HTTP server.'

4.20　Companies using or retaining 'big data' must be aware that any damage to an individual is actionable under the DPA 1998 if the processing of personal data is conducted in a way that is contrary to the data protection principles (see DPA 1998, Sch 1–4, and Chapter 2 (Civil Liability under the Data Protection Act)).

DAMAGES

4.21　Compensation is recoverable under s 13(1) for any damage suffered as a result of a contravention by a data controller of any of the requirements of the DPA 1998 whether pecuniary or non-pecuniary loss.[16]

4.22　The Court of Appeal has concluded that this is the correct interpretation of the Personal Data Directive using the principle in *Benkharbouche*:[17]

---

[13]　The Working Party on the Protection of Individuals with regard to the Processing of Personal Data, Opinion (No 4/2007) on the concept of personal data (WP 136 adopted on 20 June), at p 14.

[14]　'In general terms, a natural person can be considered as 'identified' when, within a group of persons, he or she is 'distinguished' from all other members of the group. Accordingly, the natural person is 'identifiable' when, although the person has not been identified yet, it is possible to do it ...' ibid, at p 12.

[15]　Ibid, at p 16.

[16]　See *Vidal-Hall*, at [105].

[17]　[2015] 3 WLR 301.

'Since what the Directive purports to protect is privacy rather than economic rights, it would be strange if the Directive could not compensate those individuals whose data privacy had been invaded by a data controller so as to cause them emotional distress (but not pecuniary damage). It is the distressing invasion of privacy which must be taken to be the primary form of damage (commonly referred to in the European context as "moral damage") and the data subject should have an effective remedy in respect of that damage. Furthermore, it is irrational to treat EU data protection law as permitting a more restrictive approach to the recovery of damages than is available under article 8 of the Convention. It is irrational because, as we have seen at paras 56-57 above, the object of the Directive is to ensure that data processing systems protect and respect the fundamental rights and freedoms of individuals "notably the right to privacy, which is recognised both in article 8 of the [Convention] and in the general principles of Community law": recital (10). The enforcement of privacy rights under article 8 of the Convention has always permitted recovery of non-pecuniary loss.'[18]

4.23 In most instances, processing personal data in a manner which contravenes a data protection principle will not result in pecuniary loss. Previously the courts would find nominal damages, in accordance with DPA 1998, s 13(2)(a), that that claimants might also be awarded damages in relation to distress.[19]

4.24 *Vidal-Hall* has now clarified the position. Non-pecuniary loss can now be claimed even where there is no pecuniary loss, or the contravention relates to the processing of personal data for the special purposes. Processing personal data in accordance with the data protection principles is essential to avoid the risk of litigation.

INTERCEPTION OF TELECOMMUNICATIONS

4.25 In 1997 the European Parliament and Council issued Directive 97/66/EC concerning the processing of personal data and the protection of privacy in the telecommunications sector (the 1997 Directive). The Regulation of Investigatory Powers Act 2000 (RIPA 2000) was, in part, enacted to implement Art 5 of the 1997 Directive, which required member states to safeguard the confidentiality of communications:

Article 5 Confidentiality of the communications

1. Member States shall ensure via national regulations the confidentiality of communications by means of a public telecommunications network and publicly available telecommunications services. In particular, they shall prohibit listening, tapping, storage or other kinds of interception or surveillance of communications, by others than users, without the consent of the users concerned, except when legally authorised, in accordance with Article 14(1).

---

[18] See *Vidal-Hall*, at [77].
[19] See *Halliday v Creation Consumer Finance Ltd* [2013] 3 CMLR 4.

2. Paragraph 1 shall not affect any legally authorised recording of communications in the course of lawful business practice for the purpose of providing evidence of a commercial transaction or of any other business communication.

4.26 In accordance with RIPA 2000, s 1, it is a criminal offence to intercept private information, which is transmitted through a public telecommunication system. The definition of interception is provided at RIPA 2000, s 2(2):

2 Meaning and location of 'interception' etc

(2) For the purposes of this Act, but subject to the following provisions of this section, a person intercepts a communication in the course of its transmission by means of a telecommunication system if, and only if, he –

(a)   so modifies or interferes with the system, or its operation,
(b)   so monitors transmissions made by means of the system, or
(c)   so monitors transmissions made by wireless telegraphy to or from apparatus comprised in the system,

as to make some or all of the contents of the communication available, while being transmitted, to a person other than the sender or intended recipient of the communication.

4.27 Following the enactment of RIPA 2000, in 2002 the European Parliament and Council adopted Directive 2002/58/EC concerning the processing of personal data and the protection of privacy in the electronic communications sector (the 2002 Directive) which repealed the 1997 Directive. The 'Scope and Aim' of the 2002 Directive is copied below:

Article 1

Scope and aim

1. This Directive harmonises the provisions of the Member States required to ensure an equivalent level of protection of fundamental rights and freedoms, and in particular the right to privacy, with respect to the processing of personal data in the electronic communication sector and to ensure the free movement of such data and of electronic communication equipment and services in the Community.

4.28 The 2002 Directive defined 'communication' to included 'any information exchanged or conveyed between a finite number of parties by means of a publicly available electronic communications service' and extended the scope to 'electronic mail', which included 'any text, voice, sound or image message sent over a public communications network which can be stored in the network or in the recipient's terminal equipment until it is collected by the recipient'. (See Art 2.)

4.29 Article 5 in the 2002 Directive, like the 1997 Directive, prohibits 'listening, tapping or storage' of communications; however, provides an exception for 'technical storage' which is necessary for the conveyance of a communication, as long as there was no prejudice to the principle of confidentiality. The storage of voicemail messages or emails on a central system would, therefore, be permissible.

4.30 The interception of a communication in the course of its transmission by means of a telecommunication system has been interpreted to include accessing emails,[20] and may extend to a period after the intended recipient has read or listened to the communication.[21] However, in *Coulson*, the Court of Appeal (Lord Judge LCJ, Lloyd Jones LJ, Openshaw J) held that whether a communication was in the course of transmission will depend on the technology used. In that case, journalists were *'accessing'* voicemail messages from the answerphone systems of famous individuals. Approving the comments of Fulford LJ, the court drew a distinction with emails that are 'collected'. If an email has been downloaded from a central server onto a computer it has ceased to be 'in the course of transmission' and therefore does not fall within the s 1 offence. With a voicemail, which can be accessed repeatedly and is never downloaded onto a mobile telephone, it remains 'in the course of transmission' until it is deleted (see *Coulson*, at [22]).

4.31 Arguably therefore, an email which is accessed from a central server, for example when using an online Gmail or Yahoo account, is always in the course of transmission, and anyone accessing that account without the permission of the owner would be committing the interception offence by monitoring transmissions made by means of the system.

4.32 The Investigatory Powers Act 2016 (IPA 2016) will repeal and replace the s 1 offence in RIPA 2000. It is worth noting that when the relevant provisions of the IPA 2016 come into force (IPA 2016, ss 3–6) the offence will be extended to include the interception of transmissions by means of 'a private telecommunication system' (see IPA 2016, s 3(1)(a)(ii)). An individual is not guilty of the offence if they have a right to the use the system or express or implied consent; however, this may still have significant implications for those within a company who seek to access employee emails. It may be the case that specific provisions are added to employee contracts to provide explicit consent to access.

Compulsion to provide private information

4.33 As well as enforcing a prohibition on the access of private information, Part III of RIPA 2000 provides a power to compel a person to provide private information if served with a 'notice requiring disclosure'. A disclosure requirement in respect of any protected information may be made if it is necessary in the interests of national security; for the purpose of preventing or detecting crime; or in the interests of the economic well-being of the United

---

[20] See *R (Ntl Group Ltd) v Crown Court at Ipswich* [2002] EWHC 1585 (Admin).
[21] See *Coulson* [2013] EWCA Crim 1026, [2014] 1 WLR 1119.

Kingdom (see RIPA 2000, s 49(3)). Once a disclosure notice has been served on an individual it is a criminal offence not to abide by the notice (see RIPA 2000, s 53).

4.34 The Court of Appeal (Sir Igor Judge PQBD, Penry-Davey J, Simon J) in *R v S*[22] held that a person served with a notice requiring disclosure could not rely on the principle against self-incrimination, which is incumbent within the right to a fair trial protected by Art 6 of the ECHR.

4.35 In *Padellec*,[23] the Court of Appeal (Sir John Thomas PQBD, Collins J, Singh J) held that where a disclosure notice had been served for the purpose of preventing or detecting crime, and the person upon whom the notice had been served had disregarded it, the sentence to be imposed should be greater than that for the suspected underlying offence:[24]

> 'The offence in question, as the learned judge indicated in the course of his sentencing remarks, had some analogy to the offence of failing to provide a specimen in relation to a breathalyser. In that sort of situation the court would be bound to assume the worst because otherwise, unless of course there was some excuse put forward which was honestly held, even if unreasonable, the failure to give access was because there was a need to hide something which was there, in the knowledge that what was there might well produce a substantial penalty.
>
> It follows from that that it is appropriate to impose a higher sentence than would be according to the guidelines in relation to the indecent material. As we say, the assumption will inevitably be that there is a need to hide because there is material which is clearly such as would produce a serious penalty.'

THE FREEDOM OF INFORMATION ACT 2000

4.36 The Freedom of Information Act 2000 (FIA 2000) is another route through which private information can be accessed when held by a public authorities. The purpose and rational is that the public have a right to access official information. This differs from the request for access to personal information that might be made by means of a subject access request under the DPA 1998 (see Chapter 2 (Civil Liability under the Data Protection Act)). The FIA 2000 does not give people access to their own personal data, such as their health records or credit reference file, but instead places an obligation on public authorities to publish certain information about their activities. Individuals are entitled to request this information from public authorities. Public authorities include government departments, local authorities, the NHS, state schools and police forces. However, the Act does not necessarily cover every organisation that receives public money.

---

[22] [2008] EWCA Crim 2177.
[23] [2012] EWCA Crim 1956.
[24] See *Padellec*, at [8]–[9].

4.37 Pursuant to s 1(1):

> Any person making a request for information to a public authority is entitled –
>
> (a) to be informed in writing by the public authority whether it holds information of the description specified in the request, and
> (b) if that is the case, to have that information communicated to him.

4.38 This right is subject to extensive exemptions and considerations that allow the refusal of a request. Part II of the Act sets out a lengthy list of exempt information that need not be provided including, *inter alia*, information that is already accessible; will cause prejudice to an audit function; or will prejudice commercial interest. Request can also be refused on the grounds that: it would cost too much or take too much staff time to deal with the request; the request is vexatious; or the request repeats a previous request from the same person.

4.39 It is worth noting that the obligations of a data controller, under the DPA 1998, are not overridden by the FIA 2000. An FIA 2000 application from a third party that results in the release of personal data is actionable by an individual that has suffered damage, under s 13 of the DPA 1998.

CHAPTER 5

EMPLOYER LIABILITY AND PROTECTION

INTRODUCTION

5.01 The single biggest threat to a business's confidential information is from its employees or other insiders. Empirical data provides a comprehensive illustration of employees acquiring and removing information whether to secure future employment or to use in direct competition to an employer.

5.02 In the 2014 Verizon 'Data Breach Investigation Report',[1] the authors identified that in 95% of cases, misappropriation of data by an employee was to 'secure their next move'. The Data Breach Investigation Report, relied upon the statistics contained in 'The Recover Report', published by Mishcon de Reya, which established that in 65% of cases 'information theft by rogue employees' was undertaken to use the information in a new role with an existing competitor. In 30% of cases, the thief planned to use the data to set up a competing business.[2]

5.03 The prevalence of such employee action is not uncommon. The vast majority of those taking information (two-thirds) felt that they had a right to remove the data because they had been 'involved in the creation'; with a third believing that there would be an expectation to bring such information with them to a new employer. An earlier study into UK-based employees found that

---

[1] Verizon Enterprise Solutions, *Data Breach Investigation Report* (2014), p 24.
[2] Mishcon de Reya, *The Recovery Report* (2014), p 3.

58% of workers said that they would take confidential data if faced with redundancy, and 40% were already storing confidential information to enhance their value in the job market.[3]

5.04 Anecdotally, case-law further demonstrates that existing employees may stockpile information not only for future use in competition but potentially to illegitimately secure their current position through threats and extortion.[4] This chapter seeks to identify the methods by which employers can protect information, and immediate practical steps when a data breach is discovered.

5.05 The common online nature of most businesses presents an increased danger to employers through the vicarious liability of their employees. In the context of cyber law, this could include the act of an employee visiting a particular offending website, to emails containing inappropriate content.

5.06 Cases which have resulted from such computer misuse by employees have included claims for discrimination in the workplace, health and safety breaches and harassment. Matters outside the scope of this work also include the sharing of unwanted sexually explicit material to individuals and even defamatory statements.

5.07 An employer is unable to utilise current statute law to seek protection from such activity. A company cannot intercept emails, for example, and compliance departments are left to use a monitoring role to seek to control such misuse. The only effective recourse is for an employer, by virtue of incorporation into the contract of employment with its employees, to obtain acceptance of the proper use of the internet and email whilst at work, with the ultimate sanction for breach being disciplinary action and ultimately summary dismissal.

CONFIDENTIAL INFORMATION

5.08 In determining the type of information which is 'confidential' to the employer, there is a difference between information which can be regarded as the employer's property, and that which has become part of the employee's general knowledge through his increased skills and experience gained simply as a result of working for the employer. In *FSS Travel & Leisure Systems Ltd v Johnson*,[5] the Court of Appeal (Lord Woolf MR; Millett LJ, Mummery LJ) observed that it must be possible to identify how the information is used in the relevant business, and that the use and dissemination will likely cause to harm the employer:[6]

---

3   John Hull, 'When your employees leave, so does your data: a case note on Intercity Telecom Limited v Solanki, Computer and Telecommunications Law Review' [2015] CTLR 129.
4   See *Brandeaux Advisers (UK) v Chadwick* [2010] EWHC 3241 (QB), [2011] IRLR 224.
5   [1999] FSR 505.
6   See *FSS Travel & Leisure Systems Ltd*, at 512.

'[T]he problem in making a distinction between general skill and knowledge, which every employee can take with him when he leaves, and secret or confidential information, which he may be restrained from using, is one of definition. It must be possible to identify information used in the relevant business, the use and dissemination of which is likely to harm the employer, and establish that the employer has limited dissemination and not, for example, encouraged or permitted its widespread publication.'

5.09 Often an employer seeks to protect against the disclosure of confidential information by relying on an implied obligation of confidentiality both during the currency of employment and post-termination. In *Faccenda Chicken Ltd v Fowler*[7] the Court of Appeal (Kerr LJ, Neill LJ, Nourse LJ) held that, in order to determine whether information could be protected after termination of employment, under the implied duty of confidentiality, a court should have regard to 'the nature of the employment' and 'the nature of the information':[8]

'In order to determine whether any particular item of information falls within the implied term so as to prevent its use or disclosure by an employee after his employment has ceased, it is necessary to consider all the circumstances of the case. We are satisfied that the following matters are among those to which attention must be paid:

(a)   The nature of the employment. Thus employment in a capacity where 'confidential' material is habitually handled may impose a high obligation of confidentiality because the employee can be expected to realise its sensitive nature to a greater extent than if he were employed in a capacity where such material reaches him only occasionally or incidentally.

(b)   The nature of the information itself. In our judgment the information will only be protected if it can properly be classed as a trade secret or as material which, while not properly to be described as a trade secret, is in all the circumstances of such a highly confidential nature as to require the same protection as a trade secret eo nomine. The restrictive covenant cases demonstrate that a covenant will not be upheld on the basis of the status of the information which might be disclosed by the former employee if he is not restrained, unless it can be regarded as a trade secret or the equivalent of a trade secret.'

5.10 The duty of confidentiality will arise where the employee's role requires routine handling of confidential information, so that he ought to be aware of its sensitivity, and the employee has been informed as to the confidentiality of the information. The information itself must properly be characterised as a trade secret or similarly highly confidential to be protected post-termination, and be separable from other information which the employee would be free to use or disclose.

5.11 An employer can have no legitimate interest in protecting information which is not confidential because, for example, it has already been published or where publication would not harm the employer's business interests. The High

---

[7]   [1987] Ch 117.
[8]   See *Faccenda Chicken Ltd*, at 137.

Court (Sir Robert Megarry VC), in *Thomas Marshall (Exports) Ltd v Guinle*,[9] provided a four-part test for confidential information or trade secrets which the court will protect:[10]

> 'First, I think that the information must be information the release of which the owner believes would be injurious to him or of advantage to his rivals or others. Second, I think the owner must believe that the information is confidential or secret, i.e., that it is not already in the public domain. It may be that some or all of his rivals already have the information: but as long as the owner believes it to be confidential I think he is entitled to try and protect it. Third, I think that the owner's belief under the two previous heads must be reasonable. Fourth, I think that the information must be judged in the light of the usage and practices of the particular industry or trade concerned. It may be that information which does not satisfy all these requirements may be entitled to protection as confidential information or trade secrets: but I think that any information which does satisfy them must be of a type which is entitled to protection.'

5.12 Whether an employer can protect information will depend on the nature of the information, the commercial damage which might be done to the employer and the extent to which the confidentiality of the material was explained to the employee or would have been apparent. If an employer can establish that information was confidential the misuse of that information, for example, by providing it to a competitor is readily actionable within the courts.

Crowson Fabrics Ltd v Rider[11]

5.13 In *Crowson v Rider*, Crowson Fabrics Ltd, the claimant, was engaged in the design, production and supply of fabrics for home and commercial furnishings and decoration. The chairman and sole shareholder, did not attend to the business full time but maintained hands-on control by proxy. In effect, all the important decisions about the business were made by him, albeit from afar. The first defendant, Paul Rider, was the Product and Distribution Director although it was suggested that he had 'no legal responsibilities'.[12] He was part of the senior management of the company and was one of the inner circle on whom the chairman relied. The second defendant, Warren Stimson, was the UK and Export Sales Manager. His salary was greater than the first defendant's; however, he was not invited into strategic meetings by the chairman. There were no restrictive covenants within the employment contracts of either defendant.

5.14 The claimant asserted that both defendants had access to confidential information, specifically customer contact and supply information, and that a database right subsisted in the systematic and methodical arrangement of this information.

---

9   [1979] Ch 227.
10   See *Thomas Marshall (Exports) Ltd*, at 248.
11   [2007] EWHC 2942 (Ch), [2008] FSR 17.
12   See *Crowson v Rider*, at [21].

5.15 In January 2007, the defendants decided to set up in competition to the claimant. Whilst employed they prepared a document using the claimant's computers showing the various steps they intended to take to set up the business. The defendants sequentially handed-in their notice but did not tell the claimant of their intention to form a rival company.

5.16 While working his notice the first defendant was asked to prepare a 'Supplier Bible'. He also compiled a spreadsheet entitled 'Concept forecast sales by customer' which listed 3,500 of the claimant's customers with sales figures. The second defendant used the claimant's email system to contact customers, and notify them of the rival company. The third defendant, Concept Textiles Ltd, (Concept) was subsequently incorporated by the defendants.

5.17 The claimant contended that the first defendant as an employee owed a duty of good faith and fidelity and was subject to an implied obligation not to copy, remove or misuse any of the claimant's confidential business information. The claimant also contended that, by virtue of the seniority of his employment, the first defendant owed a fiduciary duty to act in good faith: not to act so as to place himself in a position of conflict of interest; a duty not to use or cause to be used any information or opportunity available to him by reason of his employment and his position as a fiduciary other than to further the interests of the claimant; a duty to account to the claimant for any personal gain or profit made using such information or opportunity; and a duty to disclose to the claimant any misconduct or breach of contract, or duty, by himself or the second defendant. The claimant also contended that the second defendant was subject to the same employee obligations and fiduciary duties.

5.18 In response, the defendants claimed that none of the material that they had created or used or retained at the end of their employment contained any confidential information. All of the material was, they said, available in the public domain. They also contended that all of the material was part of their own gathered knowledge acquired over the course of their employment which they were free to use after termination, and that the claimant could not prevent an ex-employee, in the absence of a restrictive covenant, from using that knowledge and experience. They further submitted that there had been no copying of the claimant's database. It was accepted, under cross-examination, that they had had discussions with a major supplier and had had dealings with one of the claimant's sales agents whilst working out their notice.

5.19 The High Court (Peter Smith J) established that the first defendant was a fiduciary, and that both the first and second defendant had breached their duties of fidelity not to copy and retain information, such as the Supplier Bible, and not to communicate with the claimant's customers to solicit them to their rival company):[13]

---

[13]   See *Crowson v Rider*, at [86]–[87].

'I doubt whether in fact there is any significance as to whether or not Mr Rider and Mr Stimson were employees or whether they owed in addition fiduciary duties save that it can be said that Mr Rider had an obligation to disclose his own breaches and those of Mr Stimson and he was in breach of that duty. I have already observed that the copying and retention of the claimant's documents was done with the intention of benefiting themselves when they set up in their new business. That in my view is a plain breach of fidelity as an employee and would clearly be a breach of any fiduciary duty owed by Mr Rider.'

5.20 However, the information identified by the claimant as being its confidential information did not have the necessary indicia of confidence. All the information was either in the public domain, was easily discoverable by the defendants, or was in their heads. The material claimed to be confidential information was information that an employee, as part of his duty of fidelity, would have to keep confidential whilst in employment or in a fiduciary relationship with the claimant. An ex-employee could not be prevented from using material that was in the public domain provided he obtained it from the public domain. It was not possible to prevent an ex-employee from using his own gathered skills and expertise earned over the period of his employment. If by using his own memory and skills he could recall materials which were confidential whilst he was an employee he could nevertheless use them post-employment. The only information that was capable of being protected post-termination was in the nature of a trade secret:[14]

'I accept the evidence of Mr Rider and Mr Stimson... that all of the information alleged to be confidential was either in the public domain or was easily discoverable by them ... or was in their heads. I do not accept it was necessarily easily discoverable. The documents they took appear to me to afford a considerable saving of time. However detailed consideration of that might well be postponed to the question of damages or other financial relief that is ultimately granted ...

The only item which I had a lingering doubt over was information about the sales figures and profit margins. The reality, however, I suspect is that the profit margins are things which they would regularly carry out in their heads and the actual prices paid to suppliers or obtained from customers would be obtained from those organisations ...

In other words I accept the defendants' submission that the confidential information so described by the claimant does not have the necessary indicia of the quality of confidence identified by Megarry V.C. in *Thomas Marshall (Exports) Ltd v Guinle* [1979] Ch. 227; [1979] F.S.R. 208, Ch D ...

Accordingly the claimant has failed to establish that any of the information that they allege to be confidential is confidential to such an extent that they can prevent the defendants from using that information post termination of their employment provided it is used in a legitimate way.'

---

[14] See *Crowson v Rider*, at [101]–[105].

5.21 In addressing whether the defendants had obtained the information in a legitimate way the judge made it clear that an employee who deliberately copies, 'or even deliberately memorises information for use post termination' has obtained that material in an illegitimate way and an order can be made for delivery of such information.[15]

5.22 Finally, the judge addressed the database right. It was not challenged that the claimant had made a substantial investment in verifying or presenting the contents of its computer database. Those contents were arranged in a systematic or methodical way and were individually accessible by electronic or other means. The claimant had established a database right and he was the owner of that right. The defendants' admitted actions amounted to extraction of a substantial part of the claimant's database, when transferring to the computer system of the new rival company, Concept:[16]

> 'The defendants submit there has been no copying of the database. However the claimant's case is based on extraction and I do not see how the admitted actions can be anything other than an extraction. Further it is clear that the extraction has been substantial. The extraction of confidential item 2 is the clearest possible example of substantial extraction. It is the act of transfer to Concept's computer that is the extraction and not as the defendants submit the minimal use they subsequently made of it. I do not accept the extent of the use by the defendants is clearly established at this stage but it does not help them if they extract substantial parts of the database. They do not take it in my view for any reason other than to use it as they need from time to time.'

5.23 *Crowson v Rider* demonstrates that establishing that information is confidential is not straightforward but that in failing to meet the required threshold tests an employer is not without protection.

Brandeaux Advisers (UK) Ltd v Chadwick[17]

5.24 In *Brandeaux v Chadwick*, an employee transferred vast amounts of confidential information to her personal computer not to enter into competition but with a view to using it in the future should a regulatory dispute emerge.

5.25 In the course of a redundancy meeting the defendant threatened to report the claimant company to the industry regulator unless she was offered another role within the company. She was immediately placed on gardening leave and, upon finding that she had transferred confidential information to her personal email address, she was summarily dismissed for gross misconduct. The High Court (Jack J) ordered that the confidential information be returned to the company but that there was no award for damages because the company had not suffered any loss:[18]

---

[15] See *Crowson v Rider*, at [107].
[16] See *Crowson v Rider*, at [119].
[17] [2010] EWHC 3241 (QB), [2011] IRLR 224.
[18] See *Brandeaux v Chadwick*, at [29]–[30].

'At one point Mr Tolley seemed to advance an argument that Brandeaux had suffered no damage and so had no cause of action. That cannot be right. If A wrongly takes B's confidential information, A is entitled to have it back regardless of whether he can show loss …

What has actually happened as part of the e-mail process is that the documents have been copied electronically and the copies transferred. The order has to be in a form which is appropriate to the electronic nature of the retention of the material. There is not, I think, any real difficulty over this. The only way in which the material can be removed from the hard drive of Ms Chadwick's laptop is by the destruction of the hard drive. As the material is irretrievably on the hard drive, Brandeaux requires possession of the hard drive. But the court should exercise its discretion only to make an order for the delivery up on terms.'

5.26 Employers who carry a concern in respect of either current or recently departed employees should seek advice immediately. Those still employed can be made properly aware of the level of confidentiality that the company holds information, or reminded of their duties either as a fiduciary or their duty of fidelity under contract. Forensic evidence in relation to those employees recently departed can easily be lost once email accounts and personal desktops are deleted or removed. Investigation and advice at an early stage can allay worry in the future.

Pintorex Ltd v Keyvanfar[19]

5.27 In *Pintorex Ltd v Keyvanfar*, a former employee had misused confidential information belonging to his former employer in soliciting business for the benefit of his new employer. In doing so, he had been acting as agent of the new employer, and the new employer was jointly liable for his wrongdoing. The new employer's director was not liable as he lacked the requisite state of mind.

5.28 A first instance case, the Patents County Court (Alastair Wilson QC) held that the former employee had loaded a database of accounting information, belonging to his former employer, onto a computer owned by his new employer. He had then solicited business for his new employer based upon this confidential information. In doing so he had acted as an agent of the company, which was vicariously liable. It will not be in every case that an employee is acting for an employer but on the facts, it could not be argued that he was acting on a 'frolic' of his own:[20]

'As to the liability of the Second Defendant, it was submitted on its behalf that it was not liable for any of the activities of the First Defendant prior to his starting employment with the Second Defendant. Anything he did for the benefit of the Second Defendant prior to 1 October 2010 was, it was submitted, a mere frolic of his own. I reject this submission … It is clear, therefore, that the First Defendant was authorised by the Second Defendant (through its director the Third

---

[19]   [2013] EWPCC 36.
[20]   See *Pintorex Ltd v Keyvanfar*, at [46].

Defendant) to act on the Second Defendant's behalf well before 1 October 2010... Thus in my view, in so far as the First Defendant did anything which brought in business for the Second Defendant he did so in the capacity of agent for the Second Defendant.'

5.29   The defendant company was found to be jointly liable for the actions of the employee. In this instance, the third defendant director was not found to be personally liable because he had not known of the employee's intention to misuse the confidential information:[21]

'[T]he Third Defendant was not aware of the precise nature of the First Defendant's obligations to the Claimant. In any case even if, with a little more alertness, the Third Defendant might have appreciated the real risk that the First Defendant was in breach of his duties of good faith towards the Claimant, there was no strong enough evidence to satisfy me on the balance of probabilities that he 'dishonestly' (in the Royal Brunei sense referred to above by Lord Neuberger) turned a blind eye to or ignored the possibility that the First Defendant was also misusing the Claimant's confidential information. Still less was there any sufficient evidence that the First Defendant's relatively limited misuses of confidential information were part of a common design with the Third Defendant to misuse confidential information.'

5.30   The detrimental effect of losing confidential information is not limited to the company asserting ownership over the information. There is a risk inherent in the misuse of confidential information not only for the employee who has obtained the information, and may seek to use it, but also for the new employer and the directors of that company. The extent to which a new employer could be exposed to risk when recruiting a new employee is discussed later in this chapter.

PROTECTING CONFIDENTIAL INFORMATION

5.31   The cause of action for the misuse of confidential information is breach of confidence. The relevant test is contained in *Coco v AN Clark (Engineers) Ltd*:[22]

(1)   the information itself must have the necessary quality of confidence about it;

(2)   that information must have been imparted in circumstances imparting an obligation of confidence; and

(3)   there must be an unauthorised use of that information to the detriment of the party communicating it.

5.32   The 'quality of confidence' highlights that the legal test requires companies to apply measures, systems and procedures to protect their

---

[21]   See *Pintorex Ltd v Keyvanfar*, at [57].
[22]   [1968] FSR 415, at 419.

information. Most software companies ensure that their source code is a trade secret, and only disclose in very limited circumstances, even then only ever under a non-disclosure agreement. Third parties who are engaged to create compatible software will undertake to ensure the same or similar protective measures are in place.

5.33   For those bringing a breach of confidence action, the court will expect to see what measures were in place to keep the information in question confidential. The court will require specificity over the information that is asserted as confidential. The court will accept that the source code for a computer program is generally confidential, and the issue will be merely the circumstances imparting the obligation of confidence, and the unauthorised use causing detriment.

5.34   Source code constituents such as logic, algorithms and programming languages comprise ideas and principles which are not protected through intellectual property rights. If a company seeks to assert that these are confidential information it is vital that these have not been released, either deliberately or inadvertently, into the public domain. Test data similarly may not be covered by copyright or database protection so it is essential that confidence is maintained, and employee's obligations conveyed explicitly. Comments within the source code reminding the programmer why the code was structured in a particular way, and preparatory design plans, may be confidential but are highly unlikely to be protected by any other means.

5.35   If litigation is to be pursued, a pre-action disclosure request before the court for the specific piece of information that you allege the defendant holds can produce powerful evidence. Once granted the court would compel the defendant to admit to the possession, through production, of the relevant confidential information.

5.36   More often than not employers are vicariously liable for the actions of their employees, and will be included as a separate defendant in any action. The court may even be willing to apply personal liability to company directors. A new employer may owe a duty of confidence to the ex-employer if they knew, or turned a blind eye to, the employee abusing confidential information. Employers should be aware of the potential for secondary liability when recruiting or headhunting from a competitor.

5.37   Once in the public domain, confidential information is in the hands of competitors, and damages or delivering-up the confidential information is often ineffective. The court cannot make information secret again but can, in certain circumstances, issue a 'springboard injunction' which prevents the former employee from gaining a head start over their former employer through their use of the confidential information. Injunctive relief can restrict a competitor from entering the market by preventing them from using the information for a period of time.

TRADE SECRETS

5.38 A trade secret is a valuable piece of information for an enterprise that is treated as confidential and that gives that enterprise a competitive advantage.[23] The term 'trade secrets' can refer to both confidential processes and to confidential information (such as client lists, costings, price lists).[24] Confidential information is dealt with above.

5.39 Trade secrets that are confidential processes are normally associated with secret techniques of manufacture, design methods, or construction processes; or special formulae; chemical formulae or recipes, as opposed to information about a business' structure or solvency. The term trade secret suggests the 'highest level of secrecy'. As the Information Tribunal has explained: 'The ordinary understanding of the phrase usually suggests something technical, unique and achieved with a degree of difficulty and investment. Few would dispute that the recipe for "Coca Cola" is (or has been) a trade secret'.[25]

5.40 Like confidential information, the cause of action for the misuse of a trade secret is breach of confidence, and the same test applies.[26]

5.41 Owners are required to maintain protection over trade secrets. However, with sufficient effort, or through illegal acts, a competitor can usually obtain a trade secret. If an owner of a trade secret can prove that reasonable efforts have been made to keep the information confidential, the information remains a trade secret and generally remains legally protected. Conversely, trade secret owners who cannot evidence reasonable efforts at protecting confidential information risk losing the trade secret, even if the information is obtained by a competitor illegally. Monitoring practical steps such as shredding documents or the collection of confidential waste is important.

The Trade Secrets Directive

5.42 In November 2013, the European Union proposed a Directive to harmonise the definition of trade secrets in accordance with existing internationally binding standards. On 15 December 2015 the negotiating teams of the European Parliament and the Council reached a preliminary agreement on the text of the Directive. The Commission participated in the negotiations as a facilitator.

5.43 The agreed common approach was for a new framework that: aims at making it easier for national courts to deal with the misappropriation of

---

[23] Proposal for a Directive of the European Parliament and of the Council on the protection of undisclosed know-how and business information (trade secrets) against their unlawful acquisition, use and disclosure COM/2013/0813 final – 2013/0402 (COD).

[24] *Herbert Morris Ltd v Saxelby* [1916] 1 AC 688.

[25] See *Department of Health v Information Commissioner* (EA/2008/0018, 18 November 2008), at [52].

[26] See *Coco v AN Clark (Engineers) Ltd* [1968] FSR 415, at 419.

confidential business information; removes the trade secret infringing products from the market: and makes it easier for victims to receive compensation for illegal actions. Under the agreement, the new framework would include the following main features:

- a minimum harmonisation of the different civil law regimes, whilst allowing member states to apply stricter rules;
- the establishment of common principles, definitions and safeguards, in line with international agreements, as well as the measures, procedures and remedies that should be made available for the purpose of civil law redress;
- a limitation period of 6 years for claims or bringing actions before courts;
- the preservation of confidentiality in the course of legal proceedings, while ensuring that the rights of the parties involved in a trade secret ligation case are not undermined;
- the establishment of a favourable regime to employees in what concerns their liability for damages in case of violation of a trade secret if acting without intent.

5.44 The agreement will need to be formalised by the European Parliament and the Council and is unlikely to be finalised until 2017.

COPYRIGHT

5.45 The European Union Directive 2009/24/EC on the Legal Protection of Computer Programs (the Software Directive) requires member states to protect computer programs by copyright as literary works. Under UK law, copyright arises automatically on the creation of an original literary, dramatic, musical or artistic work by virtue of the Copyright, Designs and Patents Act 1988 (CDPA 1988). Within this jurisdiction, authorities have largely restricted the scope of copyright within computer programs to the code base, which is arguably a literary work.

The Software Directive

5.46 The 'Object of Protection' within Art 1 of the Software Directive is limited to 'expressions' within a computer program as if it was an original intellectual creation. The form or purpose of the computer program is irrelevant. The protection of copyright is over the code that creates the program. The author of the expression or code is the owner of the copyright, subject to instances of creation under contract (Software Directive, Art 1(2)):

> 'Protection in accordance with this Directive shall apply to the expression in any form of a computer program. Ideas and principles which underlie any element of a computer program, including those which underlie its interfaces, are not protected by copyright under this Directive.'

5.47 The definition of 'expression in any form of a computer program' includes the source code and object code of a computer program. The functionality that this code produces is not subject to copyright. An employee departing to a competitor is not prohibited under the Software Directive, or the CDPA 1988 within the UK, from reproducing the functionality of software developed by the previous employer provided that he does not copy the code base.

5.48 The functionality of a computer program is further defined within the Software Directive. The parts of the program which provide for such interconnection and interaction between elements of software and hardware are generally known as 'interfaces'. This functional interconnection and interaction is generally known as 'interoperability'. Interoperability can be explained as the ability to exchange information and mutually to use the information which has been exchanged. The Software Directive makes explicit that neither concept nor functionality can be protected as a literary work. Ideas or concepts which are produced as a result of the underlying source code or object code are not protected by copyright. Therefore, algorithms and programming languages which comprise merely ideas or principles are also not protected within the Software Directive (Software Directive, Recital 11):

> 'For the avoidance of doubt, it has to be made clear that only the expression of a computer program is protected and that ideas and principles which underlie any element of a program, including those which underlie its interfaces, are not protected by copyright under this Directive. In accordance with this principle of copyright, to the extent that logic, algorithms and programming languages comprise ideas and principles, those ideas and principles are not protected under this Directive.'

5.49 However, the protection of the source code extends into computer programs in any form, including those which are incorporated into hardware and those in preparatory design work, which may lead to the development of a computer program, provided that the nature of the preparatory work is such that a computer program can result from it at a later stage.

5.50 Those protections that are contained within the Software Directive can be utilised by the author of the computer program. Under Art 2, the author of a computer program is the natural person, or group of natural people, who created the program, unless the program was created under contract. This includes where a computer program was created by an employee acting within the performance of his duties (Software Directive, Art 2(3)):

> 'Where a computer program is created by an employee in the execution of his duties or following the instructions given by his employer, the employer exclusively shall be entitled to exercise all economic rights in the program so created, unless otherwise provided by contract.'

5.51 The Software Directive grants the author exclusive rights to prevent the unauthorised reproduction of his work. The unauthorised reproduction, translation, adaptation or transformation of the form of the code in which a copy of a computer program has been made available constitutes an infringement of the exclusive rights of the author.

5.52 However, a person who has legally obtained a licence to use a computer program is not prevented from performing acts necessary to observe, study or test the functioning of the program, provided that those acts do not infringe the copyright in the program. A competitor is perfectly entitled, under the Software Directive to reverse engineer a legally purchased computer program as long as the original source code is not reproduced. This could be with or without the assistance of a former employee who worked on the development of the program and subsequently moved to the competitor (Software Directive, Art 5(3)).

5.53 Copying the source code of a computer program is also permitted for lawful use after purchase, to produce a back-up copy, and to facilitate 'decompilation'. Independently produced computer programs made need to utilise copyrighted source code to interact with the protected computer program. This is permissible under the Software Directive as long as the goal is interoperability with an independently created computer program rather than the development, production or marketing of one substantially similar to the protected program (Software Directive, Art 6).

Copyright, Designs and Patents Act 1988

5.54 In the most simple terms, the CDPA 1988, as amended, establishes that copyright in protected works lasts until 70 years after the death of the creator if known, otherwise 70 years after the work was created or published. The period of protection is reduced to 50 years for computer-generated works. In order for a creation to be a work protected by copyright it must fall within one of the following categories: literary work, dramatic work, musical work, artistic work, films, sounds recordings, broadcasts, and typographical arrangement of published editions. From its inception the CDPA 1988 included 'computer program' within the definition of 'literary work'.

5.55 The provisions within the Software Directive are incorporated within the CDPA 1988. The original owner of the copyright is the author. The author of a computer-generated work, whether a computer program (literary work), musical or artistic work, is the person who undertakes to make arrangements necessary for its creation (CDPA 1988, s 9(3)). There is an exception when the work was made by an employee in the course of his employment (CDPA 1988, s 11(2)):

11 First ownership of copyright

(1) The author of a work is the first owner of any copyright in it, subject to the following provisions.

(2) Where a literary, dramatic, musical or artistic work, or a film, is made by an employee in the course of his employment, his employer is the first owner of any copyright in the work subject to any agreement to the contrary.

5.56 The owner of the copyright in a work has the exclusive right to copy the work; to issue copies of the work to the public; to rent or lend the work to the public; to perform, show or play the work in public; to communicate the work to the public; to make an adaptation of the work; or do any of the above in relation to an adaptation. These constitute the 'acts restricted by the copyright' and apply equally to computer programs as to musical or artistic works.

5.57 The CDPA 1988, ss 50A–50C, provide an exception for computer programs to be copied for lawful use after purchase, to produce a back-up copy, and to facilitate 'decompilation'. Under s 50B of the CDPA 1988, an ex-employee and/or a recruiting competitor are permitted to study how the software works with a view to replicating the functionality exactly. However, where they are trying to emulate software, s 50B(3) prohibits a lawful user to decompile a licensed copy back into the source code if it intends to create a program which is substantially similar in expression to the program decompiled, or to do any other act which is restricted by copyright.

5.58 Section 50BA makes explicit that it is not an infringement of copyright for a lawful user of a copy of a computer program to observe, study or test the functioning of the program in order to determine the ideas and principles which underlie any element of the program if he does so while performing any of the acts of loading, displaying, running, transmitting or storing the program which he is entitled to do. The copyright owner cannot contract out of this provision with a licensee or purchaser.

5.59 In order for copyright to subsist under the CDPA 1988, the author must be a 'qualifying person at the relevant time', specifically:

- a British citizen, a British overseas territories citizen, a British National (Overseas), a British Overseas citizen, a British subject or a British protected person within the meaning of the British Nationality Act 1981; or

- an individual domiciled or resident in the United Kingdom or another country to which the relevant provisions of that part of the Act extend; or

- a body incorporated under the law of a part of the United Kingdom or of another country to which the relevant provisions of that part of the Act extend.

5.60 The relevant time was either at the time of creation, for an unpublished work, or the time of publication.

5.61   Alternatively, if a computer program, or other work, is first published in the United Kingdom, the protection of the CDPA 1988 will apply. The definition of the borders of the United Kingdom, its colonies, and territorial waters is contained within ss 157–162.

5.62   Regardless of the protection afforded by the Software Directive and the CDPA 1988 an employee can easily replicate unprotected functionality without ever needing to copy the protected source code or object code. The leading authorities illustrate the limited effect of copyright.

Navitaire v Easyjet[27]

5.63   In *Navitaire v Easyjet,* the claimant was a software developer that owned the copyright in various works which made up the source code for an airline booking system known as OpenRes. The first defendant was a well-known low costs airline, and the second defendant was an America-based software company employed by the first defendant to produce a booking system called eRes. The first defendant initially used OpenRes but commissioned the second defendant to create an alternative booking system with an identical look and feel that employed the same commands. The purpose was to move from OpenRes to eRes without the customer base realising there was a change. There was never any suggestion that eRes used or copied the source code for OpenRes.

5.64   The claimant issued proceedings on the basis of 'non-textual copying'. It was suggested that eRes infringed copyright by adopting the look and feel of OpenRes; that the individual commands entered by the user to achieve particular results were protected by copyright; and that the form of screen displays, and reports displayed on the screen in response to prescribed instructions within eRes constituted an infringement. The claimant asserted that the near-identity in appearance and function could not have been achieved without a close analysis of the OpenRes system in action, and that there was non-textual reproduction of either the whole of the OpenRes software considered as a single copyright work, or of the various copyrights subsisting in 'modules' going to make up the system.

5.65   The claimant sought to use as an analogy the concept of an author 'who takes the plot of another work and copies nothing else will still infringe copyright if a substantial part of the earlier author's work is represented by that plot, and the same goes for computer programs'.[28]

5.66   In a technically detailed judgment, the High Court (Pumfrey J) found for the claimant in part but affirmed the principle that copyright in computer

---

27   [2004] EWHC 1725 (Ch), [2005] ECC 30 (Copyright).
28   See *Navitaire v Easyjet*, at [73].

programs extends only to the source code, and that imitated functionality which is derived from an alternative code base is not protected:[29]

> 'Copyright protection for computer software is a given, but I do not feel that the courts should be astute to extend that protection into a region where only the functional effects of a program are in issue. There is a respectable case for saying that copyright is not, in general, concerned with functional effects, and there is some advantage in a bright line rule protecting only the claimant's embodiment of the function in software and not some superset of that software. The case is not truly analogous with the plot of a novel, because the plot is part of the work itself. The user interface is not part of the work itself. One could permute all the letters and other codes in the command names, and it would still work in the same way, and all that would be lost is a modest mnemonic advantage. To approach the problem in this way may at least be consistent with the distinction between idea and expression that finds its way into the Software Directive, but, of course, it draws the line between idea and expression in a particular place which some would say lies too far on the side of expression. I think, however, that such is the independence of the particular form of the actual codes used from the overall functioning of the software that it is legitimate to separate them in this way, and not to afford them separate protection when the underlying software is not even arguably copied.'

5.67 The concept of 'non-textual copying' was rejected. There was no doubt that the defendants had avoided the use of the source codes in OpenRes, and it was not in dispute that in the language used, actual code and architecture, the eRes system was quite different. Even though the two different computer programs could produce identical result, this was not sufficient for a claim in copyright. The claimant's computer program, OpenRes, invited input in a manner excluded from copyright protection, output its results in a form excluded from copyright protection, and created a record of a reservation. What was left when the interface aspects of the case were disregarded was the business function of carrying out the transaction and creating the record, because none of the code was read or copied by the defendants. The court dismissed the claim for non-textual copying without reservation:[30]

> 'This does not answer the question with which I am confronted, which is peculiar, I believe, to computer programs. The reason it is a new problem is that two completely different computer programs can produce an identical result: not a result identical at some level of abstraction but identical at any level of abstraction. This is so even if the author of one has no access at all to the other but only to its results. The analogy with a plot is for this reason a poor one. It is a poor one for other reasons as well. To say these programs possess a plot is precisely like saying that the book of instructions for a booking clerk acting manually has a plot: but a book of instructions has no theme, no events, and does not have a narrative flow. Nor does a computer program, particularly one whose behaviour depends upon the history of its inputs in any given transaction. It does not have a plot, merely a series of pre-defined operations intended to achieve the desired result in response to the requests of the customer.'

---

[29] See *Navitaire v Easyjet*, at [94].
[30] See *Navitaire v Easyjet*, at [125].

5.68 The court also rejected that commands, whether individual, complex or in compilation, were literary works. A single word in isolation could not be considered a literary work taking into account the skill and labour expended, the nature of the copyright protection and its underlying policy. Individual complex commands could not be readily distinguished on the basis of an additional suffix. Compilations of commands amounted to a computer language which was not entitled to copyright protection in accordance with the Software Directive.[31]

5.69 However, the High Court held that the computer screen displays, specifically the graphical user interface (GUI) screens, attracted protection as an artistic work. It was held that the Software Directive was concerned with the protection of computer programs as literary works but did not impact upon the domestic protection provided on relevant artistic copyright.

5.70 OpenRes could be modified to the specifications of the user, utilising an 'interface builder' to produce virtual buttons that a customer could press to execute functions. The source code for the 'interface builder' would like all computer programs be protected by copyright. The functionality would not. However, Pumfrey J held that the design of the buttons produced using the functionality of the 'interface builder', when captured on the screen, were produced with sufficient skill and labour to attract artistic copyright. The replication within the eRes system of the GUI screens that were identical to that in OpenRes was a breach:[32]

> 'In my judgment, the better view is that the GUI screens are artistic works. They are recorded as such only in the complex code that displays them, but I think that this is strictly analogous to more simple digital representations of graphic works. The code constructs the screen from basic elements, and is so arranged to give a consistent appearance to the individual elements. I think, nonetheless, that to arrange a screen certainly affords the opportunity for the exercise of sufficient skill and labour for the result to amount to an artistic work. I consider that the GUI screens satisfy this requirement. There is force in the suggestion that they present a uniform appearance in layout of the elements, and so contribute to a uniformity of interface. On the whole this is sufficient skill and labour to entitle the screens sued on to artistic copyright.'

5.71 The limits of protection afforded to computer programs as literary works are clearly defined within *Navitaire v Easyjet,* and in that context copyright provides very little protection from an employee, who has assisted in developing the functionality of a computer program, moving to a competitor and replicating the software of an employer.

---

[31]   See *Navitaire v Easyjet*, at [79], [83] and [92].
[32]   See *Navitaire v Easyjet*, at [98].

Nova Productions Ltd v Mazooma Games Ltd[33]

5.72 The protection afforded artistic works within computer programs was scaled back in *Nova v Mazooma*. The claimant designed, manufactured and sold coin-operated video games including a game called *Pocket Money*, which simulated a game of pool. It claimed that its copyright in that game had been infringed in a game called *Jackpot Pool* developed by the defendants in the first action, and in a game called *Trick Shot* developed by the defendant in the second action. The claimant relied *inter alia* on its copyright in artistic works under the CDPA 1988. The claimant asserted that bitmap graphics and the sequence of frames generated and displayed to the player of the game obtained copyright protection. At first instance, the High Court (Kitchin J) held that the games played in a very different way, albeit that a few features had been derived from or inspired by the copyright work. Though he was prepared to assume that a moving image generated by a succession of still shots in one game should be compared with a similar effect in another game when considering whether there had been substantial reproduction of artistic works, he nevertheless found that there had been no infringement of copyright and no substantial reproduction. He dismissed both actions.

5.73 The Court of Appeal (Sir Andrew Morritt CJ, Jacob LJ and Lloyd LJ) dismissed the appeal, and held that although individual frames were 'graphic works' for the purpose of s 4(2) of the CDPA 1988 and were capable of protection, a series of such frames providing an illusion of movement was not a single graphic work in itself and was not therefore capable of protection under the CDPA 1988. Since there had been no frame-for-frame reproduction of the bitmap graphics, there had been no breach of the claimant's copyright in its artistic works:[34]

> 'Parliament has specifically created copyright in moving images by way of copyright in films. If Mr Howe were right, the series of still images which provides the illusion of movement would itself create a further kind of copyright work protecting moving images. It is unlikely that Parliament intended this.'

5.74 The Court of Appeal reaffirmed that ideas and principles which underlay any element of a computer program were outside the scope of copyright protection under both UK and European law, which protected the means of expression of an idea but not the idea itself:[35]

> 'To my mind these provisions are abundantly clear. The well-known dichotomy between an idea and its individual expression is intended to apply, and does, to copyright in computer software. When I say 'well-known' I mean not just known to copyright lawyers of one country but well-known all over the world. Recital 15 refers to the protection of the expression of ideas as being 'in accordance with the legislation and jurisprudence of the member states and the international copyright conventions' and is clearly a reference to this dichotomy. The Agreement on

---

[33] [2007] EWCA Civ 219, [2007] Bus LR 1032.
[34] See *Nova v Mazooma*, at [17].
[35] See *Nova v Mazooma*, at [31].

Trade-Related Aspects of Intellectual Property Rights (TRIPS) (OJ 1994 L336, p 213) likewise recognises this dichotomy: see particularly article 9(2).'

5.75 In order for artistic copyright to subsist within a computer program the image created must be identical to an existing work which was created through sufficient skill and labour to attract protection.

SAS Institute Inc v World Programming Ltd[36]

5.76 The High Court (Arnold J) in *SAS v WPL* again correctly dismissed a software developer's claims that a competitor had infringed copyright and acted in breach of a licence in creating a computer program emulating much of the functionality of its own programs.

5.77 The claimant, SAS Institute Inc, was a developer of analytical software known as the SAS System which enabled users to carry out a wide range of data processing and analysis tasks, and in particular statistical analysis. The core component of the SAS System was Base SAS, which enabled users to write and run application programs written in a language known as the SAS Language. Over the years, SAS Institute's customers had written, or had written on their behalf, thousands of application programs in the SAS Language. SAS Institute's customers had no alternative but to license use of the SAS System in order to be able to run their existing SAS Language application programs, as well to create new ones. The SAS System had been developed over a period of 35 years, and produced revenue for SAS Institute of $2.3 billion in 2009.

5.78 The defendant, World Programming Ltd (WPL) created a product called World Programming System or WPS to emulate much of the functionality of the SAS components. WPL's customers' application program executed in the same manner whether run on WPS or SAS components. WPS effectively broke the licensing monopoly which the SAS Language created. There was no suggestion that WPL had access to the source code of the SAS components, or that WPL had copied any of the text of the source code; however, WPL admitted that its programmers had used the SAS Learning Edition and Manuals as sources of information in addition to a variety of other sources.

5.79 SAS Institute contended that WPL had breached copyright in creating WPS; had contravened their licensing terms through analysing the SAS Learning Edition; had copied a substantial part of the SAS Manuals; and had breached the copyright in those Manuals.

5.80 The High Court rejected the assertion that WPS infringed on the SAS copyright. For an infringement of copyright to exist, the defendant's work had to represent the claimant's work in some real sense. The court held that copyright protection of a program is not limited to the text of the source code of the program, but extends to protecting the design of the program, that is its

---

[36] [2010] EWHC 1829 (Ch), [2010] ECDR 15.

'structure, sequence and organisation'.[37] However, there is a distinction between protecting the design of the program and protecting its functionality. The key question is 'the nature of the skill and labour'.[38] The functionality of a computer program was not a form of expression at all, and, following *Navitaire v Easyjet*, the judge considered that 'the functionality of a computer program falls on the wrong side of the line drawn by Art 1(2) of the Software Directive'.[39]

5.81 The use of the SAS Learning Edition in the creation of WPS fell outside the scope of the terms of the relevant licence. The Software Directive, Art 5(3), permitted a person with the lawful right to use a copy of a computer program to 'observe, study or test the functioning of the program in order to determine the ideas and principles which underlie any element of the program' without the authorisation of the right holder. The contractual term within the licence was null and void and SAS could not rely upon breach of contract.[40]

5.82 However, the High Court held that the manuals that accompanied the WPS software did infringe upon the copyright that protected the SAS Manuals. WPL had infringed copyrights in the SAS Manuals by substantially producing them in the WPL Manual:[41]

> 'I am prepared to accept that WPL's manual writers did not copy directly from the SAS Manuals in the sense of having one of the SAS Manuals open in front of them when writing the WPS Manual and intentionally either transcribing or paraphrasing the wording. I also accept that a considerable degree of similarity in both content and language between the SAS Manual entries and the WPS Manual entries is to be expected given that they are describing identical functionality. Nevertheless, in my judgment the degree of resemblance in the language goes beyond that which is attributable to describing identical functionality. Moreover, it is plain that the reason for this is that WPL's writers had the language of the SAS Manuals firmly in their minds when writing the WPS Manual entries. Although they tried to avoid describing the functions in the same language, they did not succeed in avoiding the use of very similar language.'

5.83 In relation to the reproduction of a substantial part, the court referred to the decision of the Court of Justice of the European Union in *Infopaq*,[42] and held that when considering whether a substantial part has been reproduced, it is necessary to focus upon what has been reproduced and to consider whether it expresses the author's own intellectual creation. The Court of Appeal (Tomlinson LJ, Lewison LJ, Vos LJ) upheld the High Court's decisions,[43] and held that in deciding whether the reproduction of elements described in the SAS

---

[37] See *SAS v WPL*, at [232].
[38] See *SAS v WPL*, at [233].
[39] See *SAS v WPL*, at [236].
[40] See *SAS v WPL*, at [313]–[314].
[41] See *SAS v WPL*, at [148].
[42] *Infopaq International A/S v Danske Dagblades Forening* [2009] ECR I-6569, [2009] ECDR 16.
[43] *SAS Institute Inc v World Programming Ltd* [2013] EWCA Civ 1482, [2015] ECDR 17.

Manuals constituted the reproduction of the expression of the intellectual creation of the author of the user manual, what was relevant was not the intellectual creation, but the expression of the intellectual creation of the author of the manual.

5.84 The courts have repeatedly stated that the functionality of a computer program is not a form of expression that can be protected through copyright. The Software Directive explicitly excludes ideas and principles which underline any element of a program including those which underline the interfaces. Copyright protects the source code within a computer program but an ex-employee is perfectly entitled to reproduce the functionality of valuable assets, without using the original source code, either in competition or for a competitor.

5.85 The Software Directive does not limit other forms of copyright protection which might apply to elements associated with computer programs. The courts have found for claimants on the basis of protected artistic works, and with literary works within associated program manuals. Arguably similar claims in relation to musical works, sounds recordings, or even typographical arrangement within publish works could potentially be successful. Copyright infringement requires an ex-employer to prove a causal connection between the original work and the copy. Therefore, a forensic expert is essential to assist in any internal investigation into copying of software in order to preserve an evidential link.

DATABASES

5.86 The making of a database can require considerable investment into human, technical and financial resources while such a database can be copied or accessed at a fraction of the cost needed to design it independently. The Directive 96/9/EC of the European Parliament and of the Council on the legal protection of databases (the Database Directive) was introduced to prevent unauthorised extraction or re-utilisation of the contents of a database which could have serious economic and technical consequences. The protection of the Database Directive, and the corresponding protection in UK law introduced by the Copyright and Rights in Databases Regulations 1997,[44] provides a separate means of potential enforcement for an employer from that contained within the Software Directive.

5.87 A 'database' is 'a collection of independent works, data or other materials arranged in a systematic or methodical way and individually accessible by electronic or other means'.[45] Within a computer program, databases may feature as a look-up table or catalogue, such as a compilation of data accessed by a software routine in the underlying object code of the program; or through carefully selected algorithms, mathematical methods and

---

[44] 1997/3032, Pt III.
[45] Database Directive, Art 1(2).

user commands within the code base. The Software Directive, Recital 11, specifically excludes logic, algorithms and programming languages as ideas and principles; however, these may find some protection if compiled into a relevant database. Databases in themselves may have a commercial value to be protected. Legal databases such as LexisNexis and Westlaw have been created through extensive skill and labour and would likely be protected under the Database Directive.

5.88 The Database Directive defines two independent protections. Member states are required to protect by copyright a database which, by reason of the selection or arrangement of their contents, 'constitute the author's own intellectual creation'.[46] This was incorporated into the CDPA 1988 by expanding the definition of 'literary work' to include 'a database', and with the inclusion of a new s 3A:

3A Databases.

(1) In this Part 'database' means a collection of independent works, data or other materials which –

(a)   are arranged in a systematic or methodical way, and
(b)   are individually accessible by electronic or other means.

(2) For the purposes of this Part a literary work consisting of a database is original if, and only if, by reason of the selection or arrangement of the contents of the database the database constitutes the author's own intellectual creation.

5.89 The definition of an author of a database is the same as for any other form of copyright under the CDPA 1988. It is not an infringement of copyright in a database for a person who has a right to use the database or any part of the database (whether under a licence to do any of the acts restricted by the copyright in the database or otherwise) to do, in the exercise of that right, anything which is necessary for the purposes of access to and use of the contents of the database or of that part of the database. Any contractual term which seeks to negate this permission is void.

5.90 Article 7 of the Database Directive creates a *sui generis* right where a maker of a database can show that there has been qualitatively and/or quantitatively substantial investment in either the obtaining, verification or presentation of the contents. The *sui generis* right grants protection from extraction and/or re-utilisation of the whole or of a substantial part of the contents of that database, regardless as to whether copyright protection subsists in the individual components of that database. Part III of the Copyright and Rights in Databases Regulations 1997 incorporates the *sui generis* right into UK law.

---

[46]   See Database Directive, Art 3.

Copyright and Rights in Databases Regulations 1997, Part III

5.91 Part III transposes the requirements within the Database Directive directly into domestic law. Regulation 13 creates the *sui generis* database right:

13 Database right

(1) A property right ('database right') subsists, in accordance with this Part, in a database if there has been a substantial investment in obtaining, verifying or presenting the contents of the database.

(2) For the purposes of paragraph (1) it is immaterial whether or not the database or any of its contents is a copyright work, within the meaning of Part I of the 1988 Act.

5.92 The owner of the right is the person who takes the initiative in obtaining, verifying or presenting the contents of the database, and who assumes the risk of investing in that obtaining, verification or presentation. Where a database is made by an employee in the course of his employment, his employer shall be regarded as the maker of the database, subject to any agreement to the contrary. The maker must have been resident within the European Economic Area, or the Isle of Man, when the database was compiled.

5.93 Regulation 16 defines actions which would contravene the *sui generis* right:

16 Acts infringing database right

(1) Subject to the provisions of this Part, a person infringes database right in a database if, without the consent of the owner of the right, he extracts or re-utilises all or a substantial part of the contents of the database.

(2) For the purposes of this Part, the repeated and systematic extraction or re-utilisation of insubstantial parts of the contents of a database may amount to the extraction or re-utilisation of a substantial part of those contents.

5.94 'Extraction', in relation to any contents of a database, means the permanent or temporary transfer of those contents to another medium by any means or in any form. 'Re-utilisation', in relation to any contents of a database, means making those contents available to the public by any means. The lawful use of a database following purchase or license; academic referencing; and copying of a work from the internet by a deposit library do not breach the *sui generis* right.

5.95 The database right expires after 15 years, from the end of the calendar year in which the making of the database was completed, unless the database undergoes substantial change, either cumulatively or on a single occasion, so that a new substantial investment qualifies the change to the database for its own term of protection. In practice additions or changes to a database which are substantial will create a new 15-year period of protection from the point of investment.

Databases to protect software

5.96 The success of utilising database protection is mixed. At first sight the database rights, whether through copyright or the *sui generis* right, appear to provide an additional cause of action for a company to prevent a former employee from utilising what could be valuable information.[47] However, the courts appear reluctant to allow a claim in copyright when the underlying material within the dataset is not protected, or when the company can more properly rely on a breach of confidence.

Cantor Gaming Ltd v GameAccount Global Ltd[48]

5.97 The claimant in *Cantor Gaming* was a subsidiary of BGC International (BGC). BCG was a substantial undertaking involved in financial services and related activities. In 2000 it was approached by two people with an idea for developing and commercialising online games. BGC arranged to employ them to run the project as a business which would be majority owned by the claimant. For the purposes of the venture, BGC and the individuals concerned incorporated a company called GameAccount Ltd as the corporate vehicle for the project. This company subsequently changed its name to Cantor Gaming Ltd, the claimant. The individuals entered into contracts of employment under which they were appointed joint chief executive officer (CEO) and chief financial officer (CFO). Three consultants were also engaged.

5.98 The CEO and CFO were not software engineers, so the software development was carried out by employees or contractors. The employment structure for these developers was convoluted; however, the copyright to the programs were vested in the claimant. In particular, they owned the copyright in GAMoney, which was a database designed to hold details about customers' accounts and the online games that they had played.

5.99 In 2002 the relationship between the claimant, the CEO and CFO broke down as a result of differences over how the project should develop. An agreement was reached where the CEO and CFO would terminate their contract of employment and would be permitted to license software from the claimant as GameAccount Global Ltd, the defendant. A clause in the licence agreement provided that the defendant would be in material breach if the company used GAMoney and became associated with a third party bookmaker directly or indirectly. The clause was breached and the agreement was brought to an end. The defendants gave an undertaking not to use and to return the

---

[47] See *Crowson v Rider*, above at **5.13**.
[48] [2007] EWHC 1914, [2007] ECC 24.

GAMoney database. Regardless, the claimant pursued a claim and an investigation discovered that the GAMoney was cached on the defendant's servers.

5.100 The High Court (Mr Daniel Alexander QC) found in favour of the claimant. It was held to be highly unlikely that, had the parties turned their minds to the matter when the contract was made, they would have regarded the mere caching of otherwise unused procedures to be caught by the term 'use'. However, it was not possible to accept the defendant's submission that the transient copies of GAMoney were functionally redundant in that they did not contribute to the operation of any software. Once it was shown that a part of a work literally reproduced was not functionally useless, it was a short step to showing that a sufficiently substantial part had been reproduced, which was the case here:[49]

> '[I]t is necessary to step back from the detail of individual uses and ask an overall question: would a person skilled in the art of software design consider that GAMoney was being "used", perhaps unimportantly, but nonetheless, materially, in the operation of the software overall for Bookmakers between 2004 and 2006? In my judgment, the answer to that question is "yes". Although not performing the function for which it was designed, namely a full-function database, overall, GAMoney was not useless for the operation of GA's software. To the contrary, it was used and GAMoney was stored in memory, backed up, parts of it were further reproduced and it was regularly accessed in order that GAMoney could perform the limited function for which it was still deployed by GA between 2004 (following the arrangements with the Bookmakers) and 2006 (when it was removed).'

5.101 *Cantor Gaming* suggests that the database right may be a useful protection to prevent competition from illegitimate actions with protected material. In this case merely possessing the database was sufficient to infer use. It is worth noting that copyright did not subsist in the material contained within the database.

Navitaire v Easyjet[50]

5.102 An alternative approach to databases was adopted by the High Court in *Navitaire v Easyjet*. In addition to those claims in copyright considered above, the claimant suggested that eRes was created based upon databases copied directly from OpenRes. It was accepted that Easyjet were anxious to maintain the record of every reservation undertaken through OpenRes, and that this information needed to be migrated to the eRes system. The judge concluded that there was no doubt that databases were copied but this 'did not influence the design of the eRes database to a substantial extent'.[51] The High Court held that a considerable amount of extraneous information was necessary to before the OpenRes database could be usefully interpreted, and that the allegation of

---

[49]   See *Cantor Gaming*, at [96].
[50]   [2004] EWHC 1725 (Ch), [2005] ECC 30 (Database Right).
[51]   See *Navitaire v Easyjet*, at [162].

copying only represented a small proportion of the relevant database.[52] The judge concluded that the schema (structure) of the databases had not been copied to the extent that there had been an infringement of copyright.[53]

5.103 A distinction was drawn between a database constituting the dataset contained and the schema which defined the limits of the database. The judge held that the schema for an electronic database was a computer program, which would be protected by the Software Directive, whereas the dataset was protected by the Database Directive. In either case the defendant had not infringed the relevant copyright. Mere possession of part of the database was not sufficient to constitute extraction or use.

Flogas Britain Ltd v Calor Gas Ltd[54]

5.104 Flogas Britain Ltd (Flogas) and Calor Gas Ltd (Calor) operated in the market for liquid propane gas (LPG). Flogas maintained a database with information on its customers. In January 2010, a former sales director at Flogas joined Calor as an area sales manager. The former employee passed to Calor's head of marketing the Flogas database. In September 2010, Flogas told its customers of an intended price increase and the head of marketing planned to use the Flogas database to send three mail shots seeking to win Flogas' customers. These contained an invitation to switch to Calor as their LPG supplier and offering £100 of free LPG to those who switched. Flogas received a surge of telephone calls from its customers about Calor's mail shot requiring Flogas match the offer. When Calor's managing director was notified the head of marketing was dismissed immediately. The final mail shot was destroyed, and the database deleted. Calor admitted liability for breach of confidence but Flogas asserted vicarious liability through breach of database rights, and sought additional damages. It was claimed that there had been a substantial investment in obtaining, verifying and presenting the customer database and that the *sui generis* right existed under reg 13 of the Copyright and Rights in Databases Regulations 1997.

5.105 The High Court (Proudman J) found that the database right subsisted in relation to the Flogas database. It was a collection of information which included information that had previously existed, such as the names and addresses of the customers, as well as comments made using a function within the system. The former employee sent a copy of the Flogas database to his Calor email address, and supplied the information to the head of marketing. This was a permanent or temporary transfer of all or a substantial part of the contents of a database to another medium, and as such amounted to 'extraction' within the meaning of the Database Directive, Art 7(2). The investment that the claimant had made in the Flogas database was undoubtedly one that had been great: it was an integral part of its business intelligence, containing detailed customer information. The information was collected over

---

[52] See *Navitaire v Easyjet*, at [170]–[171].
[53] See *Navitaire v Easyjet*, at [260].
[54] [2013] EWHC 3060 (Ch), [2014] FSR 34.

time and required significant effort in creating and maintaining it. Infringement of the database right was established; the defendant was vicariously liable for the infringement.

5.106 The extractions complained of had a close connection to the employment by Calor of the former employee. It related to business intelligence that was closely linked to the conduct of Flogas and that connection was so close that it would not be unjust to impose vicarious liability on the defendant. However, the infringement of the claimant's database right arose on exactly the same facts as the liability for breach of confidence, which was admitted. The loss had already been compensated for and the claimant could not recover twice:[55]

> 'I conclude that the defendant is vicariously liable for the infringement of Flogas's database right. I therefore go on to consider damages. The question of ordinary damages can be settled relatively simply: the infringement of Flogas's database right arose on exactly the same facts as the liability for breach of confidence. Flogas is already being compensated for the loss it has suffered. Flogas cannot recover twice.'

5.107 The decisions in *Cantor Gaming* and *Flogas v Calor* illustrate that an additional protection can be invoked to prevent the use of database material from being utilised by former employees. When an ex-employee departs to a competitor to create a functionally similar piece of software to that sold by his former employer, even if there is no evidence of source code copying, it may be that the ex-employee has secured a commercial advantage by copying a database that is functionally important to the software. Alternatively, the *sui generis* right will subsist where the former employer can demonstrate a substantial investment which the competitor has avoided through tempting an ex-employee to disclose the database.

5.108 It is worth noting that the *sui generis* right arises when a former employer undertook a substantial investment in order to obtain, verify or present data. If a software company creates data itself, including test data, that data is unlikely to be protected by the *sui generis* database right which extends to substantial investment in obtaining, verifying or presenting not in creating the data.

5.109 *Navitaire v Easyjet* appears to impose similar limits to this protection as that for the reproduction of functionality. If the database could be reproduced without applying a protected structure, or through independent work, then the protection may not apply. Copyright protection is not in the data itself but only the way the data is selected or arranged. The authorities also seem to demonstrate a reluctance to rely on the database right, preferring instead an alternative means of protection such as a breach of confidence or more clearly defined copyright.

---

[55]   See *Flogas v Calor*, at [127]–[128].

EMPLOYER LIABILITY

5.110 The unlikelihood of receiving sufficient compensation in damages from an employee who has misused confidential information, or utilised protected material without permission, renders the joinder of the new employer or competitor that has recruited the employee almost inevitable. Whether through direct or vicarious liability, a new employer will generally be liable.

5.111 However, the potential liability for an employer does not stop with a new recruit, or even with the inappropriate use of information. Employers must be aware that their cyber systems, whether email, websites, or staff internet searches, can facilitate discrimination in the workplace, health and safety breaches and harassment. Employers must be aware of how they may be liable, and put in place procedures that will mitigate unwanted behaviour.

Direct liability

5.112 Direct liability is the liability that attaches to a company or organisation when the employer directs or authorises the performance of the act by the employee. In *Tesco Supermarkets Ltd v Nattrass*,[56] provided the context through which a limited company could be directly liable for an act perpetrated by a natural person:

> 'I must start by considering the nature of the personality which by a fiction the law attributes to a corporation. A living person has a mind which can have knowledge or intention or be negligent and he has hands to carry out his intentions. A corporation has none of these: it must act through living persons, though not always one or the same person. Then the person who acts is not speaking or acting for the company. He is acting as the company and his mind which directs his acts is the mind of the company. There is no question of the company being vicariously liable. He is not acting as a servant, representative, agent or delegate. He is an embodiment of the company or, one could say, he hears and speaks through the persona of the company, within his appropriate sphere, and his mind is the mind of the company. If it is a guilty mind then that guilt is the guilt of the company. It must be a question of law whether, once the facts have been ascertained, a person in doing particular things is to be regarded as the company or merely as the company's servant or agent. In that case any liability of the company can only be a statutory or vicarious liability.'

5.113 For a company, the person 'speaking as the company' is normally a director or individual in upper management. However, a director can delegate their functions, so direct liability can extend to employees acting with delegated authority.

5.114 Direct liability is unlikely to arise in relation to instances of online harassment or discrimination. It would be unthinkable that company directors, speaking for the company, would encourage an employee to engage in racial or sexual abuse. However, email traffic will be highly relevant when considering

---

[56] [1972] AC 153, per Lord Reid, at 170.

misuse of information, competitive tendering, or even allegations under the Bribery Act 2010. A company director may certainly encourage an employee or agent to aggressively tender for work, and it is certainly plausible that direct liability for the company could arise if the employee's behaviour crosses an acceptable line.

5.115 A company's online presence may also potentially facilitate breaches of health and safety or advertising regulations. A company will likely be directly liable for online advertising instigated by an employee regardless as to whether the specific content was approved by a director, if compliance had been delegated without proper procedures in place.

5.116 In *Tesco Supermarkets Ltd v Nattrass*, the House of Lords (Lord Reid, Lord Morris of Borth-y-Gest, Viscount Dilhorne, Lord Pearson, Lord Diplock) held that a limited company can establish a defence against certain statutory offences if it has set up an efficient system for preventing the commission of offences, and the offence is committed because of the default of one of its employees, even if he is an employee responsible for the supervision of other employees. The Bribery Act 2010, s 7, imposes criminal liability on a company for failing to prevent bribery but it is a defence for the company to prove that adequate procedures were in place designed to prevent employees from undertaking such conduct. Companies need well-formulated compliance procedures which, so far as is reasonable, contemplate the cyber systems in place and prevent instances of information misuse, bullying and improper behaviour, both within and outside the company.

Vicarious liability

5.117 Vicarious liability is the imposition of liability on one person for the actionable conduct of another, based solely on the relationship between the two persons. Vicarious liability for the actions of employees is imposed on an employer either at common law or by statute. The test for vicarious liability is that the action of the employee must have been committed in the course or scope of their employment. An act is within the scope of employment if the employee was retained to perform the act, or if its performance is reasonably incidental to the matters which the employee was retained to do. It is important to note that 'within the scope of employment' is a broad term.

5.118 Misuse of confidential information and infringements of copyright have long been considered tortious, and it follows that the principles of vicarious liability apply to this behaviour.[57]

5.119 Harassment is a statutory tort to which vicarious liability equally applies. In *S&D Property Investments Ltd v Nisbet*,[58] the claimant was entitled to damages for anxiety as a result of harassment by a company director in the

---

[57] See *Pintorex Ltd v Keyvanfar*, at [46].
[58] [2009] EWHC 1726 (Ch).

course of seeking to recover a debt to the company. The director had sent emails to the claimant suggesting he should sell his property to meet the debt. The company was vicariously liable for the director's actions and it was equitable for those damages to be set off in diminution of the principal sum claimed from the claimant in the company's original debt action.

5.120 The Equality Act 2010, s 109, extends vicarious liability for employers through discrimination. Anything done by a person in the course of their employment is also treated as being done by the employer, even in circumstances where the employer had no knowledge or otherwise disapproved of the conduct in question.[59] The ambit of what falls within the course of employment has been considered and defined by the courts. In *Waters v Commissioner of Police of the Metropolis*,[60] an employer was not liable for an assault occurring to an employee who was off-duty but on a premises controlled by the employer. In *Chief Constable of Lincolnshire v Stubbs*,[61] it was held that an employer could be liable for discriminatory behaviour occurring during a social gathering which was an extension of employment.

5.121 In relation to the internet, an employer is vicariously liable for emails sent by employees to other employees and customers, but may even be liable for conduct outside the hours of employment and unrelated to work (such as the sending of emails to personal friends after work) if facilitated through the company email account. Employers should be aware that behaviour that is prejudicial towards a protected characteristic could result in a cause of action again the company. However, like with direct liability, in certain circumstances an employer can escape liability if it can establish that it took all reasonable steps to prevent the employee from committing the act of discrimination.[62]

Directors' liability

5.122 The Supreme Court (Lord Neuberger JSC, Lord Clarke JSC, Lord Sumption JSC, Lord Reed JSC, Lord Carnwath JSC) recently considered the question of what state of mind is necessary to render a director liable for breach of confidence.[63]

5.123 A director's liability can be imposed in three ways:

(1)   contractually;

(2)   common design;

(3)   dishonesty turning a 'blind-eye'.

---

[59]   See Equality Act, s 109(3).
[60]   [1997] ICR 1073.
[61]   [1999] ICR 547.
[62]   *Croft v Royal Mail Group Plc (formerly Consignia Plc* [2003] EWCA Civ 1045, [2003] ICR 1425.
[63]   See *Vestergaard Frandsen v Bestnet* [2013] UKSC 31.

5.124 The Supreme Court was dealing with breach of confidence. Although in principle director liability could be applied to other tortious activity, whether defined in common law or statute, it is unlikely that contractual provisions would deal with tortious actions such as harassment or assault. However, contractual terms may be relevant to the use of confidential information and copyright.

5.125 In *Vestergaard Frandsen,* the claimant asserted that a senior employee was liable for breach of confidence on the basis of common design. The argument proceeded on the basis that the employee had worked with others to design, manufacture and market products, and that these products were designed by one of the group in such a way as to involve the wrongful misuse of the claimant's trade secrets. There was no doubt that the former employee was liable for breach of confidence but it was asserted that by working together, others in the group were also liable with him.

5.126 The Supreme Court held that in principle 'common design' may be invoked against a defendant in a claim based on misuse of confidential information. However, in order for a defendant to be party to a common design: 'she must share with the other party, or parties, to the design, each of the features of the design which make it wrongful. If, and only if, all those features are shared, the fact that some parties to the common design did only some of the relevant acts, while others did only some other relevant acts, will not stop them all from being jointly liable'.[64]

5.127 In this case, the defendant was not in possession of the relevant trade secrets, and more importantly did not know that they were being misused. The defendant did not have the necessary state of knowledge or state of mind. Therefore, although party to the activities which may have rendered other parties liable for misuse of confidential information, the defendant was not liable under common design:[65]

> 'A driver of the motor car who transports a person to and from a bank to enable him to rob it, would be liable in tort for the robbery under common design or some similar principle, but only if she knew that her passenger intended to rob, or had robbed, the bank. So, in this case, given the ingredients of the wrong of misuse of confidential information, and given that she never had any relevant confidential information, Mrs Sig cannot be held liable in common design for exploiting with others, on behalf of Intection and then Bestnet, a product which, unknown to her, was being and had been developed through the wrongful use of Vestergaard's trade secrets.'

5.128 A director cannot evade liability by avoiding the requisite state of mind if 'blind-eye knowledge' can be inferred. A director cannot merely turn a blind-eye to obvious misuse of information to negate liability. However, in

---

[64]   See *Vestergaard Frandsen,* at [34].
[65]   See *Vestergaard Frandsen,* at [35].

order to infer such knowledge, the Supreme Court, per Lord Neuberger, held that the director must be found to be dishonest:[66]

'So far as argument (i) is concerned, it cannot succeed without a finding against Mrs Sig of dishonesty of the sort characterised by Lord Nicholls in Royal Brunei, as discussed in para 26 above. There is no such finding, and it seems to me clear from the conclusions which the Judge did reach, as summarised in para 15 above, that there was no basis for his making any finding of relevant dishonesty on the part of Mrs Sig.

As to argument (ii), it is not enough to render a defendant secondarily liable for misuse of trade secrets by another to establish that she took a risk in acting as she did. The fact that she took a risk might often render it easier to hold that she was dishonest, but, by definition, it is not enough on its own. To revert to the metaphor, if one plays with fire, one is more likely to be burnt, but it does not of itself mean that one is burnt.'

5.129 In *Royal Brunei Airlines Sdn Bhd v Tan*,[67] the House of Lords, per Lord Nicholls, approved the notion of 'commercially unacceptable conduct in the particular context involved', and suggested that 'acting in reckless disregard of others' rights or possible rights can be a tell-tale sign of dishonesty':[68]

'The only answer to these questions lies in keeping in mind that honesty is an objective standard. The individual is expected to attain the standard which would be observed by an honest person placed in those circumstances. It is impossible to be more specific. Knox J. captured the flavour of this, in a case with a commercial setting, when he referred to a person who is "guilty of commercially unacceptable conduct in the particular context involved:" see *Cowan de Groot Properties Ltd. v Eagle Trust Plc.* [1992] 4 All E.R. 700, 761. Acting in reckless disregard of others' rights or possible rights can be a tell-tale sign of dishonesty. An honest person would have regard to the circumstances known to him, including the nature and importance of the proposed transaction, the nature and importance of his role, the ordinary course of business, the degree of doubt, the practicability of the trustee or the third party proceeding otherwise and the seriousness of the adverse consequences to the beneficiaries. The circumstances will dictate which one or more of the possible courses should be taken by an honest person. He might, for instance, flatly decline to become involved. He might ask further questions. He might seek advice, or insist on further advice being obtained. He might advise the trustee of the risks but then proceed with his role in the transaction. He might do many things. Ultimately, in most cases, an honest person should have little difficulty in knowing whether a proposed transaction, or his participation in it, would offend the normally accepted standards of honest conduct.'

5.130 A company director may be personally liable for the tortious behaviour of an employee through common design, or if he dishonestly turns a blind eye to behaviour he knows to be unacceptable. In the context of the digital age, it is not a great leap to consider that a company director who knew of harassment

---

[66] See *Vestergaard Frandsen*, at [42]–[43].
[67] [1995] 2 AC 378.
[68] See *Royal Brunei*, at 391.

or discrimination in the workplace, by being copied into an email, but failed to take action, could potentially be held personally liable. Alternatively, the director who undertakes to meet the problem would not only be protecting themselves but if reasonable provisions were then put in place could be saving the company from secondary liability.

EMPLOYER MEASURES, SYSTEMS AND PROCEDURES

5.131 Whether measures, systems and procedures are sufficient to avoid employer liability is specific to the context of the company. Factors including the size, turnover, sector of trade or service, extent of regulation within the sector, and impact on the claimant, both actual and foreseeable, will be crucial to determine whether the company has taken 'all reasonable steps, and exercised all appropriate due diligence' to avoid secondary liability. A failure to take any steps to prevent online tortious activity will almost certainly cause the company to be liable for an employee's actions, and would likely render any claim of ignorance or good faith to be irrelevant.

5.132 The employee contract is the first and best place to protect the company from liability in relation to the misuse of online systems, including email and the internet. The employee contract is also an excellent first step to prevent the loss of confidential information and trade secrets, and to assert copyright protection.

5.133 It is unwise to underestimate the impact practical measures have in demonstrating that reasonable steps have been taken either to maintain confidence or to prevent unwanted behaviour. Written procedures are the beginning not the end of corporate governance. Reaffirmation and monitoring are equally important to introduction. Regular review and revision are essential.

5.134 Finally, a structured and utilised disciplinary procedure underlines satisfactory systems. A company director who shies away from his responsibility may potentially become personally liable for the improper conduct ignored.

Cyber terms of use and the employee contract

5.135 The employee contract marks the beginning of the working relationship and should be the foundation of the protection in place for the employer. Cyber terms of use should be clear and agreed before an employee is recruited. The review and revision of appropriate terms means that incorporation through an employee handbook is often the most efficient method for inclusion in the contract. Cyber terms of use should include an acceptable email and internet policy; data protection procedures; consideration of computer health and safety; discrimination and sexual harassment policies; and the procedures for investigation and sanction if there is a breach.

5.136 The protection of otherwise unprotected assets, such as software functionality or those elements classified as ideas and principles within the Software Directive, could potentially be achieved through appropriate contract provisions. Every basic employee contract should incorporate a condition related to the protection of confidential information while under the contract. Traditionally restrictive covenants following the contract have been limited to 'gardening leave' and the prohibition from starting employment with a competitor for a period of time. However, there is no reason why an employer's cyber terms of use could not be extended to protect defined information, whether ideas, principles or functionality, in a similar way to a restrictive covenant either for a period of time or indefinitely.

5.137 Employees must be made aware of the information that they handle which the employer considers to be confidential. This is likely to change over time, and unlike acceptable internet usage which will apply across the company, the confidential information handled within each department will vary. There is nothing to prevent the inclusion of a contract term which requires an employee to keep confidential specific material contained within an additional handbook or log. These supplementary logs could be tailored to the specific department or even individual. As long as sufficient protection was in place the content of these logs could retain the necessary indicia of confidence, and potentially could even attract protection in copyright.

5.138 Many employees are targeted with specific key performance indicators (KPIs) to update or innovate systems. The employee contract could require that ideas and principles, necessary to meet the relevant KPI, be recorded within the supplementary log. There is nothing to prevent a term which requires any innovation to be recorded within the log. The contract should be explicit that the compilation of the supplementary log constitutes a part of the employment contract, so that any right that subsists rests with the employer. The employee would then be required to agree not to copy, download,[69] or remove the log if they moved away from the company. This covenant would not extend to skills or experience obtained during the period of employment or even information retained within the employee's memory. However, illegitimate retention such as intentionally memorising the log would not be permitted by the courts.

5.139 Arguably if sufficient skill and labour was expended in the production of the log, there may be a claim in copyright to prevent reproduction of the material contained even from memory. This would be akin to a competitor copying a rival's company manual subconsciously (see *SAS v WPL*, above). Depending on the format of the log and the information contained there may even be an argument to suggest a database right exists.

5.140 The potential risk is that valuable information is being compiled into a single source. If confidentiality was lost either through competitor action or

---

[69] Proper protection of the supplementary log would be best facilitated as an encrypted and password-protected electronic document that can be accessed by the employee and the relevant management team.

employee mistake the impact could be disastrous. Further, this form of restrictive covenant is untested within the courts. The courts will look to balance the public interest in a company protecting important information in which substantial investment has been expended, and the free movement of employees and their utilisation of skill and experience legitimately obtained. Regardless, the potential for cyber terms of use goes far beyond a single term which prevents disclosure of confidential information while employed. In an age when the office environment is becoming increasingly virtual, and misconduct within the workplace which was once easily identified is becoming more concealed, the use of the employee contract, and associated documents, is important to employer protection.

Practical measures

5.141   The most straightforward measures may often have the biggest impact. Communication of information is vital to the ensuring that employees are aware of the acceptable limits. Beginning with the employee contract, neither the most basic terms nor the most innovative provisions are incorporated into the contract if the employee is not provided with the employee handbook. Ensure that employees receive and sign for receipt when they are first employed.

5.142   Notices to prompt employees to use confidential waste bins and to keep their desks clear of confidential information have the dual effect of reminding employees of the systems in place but also to identify information they are handling as confidential. The proper disposal of confidential information should be monitored. Confidential information which is released into the public domain through improper disposal will not be protected by the courts.

5.143   Employee training can address areas of potential weakness either through compulsory attendance at lectures delivered by relevant experts, or through informal sharing between employees of best practice. Reasonable training may take the form of lectures, seminars, debates, workshops or online videos or forums. The purpose is to engage employees, to require that they read relevant procedures, and monitor that there is understanding of the systems in place.

Disciplinary procedures

5.144   Disciplinary procedures are often poorly conceived and underutilised. Three-strike procedures (warning, written warning, action) can be formulaic and rigid, and prevent managers from addressing minor but inappropriate behaviour which is allowed to continue. Managerial action that records and addresses behaviour can be incorporated into ongoing professional development without stigmatising the employee as 'bad'.

5.145   Procedures should allow for every instance to be considered and dealt with quickly. Flexibility is vital within a clear and transparent system. Matters should be escalated as appropriate, and not after a prescribed number of warnings. A rigid three-strike system will often cause minor matters after an initial warning to go unrecorded because 'it's not serious enough for a formal warning or action'. All inappropriate behaviour requires an action whether it is verbal confirmation that the behaviour has been noted, or a formal disciplinary proceeding that may lead to summary dismissal.

CHAPTER 6

COMMERCIAL ESPIONAGE

INTRODUCTION

6.01 In 2013, the Commission of the European Union compiled a survey in relation to confidential business information. Three-quarters of respondents indicated that commercially sensitive information was 'strategically important to their company's growth, competitiveness and innovative performance'.[1] The loss of confidential information was a concern for 39% of those surveyed, with industrial espionage as a matter of special concern in the pharmaceutical and motor vehicle sectors.[2]

6.02 In the United Kingdom (UK) and the Republic of Ireland there is no statutory protection for trade secrets. The protection of information is achieved through a matrix of common law torts and statutory provisions. Understanding the means of protection provides those with valuable confidential information with the opportunity to achieve a competitive advantage against their company rivals. This chapter provides an overview of the statutory protection which provides a proprietary right over information. If a company cannot, or has not, asserted a proprietary right, tortious actions may still provide some protection.

6.03 The chapter begins with the classic definition of espionage being state-sponsored 'spying', as commercial espionage continues to be the pursuit of international actors.

---

[1] *Study on Trade Secrets and Confidential Business Information in the Internal Market*, published in April 2013, http://ec.europa.eu/internal_market/iprenforcement/docs/trade-secrets/130711_final-study_en.pdf (last accessed 6 September 2016).

[2] V Falce, 'Trade secrets – looking for (full) harmonisation in the Innovative Union', *International Review of Intellectual Property and Competition Law*, [2015] IIC 940, at 946.

Intelligence Services Act 1994

6.04 The extent to which state-sponsored economic espionage is carried out across the globe is difficult to estimate. Suggestions of foreign cyber-attacks on American businesses are relatively common.[3] In the UK, there is legal provision for intelligence agencies to target foreign diplomats for economic purposes.

6.05 The Intelligence Services Act 1994 (ISA 1994) placed the Secret Intelligence Service (SIS) and Government Communications Headquarters (GCHQ) on a statutory footing for the first time. In accordance with ISA 1994, s 3, GCHQ must act: 'in the interests of national security, with particular reference to the defence and foreign policies of Her Majesty's Government in the United Kingdom; in the interests of the economic well-being of the United Kingdom in relation to the actions or intentions of persons outside the British Islands; or in support of the prevention or detection of serious crime'.

6.06 The phrase 'interests of the economic wellbeing of the United Kingdom' has been criticised by European governments as appearing to authorise industrial espionage. The Regulation of Investigatory Powers Act 2000 (RIPA 2000) has given GCHQ precise tools to gather intelligence through techniques such as targeted interceptions. Under RIPA 2000, the Director of GCHQ is one among ten senior officials who can apply for a warrant, to either the foreign or home secretary, on grounds which are almost identical to those in the ISA 1994, including pursuit of national security and economic wellbeing. In 2009, 1,706 warrants for interceptions were approved by ministers for agencies including GCHQ.[4]

6.07 In 2013, it was revealed that British intelligence agencies monitored foreign leaders and diplomats at international conferences such as meetings of the G20, and that the information gathered had been used to brief senior British participants during the conferences.[5] Papers also showed that economic wellbeing was used to justify spying on Turkish and South African diplomats.[6]

---

[3] Ariana Eunjung Cha and Ellen Nakashima, 'Google China cyberattack part of vast espionage campaign, experts say', *The Washington Post*, 14 January 2010; Nicole Perlroth, 'Hackers in China Attacked The Times for Last 4 Months', *The New York Times* (retrieved 31 January 2013).

[4] 'The laws that allow intelligence agencies to spy on foreign diplomats: The Intelligence Services Act and Regulation of Investigatory Powers Act are broad enough to allow all manner of operations', *The Guardian*, 16 June 2013, https://www.theguardian.com/uk/2013/jun/16/laws-intelligence-agencies-spy-foreign?INTCMP=ILCNETTXT3487 (last accessed 27 September 2016).

[5] Ewen MacAskill; Nick Davies; Nick Hopkins; Julian Borger; James Ball, 'GCHQ intercepted foreign politicians' communications at G20 summits Exclusive: phones were monitored and fake internet cafés set up to gather information from allies in London in 2009', *The Guardian*, 17 June 2013 (last accessed 1 September 2016).

[6] 'The laws that allow intelligence agencies to spy on foreign diplomats: The Intelligence Services Act and Regulation of Investigatory Powers Act are broad enough to allow all manner of operations', *The Guardian*, 16 June 2013. https://www.theguardian.com/uk/2013/jun/16/laws-intelligence-agencies-spy-foreign?INTCMP=ILCNETTXT3487 (last accessed 1 September 2016).

6.08 The ISA 1994 is sufficiently wide to potentially allow for authorised access into computer systems within UK companies. In such cases the provisions contained within RIPA 2000 and the Police Act 1998 must be properly applied to prevent the individual undertaking the access from committing a criminal offence.

STATE IMMUNITY

6.09 Where the perpetrator is a sovereign state, the availability of a remedy will be subject to the State Immunity Act 1978 (SIA 1978), which establishes by virtue of s 1 the general proposition that the UK courts have **no** jurisdiction to adjudicate disputes against sovereign states. There are exceptions to this proposition but only if it can be shown that one of the exceptions described in ss 2–11 is engaged.

6.10 The chief exceptions are that the state in question has submitted to the jurisdiction of the UK courts; the proceedings relate to a commercial transaction entered into by the state[7] or the proceedings relate to personal injury and damage to property caused by an act or omission in the UK.[8]

6.11 Even if one of the exceptions set out above applies, the separate but related principle of non-justiciability must be considered. It is a rule of 'judicial restraint' that the following are not justiciable in UK courts:

- acts of the Crown in the course of relations with other states;
- executive acts authorised by the Crown in the exercise of foreign power;
- legislative or executive acts of foreign states.

The non-justiciable principle seeks to distinguish between disputes involving state authorities, which can only be resolved at a state-to-state level, and those actions that can be resolved judicially.[9]

6.12 A state must plead immunity from jurisdiction. Not doing so or inordinate delays in pleading immunity may be a bar; however, even if an exception to immunity from adjudication can be established, the SIA, s 13, provides for state immunity from interim and final enforcement actions against sovereign property. Further claimant parties are prevented from obtaining an injunction, an order for specific performance, or order for the recovery of land or other property, and from enforcing any judgment or arbitration award

---

[7] See *NML Capital Limited (Appellant) v Republic of Argentina (Respondent)* [2011] UKSC 31. The Supreme Court held that states cannot claim immunity when facing enforcement in England of foreign adverse judgments in commercial cases.

[8] See *Ogelegbanwei and others v President of the Federal Republic of Nigeria and others* [2016] EWHC 8 (QB).

[9] See *Kuwait Airways v Iraqi Airways* [2000] EWCA Civ 284.

against the property of the state. A state may consent to enforcement (s 13(3)) but an undertaking from a state to not appeal a costs order does not imply submission to any enforcement.[10]

6.13 Enforcement may be possible where it is against property 'for the time being used for, or intended to be used for, commercial purposes' (s 13(5)); but only if it is used or intended to be used exclusively for commercial purposes,[11] and does not belong to a state central bank or other monetary authority.

6.14 It will be possible to enforce a foreign judgment against a foreign state: s 31 of the Civil Jurisdiction and Judgments Act 1982 gives the English court an additional ground to those set out in the SIA 1978 to take jurisdiction over a sovereign and provides an alternative scheme for restricting state immunity in the case of foreign judgments. In *NML Capital Ltd v Republic of Argentina*[12] the two conditions in s 31 were met and Argentina could not assert immunity in respect of the enforcement proceedings.

6.15 In relation to emanations of the state, the Serious Crime Act 2015, s 44, amended s 10 of the Computer Misuse Act 1990 to extend the immunity of GCHQ, the police, security services and other enforcement officers from prosecution under the Computer Misuse Act 1990, the Data Protection Act 1998 and 'any other enactment or rule of law by virtue of which the conduct in question is authorised or required'. This provides an umbrella of protection for the investigative authorities from 'enactments', as defined at s 44(2)(a)–(e), where the investigator's conduct can be shown to be authorised. In the case of GCHQ, for example, where it is in the 'in the interests of national security, with particular reference to the defence and foreign policies of Her Majesty's Government in the United Kingdom; in the interests of the economic well-being of the United Kingdom in relation to the actions or intentions of persons outside the British Islands; or in support of the prevention or detection of serious crime'.

Computer Misuse Act 1990

6.16 Commercial espionage which involves the unauthorised access to a company computer system is a criminal offence whether undertaken by a rival company or a state agent. The protection provided by the Computer Misuse Act 1990 is described in detail within Chapter 1 (Cyber Crime). However, despite the action of 'hacking' being illegal, the criminal courts are unable to retrieve or restrict the use of information obtained through illegal means. Within the criminal law information is not considered to be property.

---

[10]   See *Mitchell v Dali* [2005] EWCA Civ 720.
[11]   See *Alcom v Republic of Columbia* [1984] AC 580.
[12]   [2011] UKSC 31.

Oxford v Moss[13]

6.17 It has long been established that confidential information does not constitute property. In *Oxford v Moss*,[14] the defendant, Mr Moss, was a student of civil engineering at Liverpool University, who had taken possession of a proof examination paper that he was expected to take the following month. It was accepted by all parties that the paper on which the examination was printed was property, owned by the Senate of Liverpool University, within the definition contained within s 4(1) of the Theft Act 1968:

4 'Property'

(1) 'Property' includes money and all other property, real or personal, including things in action and other intangible property.

6.18 However, it was also agreed that Mr Moss had no intention of taking the physical property (ie the paper) from the university. In fact, it was incumbent to his plan that the university know of no interference to the paper. The Court of Appeal (Lord Widgery LCJ, Smith J, Wien J) properly summarised the circumstance, at 185:

'He was borrowing a piece of paper hoping to be able to return it and not be detected in order that he should acquire advance knowledge of the questions to be set in the examination and thereby, I suppose, he would be enabled to have an unfair advantage as against other students who did not possess the knowledge that he did.'

6.19 On appeal, it was contended that Mr Moss had obtained confidential information, namely the meaning of the words printed on the examination paper, and that this was a form of intangible property. The Crown asserted that he had appropriated this property dishonestly and was therefore guilty of theft under s 1 of the Theft Act 1968:

1 Basic definition of theft

(1) A person is guilty of theft if he dishonestly appropriates property belonging to another with the intention of permanently depriving the other of it; and 'thief' and 'steal' shall be construed accordingly.

6.20 The Court of Appeal disagreed. Although in certain circumstances civil remedies may be sought to prohibit the use of information, confidential information was not property and, therefore, was not protected under the Theft Act:[15]

'The question for this Court is whether confidential information of this sort falls within that definition contained in section 4(1). We have been referred to a number

---

[13]   (1979) 68 Cr App R 1183.
[14]   (1979) 68 Cr App R 1183.
[15]   See *Oxford v Moss*, at 186.

of authorities emanating from the area of trade secrets and matrimonial secrets ...
Those are cases concerned with what is described as the duty to be of good faith.
They are clear illustrations of the proposition that, if a person obtains information
which is given to him in confidence and then sets out to take an unfair advantage
of it, the courts will restrain him by way of an order of injunction or will condemn
him in damages if an injunction is found to be inappropriate. It seems to me,
speaking for my part, that they are of little assistance in the present situation in
which we have to consider whether there is property in the information which is
capable of being the subject of a charge of theft. In my judgment, it is clear that the
answer to that question must be no. Accordingly, I would dismiss the Appeal.'

6.21 Even in a statute that defined property as 'things in action and other
intangible property' information did not fall within this definition. *Oxford v
Moss* makes clear that the courts will not assert a proprietary right over
information unless the statute enacted by Parliament is clear and explicit to this
intention. The Trade Marks Act 1994, the Copyright, Designs and Patents
Act 1988, and the Patent Act 1977 are such statutes.

6.22 The Court of Appeal identified that at common law a breach of
confidence could be actionable but it was not the information that was
property, rather that the court would restrain unfair advantage as a result of a
breach of good faith. Similarly, the court will intervene to prevent the
exploitation of another's goodwill under the tort of passing off. However, it
remains that there is no proprietary right in equity or the common law over
information.

STATUTORY PROVISIONS

6.23 At common law there is no proprietary right over information. The Trade
Marks Act 1994, the Copyright, Designs and Patents Act 1988, and the Patent
Act 1977 provide a proprietary interest. The courts will act to protect an
owner's property if infringed by a commercial rival.

Trade marks

6.24 The Trade Marks Act 1994 (TMA 1994) provides protection for trade
marks through a system of registration. The Act also deals with recognition
within the UK of a variety of international marks. Section 1 of the TMA 1994
defines a trade mark as:

> 'any sign capable of being represented graphically which is capable of
> distinguishing goods or services of one undertaking from those of other
> undertakings. A trade mark may, in particular, consist of words (including
> personal names), designs, letters, numerals or the shape of goods or their
> packaging.'

6.25 Registration of a trade mark is permitted in accordance with s 2 of the
TMA 1994, and provides for a proprietary right in the registered trade mark:

2 Registered trade marks

(1) A registered trade mark is a property right obtained by the registration of the trade mark under this Act and the proprietor of a registered trade mark has the rights and remedies provided by this Act.

6.26 In order to obtain registration, the trade mark must have a distinctive character and must not be similar to a mark already registered for the same class of goods or services. Sections 3–8 specify a list of grounds on which an application for the registration of a trade mark can be refused.

6.27 Registration is effected following an application under the TMA 1994, s 32, to the registrar. Provided that the requirements for registration are met, the registrar must grant an application and register the trade mark. Priority is provided for registration to a trade mark which has already been registered outside the UK, and once registered a registered trade mark lasts for 10 years. However, registration can be renewed. The TMA 1994 makes provision about the licensing of trade marks at ss 28–31.

6.28 Registration is overseen by the Comptroller-General of Patents, Designs and Trade Marks, with administration in accordance with the Trade Marks Rules 2008.[16]

6.29 The effect of a registered trade mark is to allow the proprietor to prevent use within the United Kingdom without consent. The proprietor of a registered trade mark has exclusive rights, which can be enforced from the date of registration (s 9). Infringement consists of using a sign or symbol which is identical to a registered trade mark, or is so similar that 'there exists a likelihood of confusion on the part of the public' (s 10). The infringing sign must be used in relation to goods or services which are the same or similar to those of the registered trade mark. Once the proprietor or their licensee puts goods on the market anywhere in the European Economic Area, the proprietary right over the trade mark on those goods is lost. The proprietor can no longer object to the use of the trade mark in relation to those goods (ss 12 and 17).

6.30 The proprietary right can be enforced through the courts with a claimant seeking relief by way of damages, injunctions, accounts or relief 'otherwise … available to him as is available in respect of the infringement of any other property right' (s 14). In addition to the traditional remedies available to the courts, the TMA 1994, ss 15–16, allow for an order that the offending sign be erased, removed or obliterated from any infringing goods, material or articles; or, if that is not reasonably practicable, for an order to secure the destruction of the infringing goods. Further an owner of a registered trade mark can apply for the infringing goods to be surrendered to the proprietor.

6.31 The TMA 1994, s 92, also creates a criminal offence of unauthorised use of trade mark. The offence criminalises applying a registered trade mark to

---

[16] SI 2008/1797.

goods, selling property displaying a registered trade mark, and even having possession of a good displaying a registered trade mark if there is an intention to sell or distribute in the course of a business, and if there is no consent from the trade mark owner. The maximum sentence for this offence is 10 years' imprisonment and an unlimited fine. Her Majesty's Revenue and Customs (HMRC) are given a range of powers in relation to infringing goods (s 89), and local weights and measures authorities also have enforcement powers (s 93). Search warrants can be obtained in relation to this offence by application of a constable to a magistrates' court (s 92A).

Trade Mark Directive

6.32 The TMA 1994 implemented within domestic legislation the European Union (EU) Directive 89/104/EEC (the Trade Mark Directive). The Trade Mark Directive was the first attempt at approximation of national laws relating to trade marks in respect of goods and services. Its aim was to set out the fundamental principles of trade mark regulation and enforcement within the EU, without imposing the harmonisation of the national systems.

6.33 Article 2 of the Trade Mark Directive gave a definition of a trade mark:

'A trade mark may consist of any sign capable of being represented graphically, particularly words, including personal names, designs, letters, numerals, the shape of goods or of their packaging, provided that such signs are capable of distinguishing the goods or services of one undertaking from those of other undertakings.'

This definition was incorporated in its entirety into the TMA 1994.

6.34 The Trade Mark Directive established grounds for refusing registration, licensing, and revoking or declaring trade marks invalid. Refusal or invalidity could be as a result of two apparently opposing grounds:

(1) The refusal or invalidity shall apply in case of 'trade marks which are of such a nature as to deceive the public, for instance as to the nature, quality or geographical origin of the goods or service' (Art 3(1)); and

(2) 'a trade mark shall not be registered or, if registered, shall be liable to be declared invalid if it is identical with an earlier trade mark, and the goods or services for which the trade mark is applied for or is registered are identical with the goods or services for which the earlier trade mark is protected' (Art 4(1)).

6.35 The aim of the Trade Mark Directive is the better functioning of the internal market. Although proprietors' rights are protected, and the circumscription of trade marks is prohibited, this is a means of maximising efficiency not as an absolute right. The Trade Mark Directive provides great discretion to national bodies in the implementation and practical registration of trade marks; however, as with the TMA 1994, many member states incorporated the provisions of the Trade Mark Directive in its entirety to avoid criticism from the EU Commission.

6.36 On 22 October 2008, Directive No 2008/95/EC of the European Parliament and of the Council was read as a consolidated version of the Trade Mark Directive and is the current Directive in force.

Trade Mark Regulation

6.37 In order to offer a uniform protection of trade marks within the EU, Council Regulation No 40/94/EC created a Community Trade Mark allowing a unitary identification of products and services by enterprises. Regulation No 40/94/EC was amended nine times between 1994 and 2005.[17] In order to promote clarity, Council Regulation No 207/2009/EC (the Trade Mark Regulation) was introduced as a codifying measure to create legal conditions to:

> 'enable undertakings to adapt their activities to the scale of the Community, whether in manufacturing and distributing goods or in providing services. For those purposes, trade marks enabling the products and services of undertakings to be distinguished by identical means throughout the entire Community, regardless of frontiers, should feature amongst the legal instruments which undertakings have at their disposal (Recital (2)).'

6.38 The registration for a Community Trade Mark can now be obtained through a single application to the Office of Harmonisation in the Internal Market (OHIM), and registration produces the same effects in all member states. Once an application for registration has been received, the OHIM (and in some instances the national industrial property offices) undertakes to check the possible existence of a conflict with earlier rights relating to a Community or national trade mark. This single procedure has the advantage of reducing costs for registration. The applicant avoids filing applications in every country within the EU; however, if the OHIM refuses the registration, the applicant cannot recover the costs of filling the Community Trade Mark application and will bear the costs of national applications in order to obtain single national registrations.

6.39 The Community Trade Mark lasts for 10 years from the date of filing and can be renewed for further periods of 10 years (Art 46). However, failure to put a trade mark to 'genuine use' in any period of 5 years can lead to 'sanction'

---

17 Council Regulation (EC) No 40/94(OJ L 11, 14.1.1994, p. 1); Council Regulation (EC) No 3288/94 (OJ L 349, 31.12.1994, p 83); Council Regulation (EC) No 807/2003(OJ L 122, 16.5.2003, p 36); only point 48 of Annex III Council Regulation (EC) No 1653/2003 (OJ L 245, 29.9.2003, p 36); Council Regulation (EC) No 1992/2003 (OJ L 296, 14.11.2003, p 1); Council Regulation (EC) No 422/2004 (OJ L 70, 9.3.2004, p 1); Council Regulation (EC) No 1891/2006(OJ L 386, 29.12.2006, p 14) Only Article 1; Annex II, Part 4 (C)(I) of the 2003 Act of Accession(OJ L 236, 23.9.2003, p 342); and Annex III, Point 1.I of the 2005 Act of Accession (OJ L 157, 21.6.2005, p 231).

(Art 15). The major sanction for non-use is the liability to revocation or cancellation of the registration (Art 51).

6.40 Registration generates a proprietary right, and gives exclusive rights to the proprietor to prohibit any third party to use identical or similar signs to the Community Trade Mark registered. This includes the right to license and transfer the rights (Arts 17–23). National courts have exclusive competence about deciding on validity and infringements of Community Trade Marks (Arts 95–96). Claims for international infringement must be brought in the courts of the member state in which the defendant is domiciled or, if he is not domiciled in any of the member states, in which he has an establishment. In an online context it may be the case that neither apply, in which case a claim can be pursued where the claimant is domiciled or established (Art 97).

6.41 Infringement proceedings may also be brought in 'the courts of the Member State in which the act of infringement has been committed or threatened' (Art 97(5)). The court in that instance is restricted to jurisdiction over the infringing acts within that member state (Art 98(2)). In *Coty Germany GmbH v First Note Perfumes NV*,[18] the European Court of Justice (ECJ) held that jurisdiction under Art 97(5) may be established solely in favour of the Community Trade Mark courts in the member state in which the defendant committed the unlawful act. The infringement in this case related to a physical sale in Belgium of counterfeit perfume. It is unclear how the case would be interpreted in an online context.

6.42 The Trade Mark Regulation sets out conditions for the refusal of registration (Arts 7–8); surrender (Art 50); and revocation and invalidity (Arts 51–55) of a Community Trade Mark within the competence of OHIM. Its decision are open to appeal before the Court of Appeal and, in certain cases, the ECJ (Arts 58–65).

6.43 There are mixed feelings about the effectiveness of the Community Trade Mark. On the 15th anniversary, the OHIM issued a press release which claimed that the system was a huge success: '320,000 companies or individuals in 190 countries have made 940,000 CTM applications, of which more than 713,000 have been registered, making the CTM a true European success story'.[19] However, some argue that the coexistence of Community and national trade marks has created confusion in trade mark registration systems. The use of the Community Trade Mark is an additional financial burden on any business who may only wish to trade within a small part of the community. As a defensive measure these businesses must seek a universal Community Trade Mark or risk

---

[18] (C-360/12) [2014] ETMR 49.
[19] http://www.liesegang-partner.eu/news/news/id/13813-ctm-turns-15.html, 5 April 2011 (last accessed 1 September 2016).

priority being claimed from another. Although applications for Community Trade Marks hve generated huge incomes for the OHIM it is arguable that the actual benefits are not so great.[20]

Internet and trade marks

6.44 The principles for trade mark protection online are consistent with that for the protection of physical or real world sales. Online content which can be considered distinctive, and is capable of distinguishing the origin of the goods and services supplied under it, can apply for protection through registration. Once registered with the relevant trade mark office the proprietor can enforce against unauthorised third party use (see Trade Marks Directive, Arts 2 and 3(1)(b); Trade Mark Regulation, Arts 4 and 7(1)(b)).

6.45 Online distinctiveness is to be assessed from the perspective of an average consumer for the goods and services. The average consumer is deemed to be reasonably observant and circumspect, albeit with an imperfect recollection, and rarely has the opportunity to compare contested trade mark material side by side.[21]

6.46 In accordance with the Trade Mark Directive, Art 12, and the Trade Mark Regulation, Art 15, online content must be subject to use provisions. Although there is no case-law directly on 'genuine use' in *Leno Merken BV v Hagelkruis Beheer BV*,[22] Advocate General Sharpston stated that mere inclusion of a trade mark on a website may be insufficient to constitute genuine use within the meaning of Art 15:[23]

> 'I therefore do not consider that use in a territory corresponding to that of only one Member State necessarily precludes the use from being characterised as genuine in the Community. At the same time, I do not consider that, for example, use of a mark on a website that is accessible in all of the 27 Member States is by definition genuine use in the Community.'

6.47 Although in that case the ECJ did not address the question of online use specifically, it broadly followed the reasoning and conclusions of the Advocate General.

6.48 The Second Chamber did hold that genuine use under the Trade Mark Regulation required that the mark must have been used to create or maintain market share for the goods and/or services protected by the registration (see *Leno Merken BV v Hagelkruis Beheer BV*, at [29]):

---

[20] http://ipso-jure.blogspot.co.uk/2011/04/15-years-of-community-trade-marks.html, 1 April 2011 (last accessed 1 September 2016).
[21] See *Lloyd Schuhfabrik Meyer & Co GmbH v Klijsen Handel BV* (C-342/97) [1999] All ER (EC) 587.
[22] (C-149/11) [2013] ETMR 16.
[23] See *Leno Merken BV v Hagelkruis Beheer BV*, at [55].

'It follows from that line of authority that there is "genuine use" of a trade mark where the mark is used in accordance with its essential function, which is to guarantee the identity of the origin of the goods or services for which it is registered, in order to create or preserve an outlet for those goods or services; genuine use does not include token use for the sole purpose of preserving the rights conferred by the mark. When assessing whether use of the trade mark is genuine, regard must be had to all the facts and circumstances relevant to establishing whether there is real commercial exploitation of the mark in the course of trade, particularly the usages regarded as warranted in the economic sector concerned as a means of maintaining or creating market share for the goods or services protected by the mark, the nature of those goods or services, the characteristics of the market and the scale and frequency of use of the mark.'

6.49 It is unlikely that the simple inclusion within a webpage or domain name would be sufficient to create or maintain market share. Therefore, even where a business could be categorised as entirely online, physical or real world use of trade marks through advertising, paper sales documentation, or commercial communications will be essential to ensure that genuine use is established.

6.50 In *Leno Merken BV v Hagelkruis Beheer BV*,[24] the court held that in certain circumstances the use of a Community Trade Mark in only one member state may suffice to satisfy use requirements. That decision has now been applied and refined by the Intellectual Property Enterprise Court in *Sofa Workshop Ltd v Sofaworks Ltd*,[25] which provided guidelines for 'genuine use', at [25]:

'(1) the question of whether there has been 'genuine use in the Community' is not to be approached from the perspective of whether there has been use of the mark in more than one, two or any other particular number of Member States. Territorial borders are to be disregarded;

(2) a Community trade mark is put to genuine use in the Community where it is used in accordance with its essential function, which is to guarantee the identity of the origin of the goods or services for which it is registered, and used for the purpose of maintaining or creating market share within the European Community for the goods or services covered by the mark;

(3) whether the mark has been so used will depend on all relevant facts and circumstances, including the characteristics of the market concerned, the nature of the relevant goods and services, the territorial extent and scale of use, and the frequency and regularity of use;

(4) purely in relation to the territorial extent of use, genuine use in the Community will in general require use in more than one Member State; and

(5) an exception to that general requirement arises where the market for the relevant goods or services is restricted to the territory of a single Member State.'

---

24   (C-149/11) [2013] Bus LR 928, [2013] ETMR 16.
25   [2015] EWHC 1773 (IPEC), [2015] ECC 25.

6.51 Within the online context these guidelines for genuine use will be equally applicable. It is therefore important for businesses with a significant online element to ensure that their websites are deemed to be targeting member states other than the UK, for example, by including prices in euros or presenting the website in different languages.

Copyright, Designs and Patents Act 1988

6.52 The protection of information by means of copyright or compilation within a database is contained within Chapter 5 (Employer Liability and Protection). Where aggressive corporate practice leads to copyright infringement, as in the TMA 1994, criminal liability can apply.

6.53 Section 107 of the Copyright, Designs and Patents Act 1988 (CDPA 1988) creates a criminal offence if a person takes possession of an article without the licence of a copyright owner, which is, and which he knows or has reason to believe is, an infringing copy of a copyright work. In the case of simple possession, the article must be held in the course of a business with a view to committing any act infringing the copyright. Similar liability applies to sale, hire, importation, or distribution (see CDPA 1988, s 107(1)):

107 Criminal liability for making or dealing with infringing articles, &c

(1) A person commits an offence who, without the licence of the copyright owner –

(a) makes for sale or hire, or
(b) imports into the United Kingdom otherwise than for his private and domestic use, or
(c) possesses in the course of a business with a view to committing any act infringing the copyright, or
(d) in the course of a business –
    (i)   sells or lets for hire, or
    (ii) offers or exposes for sale or hire, or
    (iii) exhibits in public, or
    (iv) distributes, or
(e) distributes otherwise than in the course of a business to such an extent as to affect prejudicially the owner of the copyright,

an article which is, and which he knows or has reason to believe is, an infringing copy of a copyright work.

6.54 Associated offences for making articles designed to infringe copyright, communicating copyrighted material, or performance of such material are contained within s 107(2)–(3).

6.55 The offences carry various sentences with the maximum sentence of 10 years' imprisonment and a fine reserved for making infringing articles for sale or hire, importation and distribution (s 107(1)(a), (b), (d)(iv) or (e)).

6.56 Similar to offences under the TMA 1994, the local weights and measures authorities also have enforcement powers (s 107A), and search warrants can be obtained in relation to this offence by application of a constable to a magistrates' court (s 109). Court orders can be made for infringing material to be delivered to the copyright owner (s 108).

Patents

6.57 Patent law is intended to encourage invention and innovation by allowing an inventor to register the invention as a patent and gain a 20-year monopoly over the exploitation of that invention. In securing against commercial espionage, once granted a patent can be protected through the courts of any country that the patent grant covers. The UK Intellectual Patent Office (IPO) covers the United Kingdom, the European Patent Office (EPO) covers all member states of the European Patent Organisation and the World Intellectual Patent Office (WIPO) covers all states that are signatories to the Patent Co-operation Treaty.

6.58 In the UK, the registration and protection of patents is in accordance with the Patents Act 1977 (PA 1977). In order to obtain a patent an invention must be novel, involve an inventive step, and capable of industrial application (s 1(1)). Any new application for a patent must be checked against existing patents to ensure the criteria are met. If the invention already existed or could be easily discovered from existing information ('prior art') without anything new it will not be registrable or could be challenged after registration.

6.59 The test of novelty must disclose something new, which is not contained within the sum of existing knowledge (s 2(2)). If all the steps needed to produce the invention were available in prior art then the invention may be rejected for lack of novelty. Prior art only includes knowledge available to the public. Therefore, if a previous inventor had chosen to rely on secrecy to protect their invention then a later inventor not privy to the secret could apply for a patent.

6.60 The inventive step is something that shows that the invention was not an obvious extension of prior art. An invention which was obvious to any relevantly skilled person will not meet the criteria. A relevantly skilled person is someone familiar with the kind of art in question including devices and processes (s 3).

6.61 Only an invention that can be applied in an industrial way is patentable. Agricultural business constitutes an industry for the purposes of patents. The discovery of a fact that cannot be directly applied in an industrial sense is not sufficient except in biotechnology industries. Inventions such as gene sequences may be patented even if there is not an immediate application of the technology (s 4).

6.62 For the difficulties in asserting novelty and originality see *HTC Corporation v Gemalto SA*;[26] Chapter 7 (Control Mechanisms for Embedded Devices).

6.63 Successful patents are shown on public registers which can be seen by competitors. It is not uncommon for an inventor to prefer to rely on secrecy to protect an invention, although this may risk the 'invention' and patent by another.

Difference between trade marks and patents

6.64 Novelty or distinctiveness are common between the use of trade marks and patents, as is registration within a public register marking the point of protection.

6.65 However, once a trade mark has been identified as dissimilar to any existing mark there are very few hurdles to overcome. Trade marks can be 'any sign capable of being represented graphically which is capable of distinguishing goods or services of one undertaking from those of other undertakings'. The breadth of trade marks to include: words; designs; letters; numerals or shapes; is so vast that anything sufficiently distinctive can be registered.

6.66 In comparison the requirement of 'invention' inhibits many designs or processes from achieving a patent. An inventor seeking a patent must reveal his idea to public scrutiny and risk challenge on the grounds of novelty or originality in comparison to prior art. There is a not insignificant risk to this public disclosure as concepts which fail to be patented cannot be protected as confidential information or as a trade secret. In this context it is unsurprising that in the UK only 4% of innovative companies patent, and in the US only about 5.5% of all manufacturing firms engage in patent activity.[27]

6.67 A word or design which encompasses a process can be properly protected using a trade mark; however, the underlying process has no protection from this registration. Weightwatchers, Google, Photoshop and Hoover are all properly registered trade marks which represent a process or system. Although the trade mark protects the brand name, the underlying process is open to imitation and the owner must seek alternative means of protection. The Google algorithm is a trade secret which is highly confidential. The original Hoover vacuum cleaner relied on patents to obtain competitive advantage and protect its then innovative designs. Weightwatchers is often copied and instead relies solely on the brand name to rival its competitors. When considering security from commercial rivals it is worth considering the range of protections available, and applying that which is most appropriate to the information to be protected.

---

26 [2014] RPC 9.
27 V Falce, 'Trade secrets – looking for (full) harmonisation in the Innovative Union', International Review of Intellectual Property and Competition Law, [2015] IIC 940, at 950.

COMMON LAW

6.68   At common law information *per se* is unprotected. However, the courts will intervene to protect from unfair advantage as a result of breach of confidence (see Chapter 5 (Employer Liability and Protection)); and against detriment to a trader's goodwill as a result of a misrepresentation by a competitor. In instances when there is no registration of a trade mark, the tort of passing off can constitute best protection from aggressive corporate practice.

Passing off

6.69   In the nineteenth-century case of *Seixo v Provezende*,[28] 128 years before the introduction of the Trade Marks Act 1994, the Chancery Division of the Court of Appeal (Lord Cranworth LC) held that 'one man cannot offer his goods for sale representing them to be the manufacture of a rival trader'.[29] The degree of resemblance necessary to sustain a claim in action was incapable of definition '*a priori;* however, the test to be applied was whether an ordinary purchaser, purchasing with ordinary caution, was likely to be misled.[30] The tort of 'passing off' was established.

6.70   The House of Lords (Lord Bridge of Harwich, Lord Brandon of Oakbrook, Lord Oliver of Aylmerton, Lord Goff of Chieveley, Lord Jauncey of Tullichettle) decision in *Reckitt & Colman Products Ltd v Borden Inc*[31] (known as the *Jif Lemon* case) is now the leading case, in which Lord Oliver defined the tort in a modern context:[32]

> 'The law of passing off can be summarised in one short general proposition – no man may pass off his goods as those of another. More specifically, it may be expressed in terms of the elements which the plaintiff in such an action has to prove in order to succeed. These are three in number. First, he must establish a goodwill or reputation attached to the goods or services which he supplies in the mind of the purchasing public by association with the identifying "get-up" (whether it consists simply of a brand name or a trade description, or the individual features of labelling or packaging) under which his particular goods or services are offered to the public, such that the get-up is recognised by the public as distinctive specifically of the plaintiff's goods or services. Secondly, he must demonstrate a misrepresentation by the defendant to the public (whether or not intentional) leading or likely to lead the public to believe that goods or services offered by him are the goods or services of the plaintiff. Whether the public is aware of the plaintiff's identity as the manufacturer or supplier of the goods or services is immaterial, as long as they are identified with a particular source which is in fact the plaintiff. For example, if the public is accustomed to rely upon a particular brand name in purchasing goods of a particular description, it matters not at all that there is little or no public awareness of the identity of the proprietor of the brand name. Thirdly, he must demonstrate that he suffers or, in a quia timet

---

[28]   (1865–66) LR 1 Ch App 192.
[29]   *Seixo v Provezende*, at 195.
[30]   Ibid, at 196.
[31]   [1990] 1 WLR 491.
[32]   See *Reckitt & Colman Products Ltd v Borden Inc*, at 499.

action, that he is likely to suffer damage by reason of the erroneous belief engendered by the defendant's misrepresentation that the source of the defendant's goods or services is the same as the source of those offered by the plaintiff.'

6.71 The tort of passing off protects a trader's goodwill from damage caused by misrepresentations, with the essence of the action being a deceit practised upon the public. Customers have to be taken as they are found. Where it has been shown that the public has been deceived, it is no defence to assert that with greater care, or diligence, the deception would have been overcome.

6.72 Accordingly, a misrepresentation is potentially actionable because it constitutes an invasion of the proprietary rights vested in a claimant, specifically their goodwill. However, it is a prerequisite of any successful passing off action that the claimant's goods have acquired a reputation in the market and are known by some distinguishing feature. It is also a necessary that the misrepresentation has deceived or is likely to deceive, and that the claimant is likely to suffer damage by such deception. Mere confusion which does not lead to a sale is not sufficient:[33]

'[I]f a customer asks for a tin of black shoe polish without specifying any brand and is offered the product of A which he mistakenly believes to be that of B, he may be confused as to what he has got but he has not been deceived into getting it. Misrepresentation has played no part in his purchase.'

6.73 In *HFC Bank Plc v HSBC Bank Plc (formerly Midland Bank Plc)*,[34] the Chancery Division of the High Court (Lloyd J) considered whether the rebranding of the Midland Bank to HSBC could lead to a successful claim in passing off for an existing bank within the market, HFC. It was accepted that there was a phonic similarity between HFC and HSBC which may cause some confusion. However, mere confusion between two parties' products was not sufficient. HFC were required to prove that they had obtained brand recognition, and therefore goodwill, and that the actions of the defendant impacted upon a customer who recognised that brand. The identity of the supplier of the relevant goods or service must matter to the customer for a mistake to identity to be relevant.

6.74 In this case, the High Court held that any deception was momentary or inconsequential. The relevant customers intended to engage in borrowing significant sums of money, and that in all instances any mistake was rectified before the completion of a transaction. HFC had failed to demonstrate that there was a brand recognition which raised goodwill with the relevant customers:[35]

'Clearly, in a market place in which there is an actively promoted brand somewhat similar to that of HFC, it would be the more difficult for HFC to improve its brand

---

[33] See *Reckitt & Colman Products Ltd v Borden Inc*, per Lord Jauncey, at 510.
[34] [2000] FSR 176.
[35] See *HFC Bank Plc v HSBC Bank Plc*, at 201.

recognition. That, however, only shows that HFC has had an easy task up to 1998 and will now have to try harder. It does not show that HFC is entitled to a cordon sanitaire, protecting it from such competition as the HSBC brand represents. I can quite see why HFC should regard with dismay and try to prevent a situation arising in which it has to revise its previously low-key attitude to brand awareness, but I do not consider that it has been shown that this situation has been produced in circumstances involving passing off on the part of Midland. In my judgment, no misrepresentation has been proved. Rather, these are cases of non-actionable confusion.'

6.75 The proper approach in deciding whether there is a misrepresentation carrying a likelihood of deception is an 'overall "jury" assessment', or a question of fact for the court to consider based on the evidence adduced, using its common sense and its own opinion as to the likelihood of deception. The decision of the High Court was affirmed by the Court of Appeal (Nourse LJ, Sedley LJ, Judge LJ).[36]

6.76 The proprietary goodwill protected is territorial in nature. It is important that the goodwill exists within the jurisdiction where the claim is being brought.[37]

6.77 The damage that might be suffered by a claimant in a passing off action can include, *inter alia*, diversion of sales, damage to goodwill by inferior goods or services, dilution of goodwill, or the loss of licensing income.

6.78 The proprietary right of goodwill is not limited to goods and services but extends to image rights.[38] When considering damages for a successful claim in passing off in this context, the fee that the owner of the image rights would have charged is appropriate.

6.79 As with all torts, it is a defence to show that the claimant's case does not satisfy the constituent elements of the action. A defendant may wish to attack the existence of goodwill or argue that no damage has occurred.

6.80 It may be a defence to an action for passing off to demonstrate that the goods or service at the heart of the claim consist of something either so ordinary or in such common use that it would be unreasonable for the claimant to suggest that it is solely their good. For instance, a description of goods sold cannot be the subject of an action for passing off. Where a common term can be shown to be uniquely associated with particular goods, that manufacturer may find relief but only if it can be shown that the defendant was using the term in a manner to mislead. A defendant cannot be restrained from using a common phrase but may be required to provide explanation.[39] In such instances the defendant should take care to distinguish the goods.[40]

---

[36] See *HFC Bank Plc v HSBC Bank Plc (formerly Midland Bank Plc)* [2000] CPLR 197.
[37] See *Starbucks (HK) Ltd v British Sky Broadcasting Group Plc* [2015] UKSC 31, [2015] 1 WLR 2628.
[38] See *Irvine v Talksport Ltd (Nos 1 and 2)* [2003] EWCA Civ 423, [2003] EMLR 26.
[39] See the speech of Lord Herschell in *Reddaway v Banham* [1896] AC 199, at 210, approved by

PASSING OFF AND CYBER SQUATTING

6.81 Passing off in the cyber context came to be referred to as the phenomenon of cyber squatting. Cyber squatting concerns the use of a domain name as an instrument of fraud or deception by registering a permutation so close to an existing business domain name as to pass it off as being the same.

6.82 Cyber squatting was carefully analysed by Park J in *Global Projects v Citigroup & Others*.[41] Here Global Projects (GP) acquired the internet domain name and address citigroup.co.uk, which was distinct but very close to the domain owned by Citigroup namely citigroup.com.

6.83 In two letters, dated 15 April and 15 July 2004, Citigroup's solicitors wrote to GP and complained that GP's registration of the domain name citigroup.co.uk was an act of passing off Citigroup's goodwill and Citigroup's mark as GPs own goodwill and marks. The letters threatened legal action. The letters were written on behalf of Citigroup itself and its two wholly owned subsidiaries, Citibank NA and Citicorp.

6.84 Notably s 21 of the TMA 1994, creates a cause of action for a person who has received unjustified threats of proceedings being brought for trade mark infringement. In December 2004 GP commenced an action under that section against Citigroup. It claimed damages and other relief for what GP contended were unjustified threats made in breach of the section.

6.85 Predictably Citigroup defended the claim and counterclaimed against GP alleging that the registration and ownership by GP of the citigroup.co.uk domain name constituted the tort of passing off. They also alleged that GP was in breach of registered trade marks owned by Citicorp.

6.86 In examining the position Park J identified, at [40], the core elements of cyber squatting:

---

the House of Lords in *Reckitt & Colman Products Ltd v Borden Inc*, at 506: 'The name of a person, or words forming part of the common stock of language, may become so far associated with the goods of a particular maker that it is capable of proof that the use of them by themselves without explanation or qualification by another manufacturer would deceive a purchaser into the belief that he was getting the goods of A, when he was really getting the goods of B. In a case of this description the mere proof by the plaintiff that the defendant was using a name, word, or device which he had adopted to distinguish his goods would not entitle him to any relief. He could only obtain it by proving further that the defendant was using it under such circumstances or in such manner as to put off his goods as the goods of the plaintiff. If he could succeed in proving this I think he would, on well-established principles, be entitled to an injunction'.

40 See comments, *obiter,* of Romer LJ in *Payton & Co Ltd v Snelling, Lampard & Co Ltd*, 17 RPC 48, at 56: 'when one person has used certain leading features, though common to the trade, if another person is going to put goods on the market, having the same leading features, he should take extra care by the distinguishing features he is going to put on his goods, to see that the goods can be really distinguished …'.

41 [2005] EWHC 2663 (Ch).

'The mere registration and maintenance in force of a domain name which leads, or may lead, people to believe that the holder of the domain is linked with a person (eg Marks & Spencer or British Telecom, or, I would add, Citigroup) is enough to make the domain a potential "instrument of fraud", and it is passing off.'

6.87 It should be noted that not every registration of a domain name would constitute an instrument of fraud, and the other essential elements in relation to the tort must be established. In *Marks & Spencer Plc v One In A Million Ltd*,[42] Jonathan Sumption QC, then sitting as a deputy judge of the High Court, pointed out that mere registration of a deceptive internet domain name does not of itself constitute passing off:

'The mere creation of an "instrument of deception", without either using it for deception or putting it into the hands of someone else to do so, is not passing off. There is no such tort as going equipped for passing off. It follows that the mere registration of a deceptive company name or a deceptive Internet domain name is not passing off. In both of these cases the court granted what amounted to a quia timet injunction to restrain a threatened rather than an actual tort. In both cases, the injunctions were interlocutory rather than final, and the threat is no doubt easier to establish in that context. But even a final injunction does not require proof that damage will certainly occur. It is enough that what is going on is calculated to infringe the plaintiff's rights in future.'

The factual matrix will need to be examined to establish the actual intent or purpose behind the registration, the business of the parties and whether this might lead to the belief that the domain was linked with the person bringing the complaint. In the case of *Marks & Spencer Plc*, the court held that use was calculated to infringe the company's future rights. This was sufficient to establish the common law tort. A complainant will be required to prove it had an established reputation associated with the relevant name and that the domain was indeed being used as an instrument of fraud to cause it harm by misrepresenting itself/passing itself off as the complainant.

6.88 In *British Telecommunications Plc v One in a Million Ltd*,[43] the conjoined appeal with *Marks & Spencer Plc*, the Court of Appeal (Stuart-Smith LJ, Swinton Thomas LJ, Aldous LJ) affirmed the High Court's decision. The Court of Appeal held that registration of a domain name, on the WHOIS public register of domain name registrants, could amount to passing off if the domain name incorporated an inherently distinctive sign, or was connected to or associated with the owner of the goodwill in the distinctive name, such that it constituted a false representation. The court concluded that misrepresentation eroded the exclusivity of the distinctive name and thereby caused damage to its owner even if the domain name had not been used:[44]

'It is accepted that the name Marks & Spencer denotes Marks & Spencer Plc. and nobody else. Thus anybody seeing or hearing the name realises that what is being

---

[42]   [1998] FSR 265, at 271.
[43]   [1999] 1 WLR 903.
[44]   See *British Telecommunications Plc v One in a Million Ltd*, at 924.

referred to is the business of Marks & Spencer Plc. It follows that registration by the defendants of a domain name including the name Marks & Spencer makes a false representation that they are associated or connected with Marks & Spencer Plc. This can be demonstrated by considering the reaction of a person who taps into his computer the domain name marksandspencer.co.uk and presses a button to execute a "Whois" search. He will be told that the registrant is One In A Million Ltd. A substantial number of persons will conclude that One In A Million Ltd must be connected or associated with Marks & Spencer Plc. That amounts to a false representation which constitutes passing off.'

6.89 The decision was followed by the Intellectual Property Enterprise Court (Judge Hacon) in *Vertical Leisure Ltd v Poleplus Ltd*.[45]

6.90 The principles in relation to damages in a successful action in passing off are discussed in *Harman v Burge*.[46]

Passing off and trade marks

6.91 Passing off actions are often brought in respect of signs used to distinguish goods or services in the marketplace. These signs might themselves be registered trade marks, whether in the UK or Community Trade Marks. Often where a mark is registered, a passing off action is brought in parallel with an infringement action. Where there is no registration, the passing off action is brought alone.

6.92 In the absence of a registered trade mark, a trader does not have a monopoly in a name or a logo. Accordingly, a rival is free to use an unregistered mark unless such use amounts to a representation that his goods/services are those of the claimant. If he can distinguish his own goods/services then he is entitled to use the mark. In order to succeed in a claim relating to an unregistered trade mark, the claimant must show that the mark is distinctive. In the context of passing off, distinctive means that in the eyes of the public the mark denotes the claimant and none other. This is a question of fact (an 'overall "jury" assessment').

6.93 A substantial number of potential customers for the claimant's goods or services must be liable to be deceived. Careless or indifferent persons will not suffice; however, there is no requirement for the resemblance between two marks to be so high that an ordinary purchaser would only be deceived if the marks were placed side by side.[47] There is no need for the defendant to be acting fraudulently or maliciously as confusion and misrepresentation are distinct concepts:[48]

---

[45] [2015] EWHC 841 (IPEC).
[46] [2014] EWHC 2836 (IPEC).
[47] See *Norman Kark Publications Ltd v Odhams Press Ltd* [1962] 1 WLR 380, at 393.
[48] See *Comic Enterprises Ltd v Twentieth Century Fox Film Corp* [2016] EWCA Civ 41, [2016] ETMR 22, at [159].

'In this regard it is to be noted that the scope of protection conferred by the law of passing off is not the same as that afforded by a registered trade mark. As we have seen, in considering a claim for infringement the court need not restrict its consideration to the particular way the mark has been used and the goodwill that has been generated in connection with it, and may take into account a notional and fair use of the mark in relation to all of the goods and services for which it is registered. But of course all of the other conditions for protection must also be satisfied.'

6.94 An application for a registered trade mark may be opposed if its use in the UK is liable to be prevented by the tort of passing off (see TMA 1994, s 5(4)(a)). A registered mark may be declared invalid by the registrar or the court under s 46(2)(b) if there was an earlier right to prevent passing off. A registered trade mark will not be declared invalid if it can be shown that there was acquiescence of the owner of the goodwill (see TMA 1994, s 48). A similar provision exists for opposing the registration of a Community Trade Mark under the Trade Mark Regulation, Arts 8(4) and 41. Invalidity proceedings may be used in OHIM or as a counterclaim in infringement proceedings for Community Marks already registered under Art 53.

6.95 The general effect of invalidity is retroactive, save for certain exceptions. Therefore, claiming a declaration of invalidity as a counterclaim will act as a defence to claims for infringement.

INTERNATIONAL/EUROPEAN APPROACH

6.96 In a *Study on Trade Secrets and Confidential Business Information in the Internal Market*, prepared for the European Commission, and published in April 2013,[49] 140 companies reported attempts or acts of misappropriation of trade but only 47% sought remedies in EU courts. The reasons not to engage in litigation included the difficulty in collecting evidence (43%); the impact on company reputation (30%); and the cost of litigation (30%). This is despite an international context focus towards the protection of confidential information being in place since the end of the Uruguay Round of the General Agreement on Tariffs and Trade (GATT) in 1994.

6.97 The Agreement on Trade-Related Aspects of Intellectual Property Rights (TRIPS) was the result of negotiations regarding an international agreement administered by the World Trade Organization (WTO) that sets down minimum standards for many forms of intellectual property (IP) regulation as applied to national governments of other WTO members. The TRIPS agreement introduced intellectual property law into the international trading system for the first time and remains a source of protection against commercial espionage albeit that it has been superseded in a European context.

---

[49] http://ec.europa.eu/internal_market/iprenforcement/docs/trade-secrets/130711_final-study_en.pdf.

6.98 The Trade Mark Directive and the Trade Mark Regulation provide a centralised means of protection throughout the EU. This legislation provides a means of enforcement within the national courts of its members, which seeks to address the difficulty in collecting evidence and the cost of litigation.

6.99 In Europe, jurisdiction in national trade mark infringement, passing off and unfair competition proceedings are governed by Regulation 1215/2012 on Jurisdiction and the Recognition and Enforcement of Judgments in Civil and Commercial Matters (Brussels Regulation (Recast)), which has replaced Regulation 44/2001. The Brussels Regulation (Recast) applies equally to online content as well as offline content, although internet service providers' use of multiple technologies in multiple countries means that its application to cases involving the internet is complex.

6.100 Article 4 of the Brussels Regulation (Recast) provides that persons domiciled in a member state shall be sued in the courts of that member state unless the Regulation provides otherwise. Article 7(2) provides for one such derogation from Art 4, stating that a person domiciled in a member state may be sued:

> 'in matters relating to tort, delict or quasi-delict [which includes claims for trade mark infringement and passing off], in the courts for the place where the harmful event occurred or may occur.'

6.101 In *Wintersteiger AG v Products 4U Sondermaschinenbau GmbH*,[50] the Court of Justice held that the mere accessibility of online content from within a member state did not give that member state jurisdiction to hear claims regarding the alleged infringement of national trade mark rights. Those member states competent to take jurisdiction are only those where the mark is registered or where the defendant is established. It is unlikely that a court will substantially depart from this analysis in a case involving passing off:[51]

> '[I]t must be noted at the outset that the rule of special jurisdiction laid down, by way of derogation from the principle of jurisdiction of the courts of the place of domicile of the defendant, in article 5(3) of the Regulation is based on the existence of a particularly close connecting factor between the dispute and the courts of the place where the harmful event occurred, which justifies the attribution of jurisdiction to those courts for reasons relating to the sound administration of justice and the efficacious conduct of proceedings.'

---

[50] (C-523/10) [2013] Bus LR 150.
[51] See *Wintersteiger AG v Products 4U Sondermaschinenbau GmbH* C-523/10 [2013] Bus LR 150 at [18].

CHAPTER 7

CONTROL MECHANISMS FOR EMBEDDED DEVICES

CONTENTS

INTRODUCTION

7.01 On 22 June 2016, Facebook CEO and founder Mark Zuckerberg appeared before the world's press to promote the digital content of a subsidiary company. The story changed when a photograph captured that Mr Zuckerberg had placed sticky tape over his laptop web-camera and microphone to secure the device.[1] Federal Bureau of Investigation's Director James Comey supported this approach. He said that he had taken advice to cover up the camera on his laptop to prevent people from eavesdropping on personal conversations.[2] These men were applying a control mechanism, albeit a very crude one, to ensure the security of a system embedded within their laptops.

7.02 An embedded system is an electronic product that contains a microprocessor and software to perform some constituent function within a larger entity.[3] With an increasingly large and diverse number of embedded systems used in everyday life those responsible for the protection of valuable data must consider which control mechanisms are appropriate. It is beyond the scope of this book to identify the myriad of embedded systems used for communication, to distribute control access, or for metering and billing;

---

[1] A Griffiths, 'Mark Zuckerberg seen covering up his webcam in picture celebrating Instagram milestone', 22 June 2016, (http://www.independent.co.uk/life-style/gadgets-and-tech/news/mark-zuckerberg-seen-covering-up-his-webcam-in-picture-celebrating-instagram-milestone-a7094896.html) (last accessed 14 August 2016).

[2] Ibid.

[3] D Kleidermacher, M Kleidermacher, *Embedded Systems Security: Practical Methods for Safe and Secure Software and Systems Development* (Elsevier Inc, 2012), p 3.

however, obvious examples include subscriber identity module (SIM) cards used to personalise mobile phones, smartcards for satellite TV services, and cryptographic processes used in automatic teller machines (ATMs) and point-of-sale equipment. Embedded devices are not limited to the retail sector. The rise in 'bring-your-own-device' (BYOD) within the workspace means that corporate IT managers must be equally aware of the control mechanisms necessary to protect company property and data.

7.03 This chapter outlines the legal context behind three broad control areas: technical protection; protection through litigation; and the commercial approach. System designers must first determine what threats are feasible, and then decide what security policies make economic sense relative to the value of the resources exposed to a particular threat. Those responsible for the protection of company property must have an awareness of the potential threats to an embedded system and the processes that can be put in place to negate these threats; understand the legal landscape that may through enforcement prevent further dissemination of information and data; or, in the alternative, consider means to obtain fair recompense for protected material.

7.04 Ultimately the correct approach will likely be a combination of control mechanisms which are bespoke to the embedded systems employed. This may be as complicated as digital rights management (DRM) software built into the systems, which itself can only be accessed using biometric recognition, all supported by a large legal team prepared to litigate any breach of copyright or patent. Alternatively, it may be as simple as some sticky tape placed over a camera and a microphone.

TECHNICAL PROTECTION

7.05 Technological protection measures to secure embedded devices are broadly divided into two categories: access control; and copy control. Access control measures secure the access to information and protected content and may include cryptography, passwords and digital signatures. Copy control measures such as selectable output controls (SOC) for high definition television transmissions, serial copy management systems for audio digital taping devices, and content scrambling systems for DVDs prevent third parties from exploiting the exclusive rights of copyright owners. These DRM technologies seek to control the use, modification and distribution of copyrighted works. In conjunction with the technology, a legal context has been developed at the national and supranational level to prohibit the circumvention of DRM systems.

Awareness of threats to embedded systems

7.06 Evaluating potential threats to an embedded system is vital before an appropriate control mechanism can be advanced. Threats may be external, such as a criminal with the intention to steal, modify or damage data, or may be internal, such as a fault within the software that is intrinsic to the system.

External threats

7.07 The source of an external threat will be an individual seeking unauthorised access to data. An attack on a company computer system by an individual outside of the firm, or a 'computer hacker', is the common perception of a cyber-criminal. However, external threats to data may also arise from employees within the company, who want to strike out on their own or use the information to obtain work at a rival organisation. These potential threats have been considered in detail within earlier chapters (Chapter 1 (Cyber Crime); Chapter 5 (Employer Liability and Protection)).

7.08 The use of embedded systems as access points for external threats is growing. In 2010, General Motors introduced a feature to enable car owners to manipulate the locks of a car and start the car's engine from anywhere in the world using a smartphone. The feature utilised General Motors' OnStar telematics system, which was standard in every US Ford from 2007. A team of researchers at Oakland University published a study demonstrating that using these embedded systems the car's brakes, engine and accelerator could be manipulated, potentially with malice.[4] This was a university research study, without any intention towards illegal activity; but also in 2010 the Stuxnet worm infiltrated a Siemens process control system at a nuclear power plant. It is likely that the Stuxnet worm was the first malware to directly target an embedded control system.[5]

7.09 External threats through embedded devices are not limited to large manufacturers or infrastructure. Mobile computing and BYOD are common within modern firms. In order to transfer data, and communicate by phone or email, employees, consultants and guests are invited to access computer networks. Devices with embedded systems include laptops, smartphones, PDAs, and portable universal serial bus (USB) devices which are connected using wireless local area networks (WLAN). In 2008, the US National Institute of Standards and Technology publicly recognised and extensively warned about a lack of security in WLAN technologies and standards:[6]

'Organizations employing legacy IEEE 802.11 WLANs should be aware of the limited and weak security controls available to protect communications. Legacy WLANs are particularly susceptible to loss of confidentiality, integrity, and availability. Unauthorized users have access to well-documented security flaws and exploits that can easily compromise an organization's systems and information,

---

4   K Koscher, A Czeskis, F Roesner, S Patel, T Kohno, 'Experimental Security Analysis of a Modern Automobile', Oakland, CA: 2010 IEEE Symposium on Security and Privacy; 19 May 2010.

5   D Kleidermacher, M Kleidermacher, *Embedded Systems Security: Practical Methods for Safe and Secure Software and Systems Development* (Elsevier Inc, 2012), p 15.

6   B Longu, 'Learning on the wires: BYOD, embedded systems, wireless technologies and cybercrime', LIM 2013, 13(2), 119–123, 2013, p 120.

corrupt the organization's data, consume network bandwidth, degrade network performance, launch attacks that prevent authorized users from accessing the network, or use the organization's resources to launch attacks on other networks.'[7]

7.10 Embedded systems were traditionally considered to be autonomous closed systems but are now increasingly connected to networks to undertake in-field updates and remote debugging. In 2010, a critical and widespread vulnerability was discovered in VxWorks, a real-time operating system embedded in products including: SCADA automation systems, video conferencing suites, and WiFi routers. Using the vulnerability within the VxWorks debugging interface, a remote attacker could read or write any physical memory location within the products. Administrative passwords could be extracted and malware installed. A quarter of a million devices accessible directly from the Internet were found to be vulnerable.[8] The VxWork vulnerability illustrates that IT managers must be aware that embedded systems are a point of attack for external threats, and consider appropriate control mechanisms.

Internal threats

7.11 In June 2014, the UK Government's National Cyber Security Programme (NCSP) lent support and funding to the Trustworthy Software Initiative (TSI) to meet potential internal threats. Most software has defects in the coding which can cause software to fail. 'Trustworthy Software' is software that is appropriate, free from such defects, and performs consistently. No software can be proven to be completely free of all defects, but the level of 'trustworthiness' should be appropriate for the purpose for which the software is used, and evaluated against five key indicators: safety, reliability, availability, resilience and security.

7.12 The Trustworthy Software Framework (TSF) represents the core of activity for TSI, and acts as a consensus, neutral (domain independent) way to access advice and standards of best practice. It is being built as a layered repository with increasing levels of detail to service different needs. A summary of the Comprehensive View of Level 3 of the current TSF (v3.3) is available on the TSI website (http://www.uk-tsi.org/trustworthy-software-framework—tsf). Work is currently in progress to perform the initial population of Level 4 of the TSF, which will be a maintained index into: citations; methods; and data sharing techniques. Use of the TSF is predicated upon a risk-based set of Trustworthiness Levels (TL). A Baseline View of the TSF, for use in environments with only a minimalist need for Trustworthiness, is also in development.

---

7   The National Institute of Standards and Technology, *Guide to Securing Legacy IEEE 802.11 Wireless Networks*, Special Publication 800–48 Revision 1.

8   D Kleidermacher, M Kleidermacher, *Embedded Systems Security: Practical Methods for Safe and Secure Software and Systems Development* (Elsevier Inc, 2012), p 22.

7.13 Working alongside the British Standards Institution (the UK national standards body), TSI has produced a Publicly Available Specification (PAS 754) entitled 'Software Trustworthiness – Governance and Management – Specification'. PAS 754 is applicable to any organisation aiming to adopt trustworthy software practices. The purposes of the specification are to:

- define the overall principles for effective software trustworthiness, including technical, physical, cultural and behavioural measures alongside effective leadership and governance;

- identify the necessary tools, techniques and processes required to ensure software trustworthiness and addresses issues of safety, reliability, availability, security and resilience.

7.14 Although PAS 754 does not specify the detailed processes or actions that an organisation should follow in order to achieve these outcomes, consideration of the specifications is essential when commissioning new software or implementing a new system. It is at this moment that negating internal threats is most cost efficient.

Access control

7.15 Whether a person is using an Oyster card on the London Underground, taking money from a cash point or buying a drink from a card operated vending machine, the interaction is being processed through a cryptographic application programming interface (API). The API sits on the boundary between a trusted and untrusted environment, and is the point where cryptography, protocols, access controls and operating procedures come together to enforce a security policy.

7.16 The internal cryptographic processes within any of these systems goes beyond the scope of this book; however, it is evident that the level of security required varies depending upon the process to be completed. The control mechanisms within the vending machine are likely to be less as this is potentially a closed system without remote access. Comparing the cash card with the Oyster card, withdrawal of money from a cash machine requires a personal identification number (PIN) in addition to the possession of a card. The access control for this embedded device is greater as additional security authentication is required.

7.17 Security authentication systems can be classified in terms of how many different types of checks are made of a person attempting to access a system. There are three types of security authentication which can be applied:

- what the customer has in their possession (a plastic card or other device);
- what the customer knows (a secret code or password);
- identification through monitoring aspects of who the customer is (biometric checks such as fingerprint recognition).

7.18 Taking mobile banking as an example, a one-factor authentication system is common for simple website access, and is usually a password. Physical financial services transactions have traditionally used two-factor authentication such as a cash card and a PIN. Electronic financial services similarly use two-factor authentication such as a 'key-fob' or mobile telephone to generate a one-time code that the customer has to enter along with their password. More recently fingerprint scans, using smartphone technology, are being applied for access to online banking. The strongest form of security authentication is three-factor authentication.

7.19 Greater access control should not automatically be considered an additional burdensome cost but as an opportunity to offer greater digital content. Companies utilising secure digital interfaces are challenging those that trade more traditionally from a physical premises. Online banking, trading platforms, gambling, casinos, and shopping are gaining increasing market share. However, it is diversification into areas which were previously dominated by large institutions that is now obtainable. Apple Pay, for example, will grow and compete with Visa and MasterCard.

7.20 Apple Pay uses near-field communications (NFC) found in the iPhone (from iPhone 6 onwards) and Apple Watch in a similar manner to contactless cards. However, unlike contactless cards, Apple Pay includes an extra security measure known as tokenisation, which ensures that the card details stored on a phone are never passed to the retailer. Instead, the payee receives a single-use 'token' allowing them to debit the payment only once. The payments are secured and verified by the owner's fingerprint using Apple's Touch ID system.

7.21 This level of diversification will likely require legal advice. Apple Pay is not 'a bank' within the definition of the Banking Act 2009, nor will it be regulated by the Payment Systems Regulator in accordance with the Financial Services (Banking Reform) Act 2013.[9] The European Union E-Money Directive (2009/110/EC)[10] and the first Payment Services Directive (2007/64/EC)[11] will also not apply. However, Apple Pay will likely fall within the second Payment Services Directive (2015/2366/EC) (see Art 4(15)): '"payment initiation service"

---

9   The Designation Orders for MasterCard and Visa Europe came into force on 1 April 2015 in accordance with s 43 of the Financial Services (Banking Reform) Act 2013.

10 'Electronic money' is defined under Art 2(2) of Directive 2009/110/EC as meaning: 'electronically, including magnetically, stored monetary value as represented by a claim on the issuer which is issued on receipt of funds for the purpose of making payment transactions as defined in point 5 of Art 4 of Directive 2007/64/EC, and which is accepted by a natural or legal person other than the electronic money issuer'. Apple Pay only facilitates the processing of payments by sending secure payment information. It does not involve the issue of e-money.

11 Potentially regulated payment service providers are excluded if they do not come into possession of the payment transaction funds, and provide technical services that support payment processing (see Art 3(j) of Directive 2007/64/EC): 'services provided by technical service providers, which support the provision of payment services, without them entering at any time into possession of the funds to be transferred, including processing and storage of data, trust and privacy protection services, data and entity authentication, information technology (IT) and communication network provision, provision and maintenance of terminals and devices used for payment services'.

means a service to initiate a payment order at the request of the payment service user with respect to a payment account held at another payment service provider'. The requirements of the Directive will be enforced throughout the European Union from 13 January 2018.[12]

COPY CONTROL

7.22 Copy control is synonymous with digital rights management (DRM). DRM is a system-based approach to copyright protection for digital media. The purpose of DRM is to prevent unauthorised redistribution of digital media and restrict the ways consumers can copy content they have purchased.

7.23 The success of DRM is mixed to say the least. In 2005, Sony BMG introduced new DRM technology for their audio CDs which installed DRM software on users' computers without clearly notifying the user or requiring confirmation. Among other things, the installed software included a rootkit, which created a severe security vulnerability others could exploit. When the nature of the DRM involved was made public, Sony BMG initially minimised the significance of the vulnerabilities its software had created, but was eventually compelled to recall millions of CDs, and released several attempts to patch the surreptitiously included software to at least remove the rootkit. Several class action lawsuits were filed, which were ultimately settled by agreements to provide affected consumers with compensation.[13] Sony BMG's DRM software had only a limited ability to prevent copying, as it affected only playback on Windows computers and not other equipment. Even on the Windows platform users regularly bypassed the restrictions.

7.24 The lack of success in DRM software is not limited to CDs or audio files. Computer games manufacturer Ubisoft employed DRM software which like rootkit would be automatically and mandatorily installed on the purchaser's PC when the game was used. However, the DRM required constant internet connection to send packets to Ubisoft's server to confirm that the copy of the game was genuine. This meant that customers that had legally purchased the game would not be able to access it if they had no internet connection; their connection was faulty or even if there was a problem with Ubisoft's verification servers. The DRM did not prevent any of the games from being 'cracked' and made available on file-sharing networks without the DRM. Those who decided to pirate the game were free from the onerous DRM to which paying customers were subject. Ubisoft was therefore inadvertently encouraging customers to acquire illegal copies.[14]

7.25 Apple have had greater success with their DRM system FairPlay. Prior to 2009, Apple's iTunes Store utilised FairPlay for music. In April 2009, all iTunes

---

[12] See Directive 2015/2366/EC, Art 115(1).
[13] R McMillan, 'Settlement Ends Sony Rootkit Case', *PC World Magazine*, IDG, 23 May 2006.
[14] A Royle, 'Pirates Ahoy! Copyright and Internet File-Sharing', *North East Law Review*, Newcastle University, June 2013.

music became available completely DRM-free; however, videos sold and rented through iTunes, as well as iOS apps, continue to use Apple's FairPlay DRM. There is little doubt that Apple effectively managed their music and video content, using FairPlay, to encourage the purchase of associated products, and that once the DRM was released these products became redundant: iPods are now a thing of the past.

7.26   Regardless of the DRM system employed there will be a technical method to circumvent the software within the digital file. Therefore, a legal and regulatory framework has been imposed internationally to prohibit DRM from being negated.

THE LEGAL AND REGULATORY CONTEXT

7.27   The World Intellectual Property Organisation Copyright Treaty (WIPO Copyright Treaty or WCT) is an international treaty on copyright law adopted by the member states of the World Intellectual Property Organization (WIPO) in 1996. As of February 2017, the treaty has been ratified by 95 states.

7.28   The WIPO Copyright Treaty was devised to provide additional protections for copyright deemed necessary due to advances in information technology. It ensured that computer programs were protected as literary works (Art 4), and that the arrangement and selection of material in databases was also protected (Art 5). On 16 March 2000, the Council of the European Union approved the Treaty on behalf of the European Community. Directive 91/250/EC created copyright protection for software (the Software Directive) and Directive 96/9/EC on copyright protection for databases (the Database Directive) (see Chapter 4 (Cyber property)).

7.29   Article 11 of the WIPO Copyright Treaty prohibited circumvention of technological measures for the protection of works, and Art 12 the unauthorised modification of rights management information contained in works. On 22 December 2002, the European Union implemented the Copyright Directive (Directive 2001/29/EC) to bring into force the WIPO Copyright Treaty and to harmonise aspects of copyright law across Europe.

The Copyright Directive

7.30   The Copyright Directive, also known as the Information Society Directive, was introduced to supplement rather than replace existing EU Directives (see Directive 2001/29/EC, Recital 20):

> 'This Directive is based on principles and rules already laid down in the Directives currently in force in this area, in particular Directives 91/250/EEC [The Software Directive], 92/100/EEC [The Rental Directive], 93/83/EEC [The Satellite and Cable Directive], 93/98/EEC [The Copyright Duration Directive] and 96/9/EC [The Database Directive], and it develops those principles and rules and places them in

the context of the information society. The provisions of this Directive should be without prejudice to the provisions of those Directives, unless otherwise provided in this Directive.'

7.31 The Copyright Directive grants exclusive rights to specified persons for 'reproduction rights' (Art 2), and the right of 'communication to the public' or 'making available to the public' (Art 3). Those specified included: authors; performers; phonogram producers; producers; and broadcasting organisation for their respective works. Article 3 was specifically intended to cover publication and transmission on the internet ('by wire or wireless means') and unlike Art 2 preserves the copyright after content is initially distributed online. The Art 3 right cannot be exhausted (see Directive 2001/29/EC, Recital 29):

'The question of exhaustion does not arise in the case of services and on-line services in particular.... Every on-line service is in fact an act which should be subject to authorisation where the copyright or related right so provides.'

7.32 The related right for authors to authorise or prohibit any form of distribution to the public by sale or otherwise is provided for in Art 4.

7.33 Article 5 provided a list of exceptions and limitations to copyright that applied in certain special cases, which do not conflict with a normal exploitation of the work or other subject-matter, and do not unreasonably prejudice the legitimate interests of the right holder (see Art 5(5)). Article 5(2) allows member states to establish copyright exceptions to the Art 2 reproduction right in cases of:

(a) photographic reproductions on paper or any similar medium of works (excluding sheet music) provided that the right holders receives fair compensation;

(b) reproductions on any medium made by a natural person for private use which is non-commercial provided that the right holders receive fair compensation;

(c) reproduction made by libraries, educational establishments, museums or archives, which are non-commercial;

(d) archival reproductions of broadcasts; and

(e) reproductions of broadcasts made by 'social institutions pursuing non-commercial purposes, such as hospitals or prisons' provided that the right holders receive fair compensation.

7.34 Article 5(3) allows member states to establish copyright exceptions to the Art 2 reproduction right and the Art 3 right of communication to the public in cases of:

(a) illustration for teaching or scientific research, provided the source, including the author's name, is acknowledged;

(b) use for the benefit of people with a disability;

(c) current event reporting, provided the source, including the author's name, is acknowledged;

(d) quotations for purposes such as criticism or review, provided the source, including the author's name, is acknowledged;

(e) use necessary for the purposes of 'public security' or to the proper performance or reporting of 'administrative, parliamentary or judicial proceedings';

(f) use of political speeches and extracts of public lectures or similar works, provided the source, including the author's name, is acknowledged;

(g) use during religious celebrations or official celebrations 'organised by a public authority';

(h) use of works such as architecture or sculpture located permanently in public places;

(i) incidental inclusion of a work in other material;

(j) the advertising, the public exhibition or sale of artistic works;

(k) caricature, parody or pastiche;

(l) use for demonstration or repair of equipment;

(m) use of an artistic work, drawing or plan of a building for the purposes of reconstruction; and

(n) for non-commercial research or private study.

7.35 The Copyright Directive encourages right holders to provide a voluntary mechanism in order to make available to beneficiaries the exceptions under Art 5(2)(a), (c), (d), (e), (3)(a), (b) and (e). Member states must then have in place appropriate mechanism to ensure that rights holders make these exceptions available (Art 6(4)).

7.36 The provisions contained within Art 6 relate to 'obligations as to technical measures'. This enforces throughout the European Union the prohibition on the circumvention of DRM systems, with Technological Protection Measures (TPM) and DRM systems as synonyms. The Copyright Directive requires that a member state provide 'adequate legal protection against the circumvention of any effective technological measures' (Art 6(1)). The expression 'technological measures' is defined as 'any technology, device or component that, in the normal course of its operation, is designed to prevent or restrict acts, in respect of works or other subject-matter, which are not authorised by the right holder of any copyright or any right related to copyright' (Art 6(3)).

7.37 In accordance with Art 6(2), member states must also provide adequate legal protection against the manufacture, import, distribution, sale, rental, advertisement for sale or rental, or possession for commercial purposes of devices, products or components or the provision of services which:

(a)   are promoted, advertised or marketed for the purpose of circumvention of any effective technological measures;

(b)   have only a limited commercially significant purpose or use other than to circumvent any effective technological measures; or

(c)   are primarily designed, produced, adapted or performed for the purpose of enabling or facilitating the circumvention of any effective technological measures.

7.38   The removal of rights management metadata is prohibited under Art 7.

Mens rea

7.39   The Copyright Directive requires that the legal protection impose a *mens rea* requirement that the person concerned in circumventing the DRM system knows or has reasonable grounds to know that this is the objective (Art 6(1)).

7.40   However, it is worth noting that there is no *mens rea* requirement for a facilitator who manufactures, imports, distributes, sells or rents a device that circumvents a DRM system if the device only has a 'limited commercially significant purpose other than to circumvent' (Art 6(2)(b)) or is 'primarily designed' for enabling circumvention (Art 6(2)(c)). If the devices can be shown to have an alternative legitimate or commercially significant purpose, with circumvention being a secondary one, then the facilitator who sells or advertises such a device must be shown to have an intent towards that illegitimate purpose.[15]

7.41   The rationale for this distinction is apparent when you consider those targeted by the relative provisions. The actual circumventors of a DRM system are the users of the copyright work, whether it be illegally downloaded music, 'cracked' computer games or even illegally intercepted television. The average consumer is unlikely to have the technical knowledge to circumvent the DRM system. Therefore, only intentional circumvention is prohibited.

7.42   In contrast the facilitators of circumvention devices are usually professionals or computer experts who profit from the production. The policy decision to impose liability upon the manufacturer who producers a device with no commercial purpose other than to access protected material is legitimate. The *mens rea* of a distributor is irrelevant unless it can be demonstrated that the circumvention device was not 'primarily designed, produced or adapted' for circumventing copyright and there is another legitimate commercial purpose for the device. The genuine merchant or importer remains liable unless objectively the device can be described as legitimate. The Copyright Directive deems that these unintentional facilitators should not escape liability.

---

[15]   See the insertion of 'purpose' within Art 6(2)(a) and (c), and Copyright Directive Recital 48.

7.43 The Copyright Directive was incorporated into UK legislation by the Copyright and Related Rights Regulations 2003,[16] which made amendments to the CDPA 1998.

The Software Directive

7.44 The Software Directive (Directive 2009/24/EC) requires member states to protect computer programs by copyright as literary works.[17] In order to protect this provision of copyright, Art 7(1)(c) prohibits the circulation or possession for commercial purposes of the means to remove or circumvent DRM:

> 1. Without prejudice to the provisions of Articles 4, 5 and 6, Member States shall provide, in accordance with their national legislation, appropriate remedies against a person committing any of the following acts:
>
> ...
>
> (c) any act of putting into circulation, or the possession for commercial purposes of, any means the sole intended purpose of which is to facilitate the unauthorised removal or circumvention of any technical device which may have been applied to protect a computer program.

7.45 The use of the broad wording 'any act of putting into circulation' is sufficient to cover sale, distribution and rental. Importation and manufacture may fall within the Software Directive if undertaken for the purpose of furthering distribution to the public and is deemed to be an integral to the distribution process.[18]

7.46 In contrast to the Copyright Directive, the 'sole intended purpose' of the infringing device must be the unauthorised removal or circumvention of DRM. Therefore, a computer program which permits software to operate with Windows and with Linux does not contradict this anti-circumvention provision. Under the Copyright Directive this computer program might potentially infringe Art 6(2)(c) if the copyright holder could prove that the 'primary purpose' was to remove or negate technological protective measures.

7.47 The Software Directive does not provide a definition for 'commercial purposes' but variants of 'commercial use' and 'commercial scale' are defined within the Rental and Lending Rights Directive (Directive 2006/115/EC, Recital 11), and the Enforcement Directive (Directive 2004/48, Recital 14). It has been suggested that the appropriate construction of 'commercial purposes' is in line with the Enforcement Directive, where the activity must be carried out within the framework of a business for any direct or indirect business-related economic advantage.[19]

---

[16] SI 2003/2498.

[17] The definitions within the Software Directive are provided in detail within Chapter 4.

[18] L Bently, 'Directive 91/250/EEC – Directive on the legal protection of computer programmes', in T Dreier and P B Hugenholtz, *Concise European Copyright Law* (Kluwer Law International, The Netherlands, 2006), p 234.

[19] M Walter, *European Copyright Law* (Oxford University Press, 2010), p 1459.

7.48 Websites that market circumventing devices or services do not fall within the prohibition under the Software Directive, which does not target advertising for sale or rental nor promotion through commercial communications. However, an advert online for a computer program that evades DRM would likely fall foul of the Copyright Directive.

Mens rea

7.49 The *mens rea* is ambiguous from the wording of the Software Directive. The 'sole intended purpose' imposes some form of test to the aim of the circumvention device. What is unclear is whether this test is objective or subjective to the person undertaking the act. Comparing the language within the Software Directive with the Copyright Directive, specifically 'intended purpose' with 'commercially significant purpose', the later interpretation appears the more likely and that a guilty intent is required.

7.50 On 1 October 2009, the provisions of the Software Directive were incorporated into UK legislation by amendment to the CDPA 1988. The amendments were achieved through Constitutional Reform Act 2005, Sch 11, para 1(2).

Conditional Access Directive

7.51 The Conditional Access Directive (Directive 98/84/EC) covers 'conditional access services', which are defined as television or radio broadcasts or internet services to which 'access … in an intelligible form is made conditional upon prior individual authorisation'.[20] Examples are pay-per-view and encrypted television and internet sites which charge for access. The Conditional Access Directive provides for prohibitions on activity involving 'illicit devices'. An illicit device is any equipment or software designed or adapted to give access to a protected service without the authorisation of the service provider (see Art 4):

Infringing activities.

Member States shall prohibit on their territory all of the following activities:

(a)   the manufacture, import, distribution, sale, rental or possession for commercial purposes of illicit devices;

(b)   the installation, maintenance or replacement for commercial purposes of an illicit device;

(c)   the use of commercial communications to promote illicit devices.

7.52 Unlike the Copyright Directive and the Software Directive, the Conditional Access Directive is not enforced by the author of the protected work. The Conditional Access Directive protects service providers from the unauthorised reception of their conditional access services, regardless as to

---

[20]   Directive 98/84/EC, Art 2(b).

whether they contain material protected by copyright. In practice, it is highly likely that the transmission protected by conditional access will also be an original work covered by copyright. Newspapers which publish material online, which can be accessed with a subscription, would potentially be able to seek protection under all three Directives. There is nothing to prevent the beneficiary of a right to enforce that which is most favourable in the circumstances of the alleged contravention.

7.53 The Conditional Access Directive does not target the non-commercial circulation of circumventing devices and, therefore, has a more limited scope of application in contrast to the Software Directive.

7.54 The Conditional Access Directive does not contain any exceptions or limitations in relation to copyright. Recital 21 indicates that the Directive is without prejudice to the 'Community rules concerning intellectual property rights'. It has been suggested that the exceptions found in the Copyright and Software Directive can be implied into the Conditional Access Directive. However, broadcasters enjoy a distinct right to remuneration based on a different legal basis than copyright law. The exceptions to copyright cannot be extended to an application beyond that area.[21] Therefore, the relationship between the copyright exceptions and the Conditional Access Directive are unclear. For example, a teacher who copies copyrighted material for educational purposes may utilise the exception contained within the Software Directive, or the voluntary agreements in place under the Copyright Directive. However, if the person obtains the material from an access controlled website, without proper regard to the DRM then the member state would be obliged to seek liability under the Conditional Access Directive.

Mens rea

7.55 Recital 22 provides the member state with a discretion to impose *mens rea* to the domestic legislation:

> '(22) Whereas national law concerning sanctions and remedies for infringing commercial activities may provide that the activities have to be carried out in the knowledge or with reasonable grounds for knowing that the devices in question were illicit.'

Copyright, Designs and Patents Act 1988

7.56 The Copyright, Designs and Patents Act 1988 (CDPA 1988), s 296, applies the measures to protect DRM within the Software Directive. Sections 296ZA–ZG apply the protections contained within the Copyright Directive. The protections contained within the Conditional Access Directive

---

[21] P Vantsiouri, 'A Legislation in Bits and Pieces: The Overlapping Anti-Circumvention Provisions of the Information Society Directive, the Software Directive and the Conditional Access Directive, and their Implementation in the United Kingdom', *European Intellectual Property Review*, 2012, p 593.

are within ss 297A–299. The wording of the anti-circumvention provisions of the CDPA 1988 reflect that of the three Directives, with minor exceptions.

Circumvention of technical devices applied to computer programs (s 296)

7.57   This section incorporates the Software Directive into UK Legislation. Rather than a prohibition on 'putting into circulation' as contained within the Software Directive, s 296(1)(b)(i) prohibits: 'manufactures for sale or hire, imports, distributes, sells or lets for hire, offers or exposes for sale or hire, advertises for sale or hire'.

> (1) This section applies where –
>
> (a)   a technical device has been applied to a computer program; and
> (b)   a person (A) knowing or having reason to believe that it will be used to make infringing copies –
>> (i)   manufactures for sale or hire, imports, distributes, sells or lets for hire, offers or exposes for sale or hire, advertises for sale or hire or has in his possession for commercial purposes any means the sole intended purpose of which is to facilitate the unauthorised removal or circumvention of the technical device; or
>> (ii)   publishes information intended to enable or assist persons to remove or circumvent the technical device.

7.58   Advertisement for sale or hire is not contained within the Software Directive. It is unlikely that this would render the CDPA 1988 as not compliant with the Directive.

7.59   It has been suggested that in order to ensure an interpretation of the CDPA 1988 which is consistent with the Software Directive, importation should only encompass acts carried out with the purpose of furthering distribution.[22] Otherwise the CDPA 1988 would target the possession of an illicit device for private purposes. This would be inconsistent with the use of 'possession for commercial purposes', which is also contained within the section.

7.60   Those permitted to enforce the circumvention protection measure within this section, as with ss 296ZA–ZG, extend to beyond the rights holder to those issuing public copies, communicating to the public, and an exclusive licensee (see CDPA 1988, ss 296(2) and 296ZA(3)). These rights are concurrent and can be exercised by any or all of those adorned (see CDPA 1988, ss 296(3) and 296ZA(4)).

7.61   The *mens rea* for the anti-circumvention of DRM of a computer program is identified within s 296 as 'knowing or having reason to believe'.

---

[22]   Ibid, p 589.

7.62 In *Kabushiki Kaisha Sony Computer Entertainment Inc v Ball (Application for Summary Judgment)*,[23] the defendant manufactured microchips that circumvented the claimants' copy protection device in their games consoles. This activity breached the CDPA 1988, s 296. However, the defendant argued that he did not know or have reason to believe that the chip would be used to make infringing copies and that the chips were destined for use abroad. The High Court (Liddle J) held that it could not be determined that there had been a breach of any of the claimants' rights without an examination of the details of the defendant's commercial operations, as the defendant might not have the necessary guilty knowledge. Under domestic legislation the *mens rea* for liability is an intention, knowledge or belief that a third party will circumvent DRM.

Circumvention of technological measures (ss 296Z–296ZG)

7.63 Section 296ZA and 296ZB prohibit the circumvention of technological measures contained within copyright work other than computer programs. The anti-circumvention measures apply to both users and facilitators in accordance with the Copyright Directive; however, an alternative *mens rea* is applied for each.

296ZA Circumvention of technological measures.

(1) This section applies where –

(a)   effective technological measures have been applied to a copyright work other than a computer program; and
(b)   a person (B) does anything which circumvents those measures knowing, or with reasonable grounds to know, that he is pursuing that objective.

296ZB Devices and services designed to circumvent technological measures.

(1) A person commits an offence if he –

(a)   manufactures for sale or hire, or
(b)   imports otherwise than for his private and domestic use, or
(c)   in the course of a business –
    (i)   sells or lets for hire, or
    (ii)   offers or exposes for sale or hire, or
    (iii)   advertises for sale or hire, or
    (iv)   possesses, or
    (v)   distributes, or
(d)   distributes otherwise than in the course of a business to such an extent as to affect prejudicially the copyright owner,

---

[23]   [2004] EWHC 1738 (Ch), [2005] ECC 24.

any device, product or component which is primarily designed, produced, or adapted for the purpose of enabling or facilitating the circumvention of effective technological measures.

7.64 When the anti-circumvention measure is in the possession of a user then liability can only be imposed if the person knows or has reasonable grounds to know that the device or system in question has the objective of circumventing DRM. However, where the 'primary purpose' of a device or system is circumvention, no *mens rea* is imposed.

7.65 Anti-circumvention devices are permitted in certain circumstances, including: for the purpose of research (s 296ZA(2)); and the innocent infringement of copyright (s 296ZD(7)). The innocent infringement of copyright extends the principle that a defendant who does not know or have reason to believe that copyright subsisted in the work is not liable under the CDPA 1988. Therefore, a person in possession of an anti-circumvention device is not liable if they did not know or believe their acts enabled or facilitate the infringement of copyright. In instances when the primary purpose of a device is circumvention, rather than imposing a *mens rea*, this raises a potential defence. In practical terms, it may be difficult for an individual to demonstrate that they neither knew nor had reasonable grounds to believe that their actions were prohibited, especially if the device or systems has no other purpose.

7.66 The CDPA 1988, s 296ZE permits complaints to be made to the Secretary of State if a protection measure prevents a person from carrying out a permitted action contained within Sch 5A. The Secretary of State has wide powers to issue a direction to ascertain whether voluntary measures are in place to enable permitted acts. If not, the Secretary of State can ensure that the owner of the exclusive right, whether the licensee or the copyright owner, makes available an unprotected copy to allow the permitted act to be completed. Similarly, the Secretary of State can permit the complainant to use an anti-circumvention device. If a copyright owner or licensee fails to abide by the Secretary of State's direction, then the complainant can seek a remedy for breach of statutory duty.

Unauthorised decoders: s 297A

7.67 The production and distribution of a device to circumvent technological protection measures on television broadcasts is a criminal offence. Possession of an unauthorised decoder is also a criminal offence but only if the possession is for a 'commercial purpose'.

297A Unauthorised decoders

(1) A person commits an offence if he –

(a)   makes, imports, distributes, sells or lets for hire or offers or exposes for sale or hire any unauthorised decoder;

(b)   has in his possession for commercial purposes any unauthorised decoder;

(c)   installs, maintains or replaces for commercial purposes any unauthorised decoder; or

(d)   advertises any unauthorised decoder for sale or hire or otherwise promotes any unauthorised decoder by means of commercial communications.

(2) ... [relating to sentence]

(3) It is a defence to any prosecution for an offence under this section for the defendant to prove that he did not know, and had no reasonable ground for believing, that the decoder was an unauthorised decoder.

7.68   Similar to the liability under s 296ZA, there is no *mens rea* requirement for this criminal offence; it is one of strict liability. However, a defendant able to demonstrate that he/she neither knew nor had reasonable grounds for believing that the decoder was unauthorised will be afforded a defence. This reverse burden is important when considering the prosecution of these offences. A prosecutor will be required to prove that an individual had a device in his/her possession, and that it was for a commercial purpose, but it is the defendant who will be required to prove that he/she neither knew or had reasonable grounds to believe that the decoder was unauthorised. The Human Rights Act 1998 and the incorporation of the European Convention of Human Rights (ECHR) would require that the burden on the defendant is merely an evidential one.

7.69   It is worth noting that the European Court of Justice has determined that a satellite transmission decoder licensed for use in a foreign country was not an illicit device, in accordance with Art 2(e) of the Conditional Access Directive, and a national law preventing its use infringed the freedom to provide services and breached competition law. As a result, a foreign decoder should not be considered an unauthorised decoder under s 297.[24]

7.70   Section 298(5) permits the innocent infringement of protective measures in relation to television broadcasts. This is likely to be more relevant to the s 297 offence: fraudulently receiving programmes. This is a dishonesty offence that requires the prosecution prove a user, rather than a facilitator, is dishonestly receiving broadcasts with an intent to avoid payment. The hurdles that a prosecutor is required to clear in order to prove this offence means that pragmatically the innocent infringement protections will very rarely be used.

European Union Agency for Network and Information Security

7.71   Further to the imposition of Directives, the European Union has adopted a soft approach to information security by establishing the European Union Agency for Network and Information Security (ENISA). According to its mandate, ENISA contributes to the development of a culture of network and information security for the benefit of citizens, consumers, enterprises and

---

[24]   See *Football Association Premier League Ltd v QC Leisure* (C-403/08) and *Murphy v Media Protection Services Ltd* (C-429/08) [2012] Bus LR 1321.

public sector organisations throughout the European Union. In practical terms the ENISA strives to serve as a centre of expertise for both member states and EU institutions to seek advice on matters related to network and information security. This has included facilitating the third pan-European cyber exercise, Cyber Europe 2014, which simulated a cyber-attack across the European Union.

7.72 During the first phase of the exercise, conducted on 28–29 April 2014, participants across Europe dealt with 16 different challenging technical cyber-security incidents. The second phase of the exercise was held on 30 October 2014; 29 EU and EFTA countries cooperated by using the EU-Standard Operational Procedures (EU-SOPs) to establish a common situation picture. The third phase of CE2014, which took place on 24–25 February 2015, focused on strategic-level cyber crisis management.

7.73 In effect ENISA is a communication centre for a multi-stakeholder approach to cyber-security challenges within the European Union. As a centre for developing policy ENISA is a useful tool for the European Commission but will have a limited impact on day-to-day private sector security.

PROTECTION THROUGH LITIGATION

7.74 The first alternative control mechanism, when technological protective measures have failed, is typically to rely on litigation to prevent the continued use of material that is subject of patents or protected by copyright. In a domestic context, the success of this approach can be relatively assured. However, with the global nature of the internet, particularly in relation to illegal file sharing and downloads, litigation is struggling as a control mechanism.

7.75 In April 2009, a Swedish court found that the four co-founders of the file-sharing website Pirate Bay were guilty of criminal offences of contributory copyright infringement.[25] They faced jail and were fined US$3.6 million in relation to a concurrent civil case brought by the International Federation of Phonographic Industry (IFPI), which represented the interests of media, film and television companies including Sony BMG, MGM, 20th Century Fox, Warner, EMI and Universal.

7.76 However, the website continued to operate until May 2010 when a further injunction was sought from a number of Hollywood-based film studios. Pirate Bay ceased to operate for a short time before continuing to operate through a different server hosted in Sweden. As of January 2016, PirateBay.org continues to operate providing a list of proxy websites where illegal file sharing takes place.

---

[25] A Mene, 'Piracy and illegal file-sharing: UK and US legal and commercial responses', Practical Law Company, www.practicallaw.com/1–502–7956.

7.77 This section will seek to highlight some of the legal challenges in pursuing litigation as a control mechanism.

Copyright

7.78 Suing individuals for copyright infringement under the CDPA 1988 was one of the first legal solutions used by the UK music industry to combat piracy and illegal file-sharing. The act of downloading a copyrighted work via a peer-to-peer network infringes several rights and could result in liability for the downloader, uploader, peer-to-peer network operator and the internet service provider (ISP).

7.79 An uploader who provides copyright protected files to a shared folder that can be accessed by others on a peer-to-peer network infringes the copyright holder's exclusive right to issue copies to the public. This contravenes the CDPA 1988, ss 16 and 18. The uploader's actions also infringe the s 20(2) right of communication to the public by electronic transmission. A downloader who transfers a file across the internet from a peer creates a new copy on their hard drive. This infringes the copyright holder's exclusive right to make copies contained within ss 16–17 of the CDPA 1988. The peer-to-peer network operator can be held liable under s 16(2) which provides: 'copyright in a work is infringed by a person who without the licence of the copyright owner does, or authorises another to do, any of the acts restricted by the copyright'. Finally, ISPs can now be held liable under the Digital Economy Act 2010.

7.80 While the litigation of individuals worked to some extent in raising the profile of illegal file sharing, it was impractical for any industry to pursue in the long term given the number of people engaged in online infringement. The costs in pursuing every infringer through legal action would be vast as such actions are expensive to use in respect of every infringement.

7.81 Instead industries sought to use 'volume litigation' to reduce these costs. Volume litigation involves copyright owners banding together, and going onto the file-sharing networks to discover the Internet Protocol (IP) addresses that are infringing copyright. The copyright holders will then seek a court order requiring the internet service providers (ISPs) to provide them with the personal details of those infringing customers. The copyright owners will then typically contact those customers, which can number in the thousands, through lawyers, who warn them that they face potential court action unless they pay a large settlement sum that may range up to £700.[26]

7.82 An alternative to suing individuals is to target the owners of the pirate sites that enable and encourage infringement to occur. The Pirate Bay case is considered to be a successful application of this approach. However, with

---

[26] A Mene, 'Piracy and illegal file-sharing: UK and US legal and commercial responses', Practical Law Company, www.practicallaw.com/1-502-7956.

websites based outside the EU, it can be difficult to litigate because of poor copyright enforcement in some jurisdictions.

Digital Economy Act 2010

7.83 The Digital Economy Act 2010 (DEA 2010) was one of the outcomes of the Digital Britain Report[27] which recommended improving the UK's communications infrastructure in order to increase competitiveness in the global digital economy. Although primarily concerned with provisions regarding digital infrastructure, ss 3–18 were measures to address online copyright infringement. These were incorporated as amendments to the Communications Act 2003, ss 120A–120N.

7.84 Under the DEA 2010, a rights holder can report a website hosting any online infringing material to the ISP. The rights holder must report the IP address to the relevant ISP within a Copyright Infringement Report (CIR). This will include details of the alleged infringements. Under s 3 of the DEA 2010 the ISP is then obliged to notify the subscriber of the IP address that they are hosting copyright material. Under s 4, the ISP is then obliged to provide the rights holder with a Copyright Infringements List (CIL) which details the alleged infringements under the IP address of the anonymous subscriber. The CIL can then be used by the rights holder to obtain a court order to reveal the subscriber's identity and to bring action for copyright infringement.

7.85 The concern with the powers under the DEA 2010 is that those with the technical ability and desire to host infringing copyright material and distribute to a commercial scale may not allow their IP address to be easily discoverable. Proxies and virtual private networks are available to mask a user's IP address. Those more determined and criminally minded may even hijack the IP address of an innocent and unknowing subscriber.

7.86 In *Media CAT Ltd v Adams*,[28] Judge Birss QC considered the problem of using an IP address to identify a defendant, and concluded that the process is at least uncertain:[29]

> 'All the IP address identifies is an internet connection, which is likely today to be a wireless home broadband router. All Media C.A.T.'s monitoring can identify is the person who has the contract with their ISP to have internet access. Assuming a case in Media C.A.T.'s favour that the IP address is indeed linked to wholesale infringements of the copyright in question (like the *Polydor* [2005] EWHC 3191 (Ch) case), Media C.A.T. do not know who did it and know that they do not know who did it …

---

[27]　https://www.gov.uk/government/uploads/system/uploads/attachment_data/file/228844/7650. pdf.

[28]　[2011] EWPCC 6, [2011] FSR 28.

[29]　See *Media Cat Ltd*, at [28]–[30].

What if the defendant authorises another to use their internet connection in general and, unknown to them, the authorised user uses P2P software and infringes copyright? Does the act of authorising use of an internet connection turn the person doing the authorising into a person authorising the infringement within s 16(2) [CDPA]? I am not aware of a case which decides that question either. Then there is the question of whether leaving an internet connection "unsecured" opens up the door to liability for infringement by others piggy-backing on the connection unbeknownst to the owner. Finally what does "unsecured" mean? Wireless routers have different levels of security available and if the level of security is relevant to liability — where is the line to be drawn?'

7.87 A person or company may still be liable under the DEA 2010, s 3, if they 'allow infringement'. This raises great uncertainty for those providing WiFi networks, who typically receive their connection through a larger ISP. For the purposes of the DEA 2010 is the WiFi provider an ISP or a subscriber? If categorised as an ISP to users then there is an obligation on the provider, whether it is a coffee shop or a multinational company, to monitor the compile CILs if infringing material is shared through their service. What is more likely is that a WiFi provider will be deemed to be a subscriber, in which case they are potentially liable to sanction for allowing infringement. At the time of publication, a rights holder has not sought to impose an obligation on a WiFi provider that is not also a larger ISP provider.

7.88 Sections 5–7 require that Ofcom, the enforcement body for the DEA 2010 under the Communications Act 2003, publish two codes in relation to implementation and then technical measures in relation to certain material online: the Initial Obligations Code (IOC) and Obligations to Limit Internet Access (Technical Measures). In 2010, a draft version of the IOC was published. This proposed that initially the IOC should only apply to ISPs with 400,000 subscribers or more. This represented the seven largest ISPs in the UK, which accounted for approximately 93.4% of subscribers.[30] Ignoring this would again permit an organised and determined infringer from avoiding the provisions of the DEA 2010 by using a smaller ISP, the draft IOC inspired TalkTalk and BT to judicially review the DEA 2010.

7.89 In *R (British Telecommunications Plc) v Secretary of State for Business, Innovation and Skills*,[31] the claimant internet service providers applied for judicial review of the DEA 2010 and the draft Copyright (Initial Obligations) (Sharing of Costs) Order 2011, which proposed to make ISPs liable for 25% of the costs incurred by Ofcom in carrying out functions under the contested provisions. The Administrative Court (Kenneth Parker J) held that the online infringement of copyright provisions in the DEA 2010 were not incompatible

---

[30]   A Royle, 'Pirates Ahoy! Copyright and Internet File-Sharing', North East Law Review, Newcastle University, June 2013, p 63.

[31]   [2011] EWHC 1021 (Admin).

with EU law; however, the draft Copyright (Initial Obligations) (Sharing of Costs) Order 2011 did infringe Directive 2002/20 (the Authorisation Directive), Art 12.[32]

7.90 The ISPs argued that the DEA 2010 infringed the Authorisation Directive because it discriminated against larger ISPs compared to smaller ones, and mobile network operators, which are not subject to the provisions of the Act. The court rejected this, holding it is reasonable and proportional to target large ISPs first. However, Parker J ruled that ISPs should not be required to bear any part of Ofcom's or the appeals body's costs of setting up, monitoring and enforcing the scheme: these would amount to administrative charges on ISPs, extending beyond the exhaustive description of recoverable administrative charges under Art 12.

7.91 The Administrative Court was reluctant to find the legislation disproportionate as Parliament had engaged in a 'lengthy process of consultation with all interested parties, which took account of the representations made by those parties, and after a voluntary, non-legislative scheme was tried out'.[33]

7.92 Interestingly the first reading of the Digital Economy Bill was on 16 March 2010 and the DEA 2010 was enacted on 8 April 2010, just 23 days later. Whether there was lengthy consultation or not in advance, the actual Bill was subject to very little debate, especially as Parliament was dissolved on 12 April 2010 for the upcoming election. It may be for this reason that controversial technical measures contained within ss 17 and 18 were never enforced.

7.93 A second consultation in relation to the IOC was issued in June 2012 but to date there is no definitive IOC. As a result, the extent of the provisions is moot. The Court of Appeal (Arden LJ, Richards LJ, Patten LJ) held that the legislation created a scheme of regulation that was conditional or contingent on future rules both for its detailed content and for it to have any legal effect; that that being so, until the code was in force there were no actual obligations or legal effects on the ISPs:[34]

> 'The judge was right to find that the contested provisions do not have the "legal effects" described by the court's case-law. The 'initial obligations' of ISPs under sections 124A and 124B are conditional on there being a code in force under sections 124C or 124D. The word "if" in section 124A(2) is important, even though the provisions contemplate that there must in due course be a code: until such time as the code comes into being, the provisions impose no obligations on ISPs. Moreover the code is to be made for the purpose of regulating the initial obligations, and the scope of those obligations will be dependent on the detailed

---

[32] See *R (British Telecommunications Plc) v Secretary of State*, at [107].
[33] Ibid at [212].
[34] See *R (British Telecommunications Plc) v Secretary of State* [2012] EWCA Civ 232, [2012] Bus LR 1766, at [42].

content of the code. Whilst the statute prescribes various basic features of the code, it leaves very considerable freedom for the working out of the detail. (The fact that the contested provisions have legal effects for Ofcom, in relation to matters such as the approval or making of the code, is irrelevant. What matters is whether there are legal effects for individuals, capable of affecting the freedom of movement of services or freedom of establishment.)'

7.94 After a period of at least 12 months, when the initial obligations have been in force, the Secretary of State can commence plans to impose technical obligations on ISPs but only if the initial obligations appear unsuccessful in reducing online copyright infringement. These plans can only come into force after a 60-day consultation period and with the approval of both Houses of Parliament. The DEA 2010 does not specify the precise mechanism for the implementation of these measures, which are to be determined within the second Ofcom Technical Measures Code.

7.95 Utilising ss 9–12, the ISP may be required to limit the speed or other capacity of the service provided to a subscriber; prevent a subscriber from using the service to gain access to particular material or limit such use; suspend the service provided to a subscriber; or limit the service provided to a subscriber in another way. The Technical Measures Code would be subject to the super-affirmative procedure in Parliament.

7.96 The provisions of the DEA 2010 are controversial and have never been properly implemented or utilised. Providing a legislative system to obtain information on individuals and companies involved in potential online copyright infringement is a positive step. The data protection issues surrounding the gathering of information on individual users are unclear under the Data Protection Act 1998 (DPA 1998). The DPA 1998 states that personal data about a subject cannot be processed without a person's consent, unless it falls into one of the exemptions. It is unclear whether one of these exemptions might apply to rights-holders and ISPs. However, the burden on ISPs to monitor their subscribers and then divulge this information to the government is great, and the impact on users is potentially draconian. In France, a similar piece of legislation which provided for an individual's internet connection to be disconnected if the IP was associated with copyright infringement was deemed to be unconstitutional. On 9 July 2013, the French Ministry of Culture published official decree No 0157, removing from the law 'the additional misdemeanour punishable by suspension of access to a communication service'.[35] Like the DEA 2010 the French legislation was scarcely used. Between the law's approval in 2009 and the abrogation of the suspension of access to a communication service in 2013, only one user had been sentenced to suspension (for 15 days). The sentence was never applied because of the

---

[35]　https://torrentfreak.com/three-strikes-and-youre-still-in-france-kills-piracy-disconnections-130709/ (last accessed 24 August 2016).

abrogation some days after. The DEA 2010 may similarly flounder if the provisions were scrutinised closely in the context of Arts 6 and 8 of the ECHR.[36]

7.97 In *Twentieth Century Film Corporation v Newzbin Limited*,[37] a collective of distributors and film-makers, including Twentieth Century Film Corporation, successfully brought a case of copyright infringement in the High Court against a website, Newzbin. Newzbin operated as an indexing network that users could use as a database to store large files containing copies of films. The case was the first to establish that a website could commit copyright infringement, under s 16 of the CDPA 1988, on the internet by authorising, enabling and encouraging its users to copy and infringe films.

7.98 *Gilham*,[38] established that playing games enabled by a modification computer chip (modchips) involved a substantial breach of copyright. The offences arose from the appellant's commercial dealing in modchips for use in conjunction with various games consoles. Gilham had operated a business for just over 2 years selling components and devices for such games consoles. Once installed the modchips enabled counterfeit games to be played on the consoles. The Court of Appeal (Stanley Burnton LJ, Penry-Davey J, Sharp J) held that the game as a whole was not the sole subject of copyright, and various drawings that resulted in the images shown on the television screens or monitors were themselves artistic works protected by copyright. The images shown on the screen were substantial copies of those works. It followed that even if the contents of the RAM of a game console, at any one time, was not a substantial copy, the image displayed on the screen was. The appellant had been rightly convicted for offences under the CDPA 1988, s 296ZB and for money laundering where he had dealt commercially with modification computer chips.

7.99 In *Coward v Phaestos Ltd*,[39] the claimant claimed ownership of the intellectual property rights in software used by the defendant group of companies. The claimant and his estranged wife had together been involved in the formation of the businesses, which the claimant suggested had been a joint enterprise. He claimed that the relevant software had been created before the execution of the partnership deed in December 1992; and that he personally owned the copyright. The businesses had an implied licence to use the software but the claimant had terminated the licence when he resigned from the partnership. The continued use amounted to copyright infringement.

---

[36] F R Moreno, 'Incompatibility of the Digital Economy Act 2010 subscriber appeal process provisions with Article 6 of the ECHR', *International Review of Law, Computers & Technology*, 10 January 2014; and 'The Digital Economy Act 2010: subscriber monitoring and the right to privacy under Article 8 of the ECHR', *International Review of Law, Computers & Technology*, 26 April 2016.

[37] [2010] EWHC 608 (Ch).

[38] [2009] EWCA Crim 2293, [2010] ECDR 5.

[39] [2013] EWHC 1292 (Ch).

7.100 The defendant counterclaimed on the basis that the software was partnership property and that the businesses had acquired all rights to it upon dissolution of the partnership. The High Court (Asplin J) found in favour of the defendant businesses. As a matter of necessity, and to give business efficacy to the situation, it was to be inferred that the software was a partnership asset, because trading could not have taken place without it and because to have retained ownership of it would have conflicted with his duty of good faith to the other partners.

Patents

7.101 The use of patents as a control mechanism is equally fraught with problems. The cost of litigation is incredibly high and the use of patents to enforce protection can lead to counterclaims. Since 2009, the 'smartphone wars' or smartphone patents licensing and litigation has been raging between Sony, Google, Apple Inc., Samsung, Microsoft, Nokia, Motorola, Huawei, and HTC, among others. The law in relation to patent litigation is extensive and cannot be encapsulated within a few paragraphs. Patents can be useful as a control mechanism to protect the design and reproduction of embedded devices but should be considered as one of many mechanisms of protection.

7.102 In *HTC Corporation v Gemalto SA*,[40] the claimant sought the revocation of two patents belonging to the defendant concerning the technology for smart cards for smart mobile telephones. The first patent (A) related to a way of running a high level programming language, Java, on a smart card or integrated circuit card using a microcontroller, with a certain memory and processor, and a converter to enable the communication of Java to the receiving device. The second patent (B) related to an invention for a smart card reader. The Patents Court had to determine whether any claim entitled to the priority date was obvious and lacked novelty over the common general knowledge and various items of prior art; and if the patents or any of their claims were valid, whether they were infringed by any of claimant's devices. The Patent Court (Birss J) held that all but one of the claims were invalid for lack of novelty or obviousness over the common general knowledge and various items of prior art. The one valid claim was not infringed by a competitor's mobile devices and smart phones. After extensive litigation the patents were insufficient as a means of protection.

THE COMMERCIAL APPROACH

7.103 Given the limited success of DRM and litigation, companies are increasingly moving towards commercial alternatives, which can be the most effective and lucrative method of tackling piracy. Apple's iTunes and the range of Amazon products, from Kindle to Amazon Music and Amazon Prime Video, are lawful alternatives for consumers to access content online.

---

[40]   [2014] RPC 9.

7.104 Within online music there are four revenue alternatives to simple purchase of online content. Spotify's advertising model allows users to stream music of their choice which is intermittently interrupted by adverts. Those who wish to listen to music without adverts can move to the subscription-based model, where music is unlimited for a monthly fee.

7.105 A US-based company, Beyond Oblivion, has proposed an alternative revenue method. Rather than collecting payment for copyright licence for the user, fees would be incorporated into the price of hardware used to access online content, for example computers, mobile telephones and MP3/MP4 players. The end user would not have to pay anything for acquiring music beyond the price of the hardware to play it on.

7.106 Social media platform mFlow is a service which incorporates music-streaming with social networking. Users are able to send (or flow) their musical preferences to friends. If they listen and then buy the music the user is credited with tokens in order to buy further content.

7.107 With the online provision of music, the most onerous aspect for music-streaming sites is the negotiation of rights clearance and licence fees. This includes the Performing Rights Society (PRS) in the UK, and various collecting societies in Europe. The length of time for negotiation, and the lack of a unified system is costly, which affects the viability of businesses such as Spotify and other start-up companies. US music-streaming site Pandora stopped operating in the UK and Europe for this reason.[41] As a result of these difficulties, arguments have been have been made to unify the system for obtaining copyright licences across Europe.[42]

7.108 The Collective Management of Copyright (EU Directive) Regulation 2016[43] (CMCR) sought to address some of these difficulties by improving market conditions for the take up of online music services across the EU. The CMCR implemented the European Union Collective Rights Management Directive 2014/26/EU, the core objective of which was to ensure that collective management organisations (CMOs) act in the best interests of the right holders they represent, and placed minimum standards of governance, financial management and transparency on all European Union CMOs. CMOs that wish to engage in the supply of multi-territorial licences in musical works for online use must abide by the level playing field imposed through the CMCR and the Directive. Part 3 of the CMCR provides obligations for CMOs seeking to engage in multi-territorial licensing. Guidance on these obligations can be obtained from the Government Intellectual Property Office.[44]

---

[41] BBC News, 'Pandora to "cut off" UK listeners', http://news.bbc.co.uk/1/hi/technology/7178699.stm, 9 January 2008.

[42] A Mene, 'Piracy and illegal file-sharing: UK and US legal and commercial responses', Practical Law Company, www.practicallaw.com/1–502–7956.

[43] SI 2016/221.

[44] https://www.gov.uk/government/uploads/system/uploads/attachment_data/file/518555/Guidance_on_CRM_Directive_implementing_regulations.pdf).

British Phonographic Industry Ltd v Mechanical-Copyright Protection Society Ltd[45]

7.109 When considering licensing agreements for online content the case of *British Phonographic Industry Ltd v Mechanical-Copyright Protection Society Ltd*[46] is essential reading. In this case, the applicants referred to the Copyright Tribunal the royalty provisions of a licensing scheme for the use of online music which had been promulgated by the respondent collecting societies (X). The new scheme set different royalty rates depending on whether services were provided by way of downloading, streaming or webcasting. The royalty was to be a percentage of the music provider's gross revenue. The applicants who had agreed to the new scheme contested the definition of 'gross revenue'. It was argued that the definition of 'gross revenue' under the new scheme was overly broad and apt to capture streams of revenue to which X was not entitled, specifically third party advertising on their websites. The following matters were in issue:

(1)　Should gross revenue ever cover more than what the consumer actually paid to purchase or use X's music in an online service?

(2)　Could it legitimately include associated advertising revenue?

(3)　Where should the line be drawn on legitimate royalty-attracting advertising revenue?

(4)　What should happen where a music service was paid for in whole or in part as a result of advertising revenue?

7.110 The Copyright Tribunal (Judge Fysh QC, J Carine, R Arnold) held that in assessing a reasonable tariff, the proper rate was that which would be negotiated between a willing licensee and a willing licensor of the copyright repertoire. A central and relevant consideration was whether there was an existing licence (particularly a recent one) that covered comparable subject matter. It was for the Tribunal in assessing cited comparators to decide to what extent the rights licensed were of the same or a similar kind, whether the transactions were concluded at arm's length with neither side affected by stress and whether they were affected by legal factors which did not apply in the case under consideration. The Tribunal then had to adapt any relevant comparators to the case under review.

7.111 Where the revenue-based approach was adopted, there had to be a sufficient nexus or direct causal connection between the use of the licensor's repertoire (in this case the music collected by X), and the revenues earned by licensees of the copyright work (the website streaming or selling the music).

7.112 The only advertising with which the definition of gross revenue was concerned was third party advertising. This had to be spelt out in the definition.

---

[45]　[2008] EMLR 5.
[46]　[2008] EMLR 5.

Where music was fully paid for by the consumer, there were three situations where advertising revenue ought to attract a royalty:

(1) where the advertising was in-stream, namely placed immediately at the start, end or during the actual delivery of work in the applicants' repertoire to the user;

(2) when the music actually offered, namely the music which was enabled or was made directly available to the consumer for downloading or streaming from any page in an online service, formed the sole content of a page on which advertising was also present; and

(3) when the music actually offered formed the predominant part of a page on which advertising was also present.

7.113 In assessing how much of a page was devoted to music actually offered, any advertising was to be disregarded. Predominant meant that 75% or more of a mixed page was devoted to music actually offered. Mathematical precision was not possible and any disagreement could be referred to the online adjudicator. If music was not actually offered on a page, then the issue of royalty on advertising revenue did not arise.

7.114 When music was free or subsidised, that very fact also fuelled an increased draw to the page from which the music was actually offered. For that reason, there was a separate close connection between free or subsidised music and advertising. When any element of subsidy or under-pricing was present in the sale or use of the repertoire online, that state of affairs was to be presumed to be due to concomitant advertising. The degree of subsidy was to be ignored: free music and subsidised music were to be treated in the same way. Accordingly, when the sole or dominant part of the page related to music actually offered, a royalty was due (regardless of whether the music was fully paid for or whether it was free or its price was artificially depressed by advertising). The sole or dominant requirement was to be understood in the same way in all cases.

7.115 Sponsored search advertising revenue had only a tenuous link with the use of the repertoire by X and could not qualify for inclusion in the definition of gross revenue. A specific exclusion was required in the final licence.

7.116 Although the provisions within this case relate to licensing for music, there is no reason why the concepts cannot apply to negotiations for a licence for any digital media or online content.

7.117 Subscription-based revenue models are not limited to music with Netflix and Amazon Prime Video examples of on-demand television and movie services. These are expanding to commission original broadcasting which cannot be obtained with other services and which challenge the traditional broadcasters. Television broadcasters are responding by providing on-demand services, such as BBC iPlayer, and 'TV Everywhere' like SkyGo. The problem then becomes how do companies limit the distribution of their content to legal recipients. For example, the content of BBC's iPlayer is free to UK-based licence payers but not those living abroad. The answer is that these companies must go full circle and apply technological protection measures as the appropriate control mechanism.

Part 2

RESPONDING TO A DATA BREACH

CHAPTER 8

RESPONDING TO A DATA BREACH

INTRODUCTION

8.01 The scope of this work is to address what entities can do in the face of a cyber-attack. Clearly there will be situations where there are data breaches which are accidental and/or otherwise innocent. This chapter does not deal with those specific occasions but of course some of the matters contained within it may well be of assistance to those trying to deal with a data breach.

8.02 One of the issues which will engage those who are the subject of a data breach will be to assess what practical steps can be taken to limit the damage which will inevitably be caused and, to consider what lawful steps can be deployed to seek redress.

8.03 A data breach by its very nature, will be almost instantaneous in its effects.

THE DATA SECURITY BREACH

8.04 In assessing the action to take in respect of a data breach, regard must be had to what can lawfully be done. The statement of the applicable law set out above, and more fully in Chapter 10, provides the context of what can be done and what redress is available. It is obvious but needs to be restated, any response to a data breach must have its foundation in law if not the entity opens itself up to potential liability.

8.05 As has been seen above, the law, whilst doing its best to keep up with rapidly changing developments in technology and the increasing ability of sophisticated hackers to access all manner of information, still retains traditional remedies to be deployed by entities subjected to attack. In that sense, the entity, in order to make maximum use of pre-emptive and/or interlocutory relief, has to have systems in place which are equipped to deal with the effects of the breach as quickly and as efficiently as possible.

8.06 It may sound an obvious point to make but it is important for every entity, whatever its size and resource, to ensure that there is a distinct chain of command defined and able to take control of the effects of a data breach. Some larger entities, even today, have data protection officers, cyber risk officers or cyber security officers. Others outsource this important function. Whatever the hierarchy which exists in any entity, what is crucial, is for certain systems to be in place. The first question to ask is 'do I know where all of the entities' data is?'

8.07 In terms of the immediate issues to be dealt with when faced with a breach, huge assistance on this matter can be gained from the ICO website www.ico.org.uk and set out there are basic questions to be asked to seek to chart a course in responding to a data breach. These include:

(1)   what type of data is involved;
(2)   how sensitive is the data;
(3)   are individuals involved;
(4)   is/was the data encrypted;
(5)   what is the scale of the breach;
(6)   what type and class of individuals are affected ie customers, staff;
(7)   are there wider risks, for example risks to public health, public confidence, serious financial harm or national security.

8.08 The reaction to a breach will aim to cater for different and sometimes conflicting aims. Clearly an entity will wish to avoid reputational risk and potential sanction by the ICO, but it must also consider its moral obligation to be as transparent as possible. A recent example of a positive approach to a data breach was that of TalkTalk. The media and communications giant chose to acknowledge a serious data breach by instant communication to its customers and to the world at large. It sought to be as transparent as possible about the effects of the breach of its large customer base and it sought to re-establish confidence in its clientele by proposing measures at its own cost to provide reassurance that the breach was an isolated incident. Market research figures tend to suggest that this approach was successful and the long-term damage was significantly mitigated.

8.09 It is submitted, that the legal framework which has to be followed to obtain injunctive and or other pre-emptive relief, lends itself to this active and transparent approach (see **8.17** et seq).

NOTIFICATION

8.10 It is a surprising but true fact that, as the law currently stands, the notification requirements of entities in the event of a data breach involving personal data are sparse.

8.11 Service providers are required to notify the ICO if a 'personal data breach' occurs. Section 5(1) of the Communications Act 2003, defines a 'service provider' as 'a provider of a public electronic communications service'. It is important to note that private communications systems are not covered by this provision. Those obliged to notify, must notify the ICO within 24 hours of becoming aware of the breach, of those matters set out by the ICO's breach notification form and communicated via that format.

8.12 Thus the application must include:

(1) name and contact details;

(2) date and time of the breach;

(3) basic information about the type of breach;

(4) basic information about the personal data concerned.

8.13 The obligation includes a requirement to notify customers without unnecessary delay if the breach is likely to adversely affect their privacy. This obligation is negated if the information was protected by encryption or is otherwise meaningless. There is also an obligation to keep a breach log.

8.14 Failure to report can result in a fine of up to £1,000. This would be in addition to any subsequent penalty imposed if fault by the entity was found for the breach.

8.15 As has been pointed out above, that is currently the extent of notification requirements in the event of a data breach. However, that is not to say that specific regulators in their respective fields do not oblige regulated entities to notify in the event of a breach and recourse should be had to the particular terms of regulation and the entity should also consider whether failure to notify the ICO of a data breach may cause transgression of the security obligations contained in the seventh data protection principle (fully discussed in Chapters 1 and 2).

8.16 It would be the submission of the authors of this work, that in order to protect reputation and to be able to make the best use of legal remedies available, that notification, even if not required, is a matter of best practice. The submission is now fortified by the change of regime which will be visited by the General Data Protection Regulation (GDPR). This is discussed fully in Chapter 12, but it is of significance to note that by virtue of Art 33 of the Regulation, a personal data breach has to be reported without undue delay and no later than 72 hours, to a supervisory authority. The Regulation also sets out the circumstances where notification is required to data subjects as defined by the Regulation (see Chapter 12). The significance of this is that the requirement to notify is extended to controllers and obligations are placed on processors. The penalties for breach of this Article, are draconian (see Chapter 12) and cannot afford to be ignored.

LEGAL REMEDIES

8.17 In order to meet the challenges of a landscape in which the wait for a final determination in damages was of limited effect, a series of what were termed 'interlocutory' remedies began to achieve prominence.

8.18 The case of *American Cyanamid v Ethicon Ltd (No 1)*[1] was of great significance in setting the boundaries between the obtaining of interim relief and the adequacy of any ultimate favourable determination. In this case, the plaintiff had brought proceedings for infringement of their patent rights. At first instance an interim injunction had been obtained. The Court of Appeal had discharged the injunction.

8.19 In allowing the appeal the House of Lords laid down the test to be employed when seeking interim injunctive relief. Lord Diplock stated that there was no special rule for cases brought for infringement of patents. The guiding principle was the balance of convenience. In order to grant injunctive relief the court must be satisfied that there existed 'a serious question to be tried'. If damages were an adequate remedy, no interim injunction should be granted notwithstanding the strength of the plaintiff's case.

8.20 This clear statement of principle was an attempt to ensure that interlocutory measures did not usurp the court's function of making a final binding determination.

8.21 However, it is submitted that, particularly in the face of a data breach, this may be of limited practical use and whilst expressly restating the position that the principles established in *American Cyanamid* remain good law and should be followed, there has, it is submitted, been a clear and growing recognition of the need for courts to be able to provide quick relief.

8.22 The courts subsequent to *American Cyanamid* have recognised the importance of immediate injunctive relief particularly in cases where there is an allegation or proved finding of breach of confidence.

8.23 In *Vestergaard Frandsen v BestNet Europe Ltd*,[2] the court (Arnold J) dealt with the state of the law in respect of the remedies available for breach of confidence through misuse of Vestergaard Frandsen (VF) trade secrets. The judge restated what he called the 'general principles'.

---

[1]   [1975] AC 396.
[2]   [2009] EWHC 1456 (Ch).

8.24 He was clear that where the claimant has 'established both the invasion of a legal right and a sufficient risk of repetition, the claimant is generally regarded as entitled to an injunction save in exceptional circumstances'. He observed that in those type of cases 'damages (were) ordinarily not … regarded as an adequate remedy'.

8.25 At para 41 of the judgment, he expressly extended his finding to specifically include breach of an equitable obligation such as misuse of confidential information.

8.26 It is submitted that these two cases, *American Cyanamid* and *VF*, clearly show how this area of law has developed in that injunctive or interim relief has become more readily available through the courts in the 30-year period between the two cases. It is right that the court expressed reservations about the availability of such relief where the misuse has been in the past, 'the duration of any injunction should not extend beyond the period for which the defendant's illegitimate advantage may be expected to continue' (para 93(iv)). However, the recognition that an injunction, an equitable as opposed to a remedy solely in damages, is an entitlement, is a hugely significant step in the extension of interlocutory relief.

8.27 In the recent case of *Allfiled UK Ltd v Eltis and others*,[3] like the *VF* case, a decision of the High Court (Hildyard J), the claimant sought interlocutory injunctive relief against the respondents in order to prevent disclosure of confidential information. The judge restated the law on the exercise of the jurisdiction to grant interim injunctions citing the Senior Courts Act 1981 and CPR r 25.1, and reiterating that the court should 'ordinarily follow the approach laid down … in *American Cyanamid* (para 65). Significantly in dealing with the principles, the judge quoted the judgment of May LJ in *Cayne v Global Natural Resources PLC*[4] that when assessing the adequacy of damages the phrase 'the balance of the risk of doing an injustice' 'was an apt gloss on the balance of convenience test laid down in *American Cyanamid*'. The judge granted interim injunctive relief but with provisos and commented upon the effect of delay in seeking such relief.

8.28 What can be gleaned from these authorities is that the legal background to seeking interim relief when faced with situations where confidential information is abused, such as would routinely be the case where there is a data breach, is that recourse to the court should be made as soon as possible and the principles stated in *American Cyanamid* will be continue to be those the court will look to. It is submitted that the more recent cases, albeit decisions of High Court judges in the Chancery Division, show a greater willingness to grant interim relief in the form of an injunction provided the threat of dissemination and misuse is continuing, and the claimants have acted expeditiously in seeking such relief. The risk of injustice by refusing interim relief pending an

---

3   [2015] EWHC 1300 (Ch).
4   [1984] 1 All ER 225, at 237.

adjudication relating to damages, has, it is submitted, shown a recognition that, particularly in breach of confidence and confidential information cases, the relief must be quick to be effective.

8.29 Indeed as discussed in Chapter 10, s 97A of the Copyright, Designs and Patents Act 1988 is an attempt by parliament to go one step further and provide proactive relief by way of so called 'blocking injunctions'. (This aspect is fully dealt with in Chapter 10.)

8.30 Chapters 1 and 10 deal with the potential criminal sanctions available to investigators and entities in the event of breaches which are deliberate and calculated, clearly the focus of these measures is deterrence and punishment as opposed to redress.

RISK-BASED APPROACH

8.31 It is submitted that the response should be comprehensive and be focussed on a risk-based approach. It is insufficient to simply do the minimum. The principles of the Data Protection Act (dealt with extensively in Chapters 1 and 2) and GDPR (Chapter 12) are clearly centred on personal data. This chapter has deliberately concentrated on avoiding reputational risk and sanctions following a breach but there may be other dangers initially unseen. The loss of intellectual property and confidential information from the entity may not attract the attention of the regulators or found a lack of trust from existing or potential customers, but may have untold detrimental consequences for the entity in the longer term.

8.32 President Donald Trump has recently said that no computer is safe (from hacking). This is undoubtedly correct and since it is so, an ability to react to a data breach will become of increasing significance for every organisation however large or small. It is also to be remembered that the new regime to be ushered in 2018 by GDPR, will mean that a failure to deal with a data breach affecting personal data could result in fines of enormous magnitude being visited on entities.

8.33 It is submitted that the watchwords of speed, clarity and transparency should become etched on the minds not only of those charged with the protection of data but also on those responsible for the overall strategy of the entity.

CHAPTER 9

INVESTIGATING INCIDENTS AND POWERS OF INVESTIGATORS

INTRODUCTION

9.01 Cyber crime and its investigation is highly demanding and technical.

9.02 All the usual rules of evidence will apply and there are additional legal considerations that will necessarily arise; if computers or portable devices are to be searched care will need to be exercised in ensuring any search and seizure is authorised and within the spirit and letter of a supporting warrant.

9.03 The risk of legally privileged communications and evidence that is inextricably linked through storage on the device will often require the presence of an independent lawyer and careful containment and separation. Add to this the dangers of illegally intercepting communications and the applications that might elicit by either service of notice or a request and one begins to realise the level of forethought and planning a thorough investigation demands.

9.04 Cyber crime is often transnational and the jurisdictional difficulties presented by the remote perpetrator are addressed in Chapter 11. Reference should also be made to Chapter 11 because the investigation, litigation and rules of evidence are so closely linked; this is especially so where, for example, the admissibility of evidence may be in question because it was obtained in a way that falls foul of search or seizure rules.

9.05 This chapter has law (statute and case-law) as its focus but regard should also be had to best practices in relation to digital evidence collation and analysis strategies.

POWERS OF AUTHORITIES

The investigating authorities

9.06 This section looks at the authorities that are tasked with investigating cyber crime, and the legislative and other tools that they have at their disposal to fulfil this task.

9.07 The National Crime Agency (NCA), which was born out of the predecessor organisation, the Serious Organised Crime Agency (SOCA), has established the National Cyber Crime Unit (NCCU). The NCCU heads up and directs UK's response to cyber crime. It provides specialist cyber capability support to other investigative agencies including regional and metropolitan police and coordinates the national response to the most serious of cyber crime threats. It will liaise and partner with industry, government and international law enforcement agencies.

9.08 The Crime and Courts Act 2013, ss 7 and 12, and Sch 7, make provision for the disclosure of information by and to the NCA and for the use of information by the Agency. However, these provisions do not extend to the Security Services, Secret Intelligence Service, or GCHQ. Sections 9 and 10 and Sch 5 provide for the operational powers of the Director General and other NCA officers, including by making provision to enable the Director General to designate NCA officers with one of more of the powers of a constable, a customs officer or an immigration officer.

9.09 Within the Metropolitan Police there is the Metropolitan Police Cyber Crime Unit (MPCCU). A team of specialist detectives within Operation FALCON, the MPCCU is employed to protect people and businesses in London from complex cyber crime and fraud. It is responsible for investigating the most serious incidents of computer intrusion, distribution of malicious code, denial of service attacks and internet-enabled fraud that would fall outside of the remit of local police forces.

9.10 Local police forces will usually have their own High-tech Crime Unit (HTCU) or other cyber unit but will often refer more serious cyber incidents to other agencies either within the NCA or the Metropolitan Police. The Police Central e-Crime Unit (PCeU) was part of the Specialist Crime Directorate of the Metropolitan Police Service in London, and was later rolled-out to hubs located in the Midlands, North West and North East; however, since 2013, has been incorporated into the NCCU.

9.11 The Serious Fraud Office (SFO) is an authority able to both investigate and prosecute. The Criminal Justice Act 1987 (CJA) was enacted in response to recommendations in the Fraud Trials Committee report. It came into force on 14 July 2008 and created the Serious Fraud Office and its primary investigative tools, often referred to as 'section 2 powers'. Section 2 of the Criminal Justice Act 1987 grants the SFO special compulsory powers to require any person (or business/bank) to provide any relevant documents (including confidential ones) and answer any relevant questions including ones about confidential matters. In relation to overseas bribery and corruption, the SFO Director may use his s 2 powers even before a formal investigation has been instigated. Moreover, the powers to question a person under investigation do not come to an end when that person is charged. This is looked at in more detail later in this chapter.[1]

9.12 The SFO's role is, in practice, arguably of limited application because it will only take on a few large economic crime cases. In considering whether to take on an investigation, the Director of the SFO applies his Statement of Principle, which includes consideration of:

- whether the apparent criminality undermines UK plc's commercial or financial interests in general and the City of London's in particular;
- whether the actual or potential financial loss involved is high;
- whether actual or potential economic harm is significant;
- whether there is a significant public interest element; and
- whether there is new species of fraud.

9.13 The SFO can and will investigate cyber crime offences but they will be small in number, of high economic value, novel and UK or City of London centric.

9.14 The Intelligence Services Act 1994 (ISA 1994) placed the Secret Intelligence Service (SIS) and Government Communications Headquarters (GCHQ) on a statutory footing for the first time. ISA 1994 enables GCHQ to conduct activities that detect and prevent crime but the Regulation of Investigatory Powers Act 2000 (RIPA 2000) has given it precise tools to gather intelligence through techniques such as targeted interceptions. Under RIPA 2000, the Director of GCHQ is one among ten senior officials who can apply for a warrant, to either the Foreign or Home Secretary, on grounds that are almost identical to those in the ISA 1994, including pursuit of national security and economic wellbeing. This particular aspect and the role of intelligence agencies is examined in more detail at Chapter 6 (Commercial Espionage).

The relevant powers

9.15 At the outset it should be noted that cyber evidence whether it be in digital, electronic or other form is subject to all the rules of evidence as would

---

[1] See *R v Director of Serious Fraud Office ex parte Smith* below.

usually apply; the legal framework for an investigation and the powers set out in the Police and Criminal Evidence Act 1984 (PACE 1984) (as amended by the Criminal Justice and Police Act 2001) and the Criminal Procedure and Investigations Act 1996 remain applicable. In relation to terrorism, regard should also be taken of the additional powers pursuant to the Terrorism Act 2000 and the Counter Terrorism Act 2008. For an examination of this evidential framework Chapter 11 (Litigating and Rules of Evidence) is recommended.

9.16 The Data Retention (EC Directive) Regulations 2009[2] (the 2009 Regulations) enacted EC Directive 2006/24 into domestic legislation. Article 3 of that Directive forced public telecoms or public communications networks providers to retain data relating to communications traffic and location and allow access to competent national authorities. Article 5 listed the data, which was wide ranging. This resulted in a challenge on the basis such requirement was incompatible with Arts 7 (respect for private life) and 8 (protection of personal information) of the European Charter of Fundamental Rights.

9.17 In *Digital Rights Ireland Ltd v Minister for Communications, Marine and Natural Resources (C-293/12)*, the Grand Chamber of the European Court of Justice (Judge Skouris (President)) held that Directive 2006/24, which required telephone communications service providers to retain traffic and location data in order to combat crime, was not compatible with the Charter of Fundamental Rights of the European Union, Arts 7 and 8.

9.18 The claimants in Ireland and Austria had brought proceedings challenging the legality of national legislation, which had transposed the Directive. The courts asked the ECJ whether the Directive was compatible with the Charter of Fundamental Rights of the European Union Arts 7 and 8. In the Preliminary ruling, the ECJ held that the obligation, under Art 3 of the Directive, on providers of publicly available electronic communications services or of public communications networks to retain the data listed in Art 5 for the purpose of making them accessible, if necessary, to the competent national authorities, raised questions relating to respect for private life and communications under Art 7 of the Charter and the protection of personal data under Art 8. The data that had to be retained made it possible to know the identity of the person with whom a subscriber or registered user had communicated and by what means, and to identify the time of the communication as well as the location from which that communication took place. It was thus possible to know the frequency of the communications of the subscriber or registered user with certain persons during a given period. The data, taken as a whole, could allow very precise conclusions to be drawn concerning the private lives of the persons whose data had been retained and accordingly affected the rights guaranteed by Arts 7 and 8. The obligation to

---

[2]   SI 2009/859.

retain the data constituted a wide-ranging and particularly serious interference with those rights. The question was then whether that interference could be justified.

9.19 Even though the retention of data was a particularly serious interference, it did not adversely affect the essence of the Art 7 right, given that Art 1(2) of the Directive did not permit access to the content of the electronic communications. Nor did it affect the essence of the Art 8 right, given that member states had to ensure that appropriate technical and organisational measures were adopted against accidental or unlawful destruction, accidental loss or alteration of the data. Furthermore, the interference satisfied an objective of general interest, which was to contribute to the fight against serious crime and thus, ultimately, to public security.

9.20 However, it was not proportionate to that objective. Although the retention of data was appropriate for attaining the objective, it applied to all means of electronic communication, thereby affecting the fundamental rights of practically the entire European population, and it was not precisely circumscribed by provisions to ensure that it was limited to what was strictly necessary. Nor did the Directive provide for sufficient safeguards, as required by Art 8 of the Charter, to ensure effective protection of the data retained against the risk of abuse and against any unlawful access and use of that data. It followed that, by adopting the Directive, the EU legislature had exceeded the limits imposed by compliance with the principle of proportionality in the light of Arts 7 and 8 of the Charter:[3]

> 'The European Court of Human Rights has for its part repeatedly held that the storing by a public authority of data relating to the private life of an individual amounts to an interference with the right to respect for his private life guaranteed by article 8.1 of the Human Rights Convention (see, inter alia, *Leander v Sweden* (1987) 9 EHRR 433) and that the use made of them has no bearing on that finding: see, inter alia, *Amann v Switzerland* (2000) 30 EHRR 843.'

9.21 However, the Court of Appeal (Patten LJ, Lloyd Jones LJ, Vos LJ) in *Secretary of State for the Home Department v Davis*[4] doubted whether *Digital Rights Ireland Ltd* lay down mandatory requirements of EU law with which national legislation had to comply:[5]

> 'On behalf of the appellant it is submitted that even if EU law is capable of imposing substantive requirements in respect of national laws governing the ability of police and other law enforcement authorities to access and use retained data, EU law simply requires Member States to comply with art.8(2) ECHR. It is submitted that there is nothing in the judgment of the CJEU in Digital Rights Ireland [2014] 3 C.M.L.R. 44 to suggest that it intended to expand the content of arts 7 and 8 of the EU Charter beyond the content of art.8(2) ECHR. In particular, it is said that the CJEU cannot be taken to have intended to go beyond established

---

3   See *Digital Rights Ireland Ltd*, at [69].
4   [2015] EWCA Civ 1185.
5   See *Secretary of State for the Home Department v Davis*, at [108].

ECHR jurisprudence either by limiting access to retained data to cases where it is justified for the purposes of the prevention, detection or prosecution of serious crime, or by requiring "a prior review carried out by a court or by an independent administrative body". This, it is said, lends further support to the view that the Court of Justice in Digital Rights Ireland was not intending to lay down mandatory requirements for national legislation.'

9.22 The UK response to *Digital Rights Ireland* was to clarify the position with the Data Retention and Investigatory Powers Act 2014 (DRIPA 2014). The explanatory note states the Act ensures that, as the original legislation intended, any company providing communication services to customers in the United Kingdom is obliged to comply with requests for communications data and interception warrants issued by the Secretary of State, irrespective of the location of the company providing the service. Both these components of the Act strengthen and clarify, rather than extend, the current legislative framework. Neither of these components provide for additional investigatory powers. The Act also provides for a review of the operation and regulation of investigatory powers in relation to communications data and interception and increased reporting from the Interception of Communications Commissioner.

DATA RETENTION AND INVESTIGATORY POWERS ACT 2014

9.23 In accordance with s 1 of the Data Retention and Investigatory Powers Act 2014 (DRIPA 2014), the Secretary of State may by notice (a 'retention notice') require a public telecommunications operator to retain relevant communications data if the Secretary of State considers that the requirement is necessary and proportionate, *inter alia*, in the interests of national security; for the purpose of preventing or detecting crime or of preventing disorder; or in the interests of public safety. The lawful purposes for which a retention notice can be issued are contained within s 22(2)(a)–(h) of the RIPA 2000.

9.24 The DRIPA 2014 only applies to *public* telecommunications operators but is very wide ranging and enables, on service of a retention notice, the retention and provision (at s 1(2)(b)) of 'all data or any description of data' to the Secretary of State.

9.25 The maximum period of retention may be varied by statutory instrument (see DRIPA 2014, s 1(3) and (4)(b)) but cannot exceed 12 months (s 1(5)).

9.26 The DRIPA 2014 does not provide a means for disclosure, only retention, and, in accordance with s 1(6), a public telecommunications operator who retains relevant communications data by virtue of this act must not disclose the data except in accordance with a lawful order either through statute or issued by the court:

(6) A public telecommunications operator who retains relevant communications data by virtue of this section must not disclose the data except –

(a) in accordance with –
  (i) Chapter 2 of Part 1 of the Regulation of Investigatory Powers Act 2000 (acquisition and disclosure of communications data), or
  (ii) a court order or other judicial authorisation or warrant, or
(b) as provided by regulations under subsection (3).

9.27 The use of the retention notices is subject to the guidance contained within the Retention of Communications Data Code of Practice which was issued in March 2015. However, the breadth of the powers contained within the DRIPA 2014 has been challenged through the courts.

9.28 In *R (Davis and others) v Secretary of State for the Home Department*,[6] the Administrative Court (Bean LJ, Collins J) were required to consider three separate claims including one brought by Conservative MP David Davies and Labour MP Tom Watson. The claimants contended that s 1 of the DRIPA 2014 was invalid as being contrary to EU law as expounded in *Digital Rights Ireland Ltd v Minister for Communications, Marine and Natural Resources*[7] since it was not accompanied by an access regime which had sufficiently stringent safeguards to protect citizens' rights under the Charter of Fundamental Rights of the European Union Art 7, concerning the right to respect for private and family life, home and communications, and Art 8, concerning the protection of personal data.

9.29 The High Court held that s 1 of the DRIPA 2014 was inconsistent with EU law and invalid in so far as it did not lay down clear and precise rules providing for access to and use of communications data retained pursuant to a retention notice to be strictly restricted to the purpose of preventing and detecting precisely defined serious offences or of conducting criminal prosecutions relating to such offences. Further, access to the data was not made dependent on a prior review by a court or an independent administrative body whose decision limited access to and use of the data to that which was strictly necessary for the purpose of attaining the objective pursued.

9.30 On appeal by the Secretary of State, the provisional view of the Court of Appeal (Patten LJ, Lloyd Jones LJ, Vos LJ) was that this was not the case. It was held that *Digital Rights Ireland Ltd* did not, in the context of the retention of, and access to, communications data, lay down mandatory requirements of EU law with which national legislation had to comply. On the basis that the EU law was unclear the Court of Appeal referred the following two questions to the European Court of Justice (ECJ) on this point:

(1) Did the CJEU in *Digital Rights Ireland* intend to lay down mandatory requirements of EU law with which the national legislation of Member States must comply?

6   [2015] EWHC 2092 (Admin).
7   (C-293/12) EU:C:2014:238.

(2) Did the CJEU in *Digital Rights Ireland* intend to expand the effect of Arts 7 and/or 8, EU Charter beyond the effect of Art 8 ECHR as established in the jurisprudence of the ECtHR?

9.31 The Grand Chamber declined to answer the second question on the basis that this did not directly affect the interpretation of Directive 2002/58, and that 'justification for making a request for a preliminary ruling is not for advisory opinions to be delivered on general or hypothetical questions, but rather that it is necessary for the effective resolution of a dispute concerning EU law'.[8]

9.32 However, the ECJ did provide guidance that a national authority must lay down the substantive and procedural conditions governing access to retained data, which was analogous to para 61 in *Digital Rights Ireland*, and that in relation to the objective of fighting crime only those directly under suspicion of the crime can be targeted:[9]

> 'In that regard, access can, as a general rule, be granted, in relation to the objective of fighting crime, only to the data of individuals suspected of planning, committing or having committed a serious crime or of being implicated in one way or another in such a crime (see, by analogy, ECtHR, 4 December 2015, *Zakharov v Russia*, CE:ECHR:2015:1204JUD004714306, § 260). However, in particular situations, where for example vital national security, defence or public security interests are threatened by terrorist activities, access to the data of other persons might also be granted where there is objective evidence from which it can be deduced that that data might, in a specific case, make an effective contribution to combating *such activities*.'

9.33 Further, the ECJ indicated that any access to retained data must be authorised by a court following application, and that those affected by any grant of access must be notified as soon as possible as long as notification does not affect the investigation:[10]

> 'In order to ensure, in practice, that those conditions are fully respected, it is essential that access of the competent national authorities to retained data should, as a general rule, except in cases of validly established urgency, be subject to a prior review carried out either by a court or by an independent administrative body, and that the decision of that court or body should be made following a reasoned request by those authorities submitted, inter alia, within the framework of procedures for the prevention, detection or prosecution of crime (see, by analogy, in relation to Directive 2006/24, the *Digital Rights* judgment, paragraph 62; see also, by analogy, in relation to Article 8 of the ECHR, ECtHR, 12 January 2016, *Szabó and Vissy v Hungary*, CE:ECHR: 2016:0112JUD003713814, §§ 77 and 80).
>
> Likewise, the competent national authorities to whom access to the retained data has been granted must notify the persons affected, under the applicable national procedures, as soon as that notification is no longer liable to jeopardise the

---

8   See *Watson in Joined Cases C-203/15 and C-698/15*, 21 December 2016, at [130]–[132].
9   See *Watson*, at [119].
10 See *Watson*, at [120]–[121].

investigations being undertaken by those authorities. That notification is, in fact, necessary to enable the persons affected to exercise, inter alia, their right to a legal remedy, expressly provided for in Article 15(2) of Directive 2002/58, read together with Article 22 of Directive 95/46, where their rights have been infringed ...'

9.34 The providers of electronic communications services must, in order to ensure the full integrity and confidentiality of that data, guarantee a particularly high level of protection and security by means of appropriate technical and organisational measures. In particular, the national legislation must make provision for the data to be retained within the European Union and for the irreversible destruction of the data at the end of the data retention period.[11]

9.35 The DRIPA 2014's 'Sunset Clause' means that this legislation expired on 31 December 2016. However, the ECJ determination in *Watson* could be a source of potential challenge to the Investigatory Powers Act 2016.

INVESTIGATORY POWERS ACT 2016

9.36 The Investigatory Powers Act 2016 (IPA 2016), colloquially coined the Snoopers Charter has, unsurprisingly, raised concerns by its perceived legislative shift away from privacy and towards mass surveillance. Supporters declare it places all investigative powers under one legislative roof, whilst detractors fear it will weaken the security of communications and allow unprecedented levels of equipment interference, which could be termed 'legal hacking'.

9.37 The Bill which led to the IPA 2016 was described by John Naughton in *The Guardian* as 'a Machiavellian masterpiece' and Edward Snowden tweeted: 'By my read, #Snoopers Charter legitimises mass surveillance. It is the most intrusive and least accountable surveillance regime in the West'. Apple were also vocal in their Bill Committee response submissions, contending that such an Act, in the belief of Apple, would be a mistake because 'it would be wrong to weaken security for hundreds of millions of law-abiding customers so that it will also be weaker for the very few who pose a threat. In this rapidly evolving cyber-threat environment, companies should remain free to implement strong encryption'.

9.38 Encryption is a thorny issue: where e-communication services, such as WhatsApp, iMessage or BBM, include end-to-end encryption, the messages are sealed and secure from monitoring; the IPA 2016 is potentially a means to prevent these secure encrypted communications as it seeks to enable all areas access to the security and intelligence services.

9.39 During the Lords' Debate, Earl Howe the Minister of State for Defence spoke in favour of the IPA 2016's approach:

---

[11] See *Watson*, at [122].

'Encryption is now almost ubiquitous and is the default setting for most IT products and online services. If we do not provide for access to encrypted communications when it is necessary and proportionate to do so, we must simply accept that there can be areas online beyond the reach of the law, where criminals can go about their business unimpeded and without the risk of detection. That cannot be right.'

9.40 In truth, much of the IPA 2016's content is a declaration or codification of powers that have been previously utilised through an array of other statutory provisions. The IPA 2016 Explanatory Note lists some of the existing legal powers available to intelligence agencies, and suggests that 'with limited exceptions, the investigatory powers provided for in this Act already existed ... The Act has to an extent consolidated these powers in one place'.[12] What the IPA 2016 does is open up the breadth and depth of those powers for scrutiny and discussion. Many railed at the now visible prospect of the bulk data gathering warrants, but bulk interception of data already takes place and is arguably an important piece in the investigative jigsaw.

9.41 There has also been an understandable expression of astonishment and fear over the retention and provision of an individual's internet connection records, which show his internet history use. Again, when held up to the light these may strike one as particularly intrusive and excessive but the authors submit this practice is not novel and has previously gone on, albeit in the shade and without fanfare. The IPA 2016 aims to place each and every power, authority and oversight relating to the evidential gathering of electronic communications on a single statutory footing. It is the authority and oversights, essentially the built-in, consolidated protections that are a departure from the current framework.

9.42 The IPA 2016 is a vast piece of legislation which could potentially warrant an entire text to itself. At the time of writing few of the actual provisions are in force, despite the Act receiving Royal Assent on 29 November 2016. As more sections are brought into force, and interpreted through in the courts, we will obtain greater understanding on the impact that this legislation will have on our privacy. Regardless, the IPA 2016 is a significant piece of legislation that will be the cornerstone of investigatory powers for many years.

9.43 It is helpful to understand how the IPA 2016 groups the different types of powers and oversights under the four main headings. The types of powers are:

(1) Interception of communications (Parts 1 and 2), which involves acquiring the content (whole or part) of communications. This then refers to acquiring content either whilst the communication is still transmitting or is present on a server. The Act represents a culmination of interception powers pursuant to RIPA 2000 (s 8) and those that might be available under the Wireless and Telegraphy Act 2006. There is a distinction throughout the Bill as to the purpose of the action (here interception) and

---

[12] See IPA Explanatory Note, at [14]–[22].

whether it is for targeted or bulk use. For interception the distinction means that only the requisite intelligence agencies (not the police or other investigative authority) can apply for, on the sole ground of national security, an interception warrant for bulk purposes. This would be where bulk information is sought for intelligence on persons who are outside the UK.

Interception warrants (all) should need to be authorised by the Secretary of State and given approval by a Judicial Commissioner prior to the warrant coming in to effect. This is examined below under 'Oversight'. The test for a warrant interception (save for bulk purposes: see above for restricted applicant and ground) is whether the applicant can demonstrate the interference with individual privacy is necessary and proportionate. Necessary would have to be founded on one of the grounds of national security, preventing/detecting serious crime or for the UK's economic well-being. Proportionate would mean weighing the intrusion and intelligence value against the privacy and individual right it intruded upon. Only nine bodies can apply for an interception warrants: HMRC, MOD, Met Police, Police Services Scotland and NI, MI5, GCHQ, SIS, NCA.

(2) Acquisition and retention of communications data (Parts 3 and 4), which involves obtaining information that relates to communications such as discovering the parties to, and the timing of, an electronic communication. This is less intrusive than interception as, unlike interception, content itself is not being exposed. The Act seeks to consolidate and replace the current diverse legislative sources which would include RIPA 2000, DRIPA 2014, Counter Terrorism and Security Act 2015, Anti-Terrorism Crime and Security Act 2001. The bodies that may apply to access communications data includes those for interception plus additional bodies such as local authorities.

The grounds on which access can be sought are also wider than for interference as they additionally include the grounds of public safety, prevention of injury in an emergency and health. A designated internal person would also be empowered to issue a data notice request to a service provider. Data is split into two types, namely entity and event. The former relates to persons and devices, the latter to actual events – incidents that have occurred. The Bill regards events data as the more intrusive type of data that may be sought.

Service providers are required to retain communications data for up to one year so that this harvested retained data is available for collection/inspection upon service of the requisite request.

Bulk communications data warrants are, as with interception, only available to the specified intelligence agencies and only for the purpose of national security. To be able to access such bulk data the intelligence agency would need to demonstrate it was a necessary and proportionate measure.

Communications data warrants (all) must be Secretary of State authorised and given the approval of the Judicial Commissioner before they can be effected.

(3) Equipment interference (Part 5), which refers to the lawful infiltration of personal equipment in order to access and acquire the private information held.

Equipment interference is wide in its terms and application, it is interception by other routes; those routes will be through interference with all manner of equipment to achieve the end.

The grounds on which warrants can be applied for and the need to demonstrate requisite necessity and proportionality, mirror those for interception. Further, if a warrant is granted and data obtained via interference then another warrant may be required to access and examine the information garnered where it relates to UK persons.

Equipment interference warrants (all) must be Secretary of State authorised and given the approval of the Judicial Commissioner before they can be effected.

(4) Provisions relating to retention and examination of 'bulk' personal datasets (Parts 6 and 7), which allows the intelligence services to obtain personal data (within the same meaning as the Data Protection Act 1998) relating to a number of individuals. The IPA 2016, s 199, provides the intelligence services are retaining a bulk personal data set when 'a majority of the individuals are not, and are unlikely to become, of interest to the intelligence service in the exercise of its functions'. The IPA 2016 therefore permits the intelligence services, with the oversight contained within the Act, to retain personal data in relation to large groups of people who are unrelated to any intelligence activity.

The IPA 2016 draws a distinction between targeted and bulk use of these powers given the intrusive nature of bulk data retrieval. Where the bulk information is within the definition of a bulk personal dataset only the specified intelligence agency can obtain or examine such dataset with a warrant that expressly permits this. Bulk personal datasets are databases containing information for a significant number of persons eg registers, electoral rolls and the like. Again these are granted by the Secretary of State and must be approved by a Judicial Commissioner before taking effect. This heightened oversight or safeguarding is an important part of the Bill and novel in the context of electronic communications investigation.

Oversight

9.44 The IPA 2016 is perhaps most novel in the level of oversight introduced. A mechanism of 'double-lock' authorisation will apply such that (with exceptions) a warrant cannot be implemented until it has been authorised by the Secretary of State and approval given by a Judicial Commissioner. No-one may be appointed as a Judicial Commissioner unless they have held a judicial position at least as senior as a High Court judge, with appointments to these positions made directly by the Prime Minister. The Prime Minister must consult the Scottish Ministers before the appointment is made.

9.45 A Judicial Commissioner must also be recommended as a candidate by the Investigatory Powers Commissioner (IPC). The Prime Minister may only appoint someone to the post of IPC after receiving a joint recommendation from the Lord Chief Justice of England and Wales, the Lord President of Scotland, the Lord Chief Justice of Northern Ireland and the Lord Chancellor. Although the IPC may delegate functions to the other Judicial Commissioners, the IPC cannot delegate the duty to make a joint recommendation to the Prime Minister about the appointment of a Judicial Commissioner.

9.46 The IPA 2016 takes account of the most urgent, life-threatening scenarios by allowing a warrant authorised by the Secretary of State to be effected immediately subject to it being reviewed by the Judicial Commissioner within a five-day period of the authorisation. Further checks and balances are provided by the creation of a new right of appeal by the Investigatory Powers Tribunal (IPT), which will continue to investigate IPA 2016 complaints against public authorities, to the Court of Appeal.[13]

9.47 The IPC Office is a result of a merger of the Surveillance and Intelligence Services Commissioners Office and the Interception of Communications Office. The IPA 2016 ensures that Judicial Commissioners are supported (within the Investigatory Powers Commissioner's Office) with information and assistance to provide a full appreciation of the intelligence agencies' work and will be able to effectively review warrants. The IPA 2016 also seeks to ensure that persons are informed in relation to defective issued warrants and that there is, to an extent, public accountability and transparency with the Investigatory Powers Commissioner having the ultimate compliance oversight and issuing in the public domain reports and guidance where appropriate.

New provisions

9.48 The IPA 2016 requires that communication service providers (CSPs) retain UK internet users' 'internet connection records', which includes the websites that were visited but not the particular pages and not the user's full browsing history, for one year. Although not technically a new provision, as it was contained within the DRIPA 2014, the continuation within the IPA 2016 constitutes the introduction of a new, permanent, requirement imposed upon internet service providers. The IPA 2016 introduces a criminal offence for a CSP or someone who works for a CSP to reveal that data has been requested.

9.49 Protection in relation to tapping the telephone conversations of Members of Parliament (known as the 'Wilson Doctrine') has been placed on statutory footing, and provision has been made for the protection of journalistic and legally privileged material.

9.50 Finally, the IPC has the power to impose fines, via a monetary penalty notice, where unlawful interception has taken place but where the person

---

[13] IPA 2016, s 242.

responsible was not intending to intercept a communication. This may be applied, for example, when a company has developed and uses a piece of software to collect information about WiFi hotspots and does not realise that it is also intercepting content sent from non-secure WiFi devices.

9.51 Until such time that the relevant provisions of the IPA 2016 are brought into force investigators can rely upon existing powers, such as those contained within the Regulation of Investigatory Powers Act 2000, which have yet to be repealed.

Regulation of Investigatory Powers Act 2000 (RIPA 2000) and interception of communications

9.52 RIPA 2000 is examined at Chapter 11 (Litigating and Rules of Evidence). Given its central importance to cyber investigations some of the provisions and considerations are further summarised below to facilitate ease of reference.

9.53 RIPA 2000 gives public authorities (for this chapter's purposes read that as investigating authorities) powers to intercept communications with and, in prescribed circumstances, without a warrant.

9.54 It will be an offence to intercept any communications (electronic, postal or other form of communication) in the course of its transmission. Here the interception will be effected when someone, other than the intended recipient, obtains whole or part of the communication sent by the sender. It will not be a criminal offence to intercept communications such as emails. This is achieved by the use of an 'interception warrant' which can only be issued pursuant to s 5 where the warrant is proportionate and necessary:

- in the interests of national security;
- for preventing or detecting serious crime;
- for the purpose of safeguarding the economic well-being of the UK.

9.55 In addition to this, s 10 permits the Home Secretary to modify the provisions of any previously signed interception warrant.

9.56 A warrant will not be required and an offence will not be committed where one party to the communication consents to the interception.

9.57 Where the interception of communications under a warrant pursuant to Part 1, Chapter 1 of that RIPA 2000 is necessary for one of the reasons prescribed in s 5(3)–(5):

> (3) Subject to the following provisions of this section, a warrant is necessary on grounds falling within this subsection if it is necessary –
>
> (a)   in the interests of national security;
> (b)   for the purpose of preventing or detecting serious crime;

(c)   for the purpose of safeguarding the economic well-being of the United Kingdom; or

(d)   for the purpose, in circumstances appearing to the Secretary of State to be equivalent to those in which he would issue a warrant by virtue of paragraph (b), of giving effect to the provisions of any international mutual assistance agreement.

(4) The matters to be taken into account in considering whether the requirements of subsection (2) are satisfied in the case of any warrant shall include whether the information which it is thought necessary to obtain under the warrant could reasonably be obtained by other means.

(5) A warrant shall not be considered necessary on the ground falling within subsection (3)(c) unless the information which it is thought necessary to obtain is information relating to the acts or intentions of persons outside the British Islands.

9.58   To acquire communications data under Chapter II, Part I of RIPA 2000, the purposes prescribed in s 22(1)–(3) are:

22 Obtaining and disclosing communications data

(1) This section applies where a person designated for the purposes of this chapter believes that it is necessary on grounds falling within subsection (2) to obtain any communications data.

(2) It is necessary on grounds falling within this subsection to obtain communications data if it is necessary –

(a)   in the interests of national security;

(b)   for the purpose of preventing or detecting crime or of preventing disorder;

(c)   in the interests of the economic well-being of the United Kingdom;

(d)   in the interests of public safety;

(e)   for the purpose of protecting public health;

(f)   for the purpose of assessing or collecting any tax, duty, levy or other imposition, contribution or charge payable to a government department;

(g)   for the purpose, in an emergency, of preventing death or injury or any damage to a person's physical or mental health, or of mitigating any injury or damage to a person's physical or mental health; or

(h)   for any purpose (not falling within paragraphs (a) to (g)) which is specified for the purposes of this subsection by an order made by the Secretary of State.

(3) Subject to subsection (5), the designated person may grant an authorisation for persons holding offices, ranks or positions with the same relevant public authority as the designated person to engage in any conduct to which this Chapter applies.

9.59   Section 26 defines the conduct that Part 2 covers, to conduct surveillance and use covert human intelligence sources:

26 Conduct to which Part II applies

(1) This Part applies to the following conduct –

(a)   directed surveillance;
(b)   intrusive surveillance; and
(c)   the conduct and use of covert human intelligence sources.

(2) Subject to subsection (6), surveillance is directed for the purposes of this Part if it is covert but not intrusive and is undertaken –

(a)   for the purposes of a specific investigation or a specific operation;
(b)   in such a manner as is likely to result in the obtaining of private information about a person (whether or not one specifically identified for the purposes of the investigation or operation); and
(c)   otherwise than by way of an immediate response to events or circumstances the nature of which is such that it would not be reasonably practicable for an authorisation under this Part to be sought for the carrying out of the surveillance.

(3) Subject to subsections (4) to (6), surveillance is intrusive for the purposes of this Part if, and only if, it is covert surveillance that –

(a)   is carried out in relation to anything taking place on any residential premises or in any private vehicle; and
(b)   involves the presence of an individual on the premises or in the vehicle or is carried out by means of a surveillance device.

(4) For the purposes of this Part surveillance is not intrusive to the extent that –

(a)   it is carried out by means only of a surveillance device designed or adapted principally for the purpose of providing information about the location of a vehicle; or
(b)   it is surveillance consisting in any such interception of a communication as falls within section 48(4).

(5) For the purposes of this Part surveillance which –

(a)   is carried out by means of a surveillance device in relation to anything taking place on any residential premises or in any private vehicle, but
(b)   is carried out without that device being present on the premises or in the vehicle,

is not intrusive unless the device is such that it consistently provides information of the same quality and detail as might be expected to be obtained from a device actually present on the premises or in the vehicle.

(6) For the purposes of this Part surveillance which –

(a)   is carried out by means of apparatus designed or adapted for the purpose of detecting the installation or use in any residential or other premises of a television receiver (within the meaning of Part 4 of the Communications Act 2003)], and

(b)   is carried out from outside those premises exclusively for that purpose,

is neither directed nor intrusive.

(7) In this Part –

(a)   references to the conduct of a covert human intelligence source are references to any conduct of such a source which falls within any of paragraphs (a) to (c) of subsection (8), or is incidental to anything falling within any of those paragraphs; and

(b)   references to the use of a covert human intelligence source are references to inducing, asking or assisting a person to engage in the conduct of such a source, or to obtain information by means of the conduct of such a source.

(8) For the purposes of this Part a person is a covert human intelligence source if –

(a)   he establishes or maintains a personal or other relationship with a person for the covert purpose of facilitating the doing of anything falling within paragraph (b) or (c);

(b)   he covertly uses such a relationship to obtain information or to provide access to any information to another person; or

(c)   he covertly discloses information obtained by the use of such a relationship, or as a consequence of the existence of such a relationship.

(9) For the purposes of this section –

(a)   surveillance is covert if, and only if, it is carried out in a manner that is calculated to ensure that persons who are subject to the surveillance are unaware that it is or may be taking place;

(b)   a purpose is covert, in relation to the establishment or maintenance of a personal or other relationship, if and only if the relationship is conducted in a manner that is calculated to ensure that one of the parties to the relationship is unaware of the purpose; and

(c)   a relationship is used covertly, and information obtained as mentioned in subsection (8)(c) is disclosed covertly, if and only if it is used or, as the case may be, disclosed in a manner that is calculated to ensure that one of the parties to the relationship is unaware of the use or disclosure in question.

(10) In this section 'private information', in relation to a person, includes any information relating to his private or family life.

(11) References in this section, in relation to a vehicle, to the presence of a surveillance device in the vehicle include references to its being located on or under the vehicle and also include references to its being attached to it.

9.60 Part I, Chapter II, is a route by which investigation authorities may obtain data by serving notice on an internet service provider requiring it to disclose identified communications data such as an IP address or other data relating to an email account.

The Investigatory Powers Tribunal

9.61 The Investigatory Powers Tribunal was established as part of the RIPA 2000 as a judicial body, independent of the British government, which hears complaints about surveillance by public bodies. The Investigatory Powers Tribunal has jurisdiction to consider complaints about the use of surveillance by any organisation with powers under RIPA 2000. It is also the only judicial body with the power to investigate the conduct of the Security Service (MI5), the Secret Intelligence Service (MI6) and the Government Communications Headquarters (GCHQ).

9.62 The Investigatory Powers Tribunal must be provided with details of complaints regarding surveillance activity by any organisation under its jurisdiction. The Tribunal will then decide whether the surveillance has been appropriately authorised and is being conducted in accordance with the applicable rules. Complaints may be dealt with on paper or by oral hearing, at the Tribunal's discretion, and may be considered in both open and closed hearings. Where a complaint is considered in an open hearing it is on the basis of a hypothetical assumption with the true position being neither confirmed nor denied (NCND).

9.63 If the Tribunal determines that the surveillance is being carried lawfully it will not confirm to the complainant that they are under surveillance but merely state that their complaint has not been upheld. The Tribunal is exempt from the Freedom of Information Act 2000 so information made available to it in the course of considering a complaint cannot be obtained under a freedom of information request. A complaint about surveillance being conducted by a private person or a company cannot be heard by the Investigatory Powers Tribunal.

9.64 In *Amnesty International Ltd v Security Service*,[14] the Investigatory Powers Tribunal (Burton J, Robert Seabrook QC, Carr J, Judge Christopher Gardner QC, Judge Rivlin QC) declared that in principle the interception of material that was subject to legal professional privilege (LPP) was unlawful as it infringed Art 8 of the European Convention of Human Rights (ECHR). This, however, led to the further application that reasons for this decision should be disclosed, which included the provision of confirmation whether named people were under surveillance. The Tribunal was required to balance the need to maintain national security with the seriousness of the infringement of Art 8, particularly as there was no lawful means for dealing with LPP material. The Tribunal were invited to give reasons for their determination to ensure their

---

[14]   (2015) UKIPTrib 13132-H.

compliance with Art 6, and concluded that when dealing with such a complaint additional transparency was required:[15]

> 'The Tribunal is persuaded by the submissions of the Claimants set out in paragraphs 16 and 17 above. We consider that it is contrary to the interests of the public and inconsistent with public confidence in this Tribunal, who are trusted to investigate matters, which investigation for the most part has to be carried out in closed proceedings, for the situation to be that the answer of no determination by reference to s 68(4)(a) could mean that there has been no interception, or could mean that there has been lawful interception (both as now, in order to preserve NCND) or could mean that there has been unlawful interception. That level of ambiguity would place the validity of all the decisions of this Tribunal in doubt. The Tribunal has been entrusted with the task of investigating complaints, to a large extent in closed proceedings, and without divulging details which might place security at risk. It would, in the Tribunal's judgment, undermine public confidence that Parliament had created a means of holding the relevant public agencies to account, if the Tribunal's findings of unlawful conduct by the Intelligence Agencies could be concealed on the basis of a non-specific submission of a risk to public safety.'

9.65   The limits of surveillance are not merely restricted to material that is subject to LPP. In *News Group Newspapers Ltd v Commissioner of Police of the Metropolis*,[16] the Investigatory Powers Tribunal (Burton J, Carr J, Charles Flint QC, Susan O'Brien QC, Graham Zellick QC) found that in respect of four authorisations under the Regulation of Investigatory Powers Act 2000, s 22, one of the authorisations was neither necessary nor proportionate to the legitimate aim which it pursued, and there had thus been an infringement of the complainant's Art 10 Convention rights.

9.66   The complainant from a newspaper group and three of its journalists was against the Commissioner for the Metropolitan Police following the investigation into an incident that took place in September 2012 when the Government Chief Whip was prevented from leaving Downing Street through the main gate on his bicycle. An article about the incident appeared on the front page of the newspaper. Four authorisations were issued under RIPA 2000, s 22 for the purpose of enabling the police to obtain communications data that might have revealed the sources of information obtained by the journalists. The issue was whether the obtaining of the communications data was prescribed by law and necessary in a democratic society so as to comply with the requirements of Art 10 of the ECHR, which protected freedom of expression.

9.67   There might have been a proper investigative purpose, but it did not justify the serious step of obtaining access to communications data that might identify a journalist's sources. The authorisation must be both necessary and proportionate to the effect of the infringement in question, not to the procedure

---

15   See *Amnesty International Ltd*, at [19].
16   [2016] 2 All ER 483.

by which an order or authorisation was obtained. It was the intrusion that had to be justified under the principle of proportionality:[17]

> 'The main submission of the Respondent was that the Complainants' argument confuses the issue of proportionality with legality. The question is whether the police used the least intrusive measure, and that test focuses on the infringement of rights, not the means by which an order or authorisation is obtained. The intrusion is the obtaining of communications data which might reveal a journalist's source, not the making of an application to a designated person under RIPA or to a judge under PACE ...
>
> The communications data obtained, whether from a judge under PACE or from a designated person under s 22 of RIPA, is data which has the same effect of potentially revealing a journalist's source and thus the intrusion on rights is the same. It is that intrusion, not the procedure used to give it legal effect, which must be justified under the principle of proportionality.'

The protection of journalistic sources may amount to a prohibition to prosecution but similar protections, for example the privilege against self-incrimination, are unlikely to constitute a defence. An offender who had been served with a notice under RIPA 2000, s 49 requiring him to disclose the password or keys to encrypted files, and who was subsequently charged with failing to comply with the notice under s 53 of RIPA 2000, could not rely on the privilege against self-incrimination as a reason for refusing to comply. The evidence on the files existed independently of the will of the offender, and the privilege against self-incrimination would be engaged only if the data itself contained incriminating material:[18]

> 'In short, although the defendants' knowledge of the means of access to the data may engage the privilege against self-incrimination, it would only do so if the data itself-which undoubtedly exists independently of the will of the defendants and to which the privilege against self-incrimination does not apply-contains incriminating material. If that data was neutral or innocent, the knowledge of the means of access to it would similarly be either neutral or innocent. On the other hand, if the material were, as we have assumed, incriminatory, it would be open to the trial judge to exclude evidence of the means by which the prosecution gained access to it. Accordingly the extent to which the privilege against self-incrimination may be engaged is indeed very limited.'

SFO SECTION 2 POWERS

9.68 The CJA 1987 was responsible for establishing and empowering the SFO. Section 2 of the CJA grants the SFO special compulsory powers to require any person (or business/bank) to provide any relevant documents (including confidential ones) and answer any relevant questions including ones about confidential matters:

---

[17] See *News Group Newspapers Ltd v Commissioner of Police of the Metropolis* [2016] 2 All ER 483, at [90]–[91].

[18] See *R v S* [2008] EWCA Crim 2177, at [24].

2 Director's investigation powers

(2) The Director may by notice in writing require the person whose affairs are to be investigated ('the person under investigation') or any other person whom he has reason to believe has relevant information to answer questions or otherwise furnish information with respect to any matter relevant to the investigation at a specified place and either at a specified time or forthwith.

(3) The Director may by notice in writing require the person under investigation or any other person to produce at such place as may be specified in the notice and either forthwith or at such time as may be so specified, any specified documents which appear to the Director to relate to any matter relevant to the investigation or any documents of a specified class which appear to him so to relate; and –

(a)   if any such documents are produced, the Director may –
    (i)   take copies or extracts from them;
    (ii)   require the person producing them to provide an explanation of any of them;
(b)   if any such documents are not produced, the Director may require the person who was required to produce them to state, to the best of his knowledge and belief, where they are.

(4) Where, on information on oath laid by a member of the Serious Fraud Office, a justice of the peace is satisfied, in relation to any documents, that there are reasonable grounds for believing –

(a)   that –
    (i)   a person has failed to comply with an obligation under this section to produce them;
    (ii)   it is not practicable to serve a notice under subsection (3) above in relation to them; or
    (iii)   the service of such a notice in relation to them might seriously prejudice the investigation; and
(b)   that they are on premises specified in the information, he may issue such a warrant as is mentioned in subsection (5) below.

(5) The warrant referred to above is a warrant authorising any constable –

(a)   to enter (using such force as is reasonably necessary for the purpose) and search the premises, and
(b)   to take possession of any documents appearing to be documents of the description specified in the information or to take in relation to any documents so appearing any other steps which may appear to be necessary for preserving them and preventing interference with them.

(6) Unless it is not practicable in the circumstances, a constable executing a warrant issued under subsection (4) above shall be accompanied by an appropriate person.

9.69   The s 2 powers were subject to challenge in *R v Director of the Serious Fraud Office ex p Smith*.[19]

9.70   In *ex p Smith*, the applicant chairman and managing director of a company, was charged that between 1 January 1985 and 29 April 1991 he had knowingly been a party to the carrying on of the business of the company with intent to defraud its creditors, contrary to s 458 of the Companies Act 1985. He was cautioned. On 7 May he was admitted to bail. The Director of the Serious Fraud Office formed the opinion that the matter was appropriate for investigation by procedures under the CJA and on 24 June served a notice on the applicant requiring him to attend for interview at her offices and answer questions or otherwise furnish information.

9.71   The applicant sought judicial review of the Director's decision to seek to enforce compliance with the requirements of the notice. The Divisional Court of the Queen's Bench Division granted the applicant a declaration to the effect that the Director was entitled to ask him questions after he had been charged but only after administering a fresh caution and that the fact of such a caution would be reasonable excuse for a refusal to answer within s 2(13) of the CJA.

9.72   The House of Lords (Lord Templeman, Lord Bridge, Lord Ackner, Lord Lowry, Lord Mustill) overturned the decision of the Divisional Court in favour of the Director of the SFO. It was held that the plain intention of the CJA was that the Director's powers should not end when the person under investigation was charged. Accordingly, the appellant could be compelled to answer questions and no fresh caution was required:[20]

> 'For these reasons I conclude that as a matter of interpretation 'that the principle of common sense, expressed in the maxim generalia specialibus non derogant, entails that the general provisions of the Code yield to the particular provisions of the Act of 1987 in cases to which that Act applies; and that neither history nor logic demands that any qualification of what Parliament has so clearly enacted ought to be implied.'

9.73   It is generally accepted that material obtained through compulsion cannot then be used against an individual within criminal proceedings as this would interfere with an individual's right to a fair trial as protected by Art 6 of the ECHR. In *Beghal v Director of Public Prosecutions*,[21] the Court of Appeal (Gross LJ, Swift J, Foskett J) indicated, *obiter*, at [138], that 'it is fanciful to suppose that permission would be granted in criminal proceedings for such admissions to be adduced in evidence'.

9.74   However, *In the Matter of L-R (Children)*[22] the Court of Appeal (McFarlane LJ, Rafferty LJ, Kitchen J) identified that evidence obtained under

---

[19]   [1993] AC 1.
[20]   See *ex p Smith*, at 44.
[21]   [2013] EWHC 2573 (Admin).
[22]   [2013] EWCA Civ 1129.

compulsion within the family court is often disclosed to criminal prosecutors. The evidence disclosed was admissible to challenge a witness, previously compelled, pursuant to s 119 of the Criminal Justice Act 2003:[23]

> 'Notwithstanding the protection provided by the terms of section 98(2), which limits the use to which any material arising in the family proceedings from evidence given can be used, the case of *Re EC* [[1996] 2 FLR 123] has established that the Family Court can and often does disclose transcripts of oral evidence given, or copies of witness statements provided by parents or other records in expert reports or social work documents of what parents have said into the criminal process. A more recent development is the enactment of section 119 of the Criminal Justice Act 2003, which provides for the deployment of inconsistent previous statements made by a party to criminal proceedings, and it is plain that that provision may apply in certain cases to material that has been disclosed from the Family Court.'

9.75   Regardless of the *obiter* comments by the Court of Appeal in *L-R (Children)* it is highly unlikely that a prosecuting authority would seek to rely at trial on inculpatory material obtained by means of s 2 powers. If they did the trial judge retains a discretion, under s 78 of PACE 1984, to exclude this material.

THE INTELLIGENCE SERVICES ACT 1994

9.76   The Intelligence Services Act 1994, s 1, provides statutory foundation for the UK secret services to 'obtain and provide information' and 'perform other tasks' relating to persons outside the British Isles. Section 3 establishes the monitoring and surveillance role of GCHQ. These are is discussed at Chapter 6 (Commercial Espionage) but s 1 is reproduced in part below:

1 The Secret Intelligence Service

(1) There shall continue to be a Secret Intelligence Service (in this Act referred to as 'the Intelligence Service') under the authority of the Secretary of State; and, subject to subsection (2) below, its functions shall be –

(a)   to obtain and provide information relating to the actions or intentions of persons outside the British Islands; and

(b)   to perform other tasks relating to the actions or intentions of such persons.

(2) The functions of the Intelligence Service shall be exercisable only –

(a)   in the interests of national security, with particular reference to the defence and foreign policies of Her Majesty's Government in the United Kingdom; or

(b)   in the interests of the economic well-being of the United Kingdom; or

(c)   in support of the prevention or detection of serious crime.

(iv)   for the purpose of any criminal proceedings; ...

---

[23]   See *L-R (Children)*, per McFarlane, LJ, at [14].

9.77 This is, unsurprisingly, widely drawn and s 2(a) 'in the interests of national security' is likely to be given a broad interpretation. This can include taking account of threats that cannot be shown to be UK specific as a global approach can be taken to national security.

9.78 In *Secretary of State for the Home Department v Rehman*,[24] the appellant was a Pakistani national (X) with alleged links to an Islamic terrorist group. He appealed against the decision of the Court of Appeal,[25] which allowed the Secretary of State's appeal against the determination of the Special Immigration Appeals Commission.[26] The Secretary of State had decided to deport X on the basis that he posed a threat to national security. The Commission had allowed X's appeal against this decision. The Court of Appeal had found that in assessing whether an individual posed a risk to national security a global approach should be taken and that on such basis a person was a danger to national security if they engaged in activities of a kind such as to create a risk of adverse repercussions on the security of the United Kingdom.[27] The Court of Appeal held that X could be deported.

9.79 The House of Lords (Lord Slynn of Hadley, Lord Steyn, Lord Hoffmann, Lord Clyde, Lord Hutton) held that a threat to the interests of national security could arise from acts taken against other states and was not limited to activities directly targeted against the UK. It was within the discretion of the Secretary of State to decide whether deportation was 'conducive to the public good' (see s 15(3) of the Immigration Act 1971, now repealed). The Secretary of State was entitled to have regard to all the information available to him relating to the actual and potential activities of an individual and in making his decision no particular standard of proof was required. It was necessary that there be material upon which he could reasonably and proportionately determine that it was a real possibility that activities that were harmful to national security might occur but there was no necessity that he be satisfied that such material was proved. It was apparent that the ascertaining of a degree of probability was not relevant when concluding whether deportation should take place for the public good:[28]

> '[15] It seems to me that the appellant is entitled to say that 'the interests of national security' cannot be used to justify any reason the Secretary of State has for wishing to deport an individual from the United Kingdom. There must be some possibility of risk or danger to the security or well-being of the nation which the Secretary of State considers makes it desirable for the public good that the individual should be deported. But I do not accept that this risk has to be the result of 'a direct threat' to the United Kingdom as Mr Kadri has argued. Nor do I accept that the interests of national security are limited to action by an individual which can be said to be 'targeted at' the United Kingdom, its system of government or its people as the Commission considered.

---

24   [2001] UKHL 47, [2003] 1 AC 153.
25   [2000] 3 WLR 1240.
26   [1999] INLR 517.
27   See [2000] 3 WLR 1240, at [39].
28   See *Rehman*, per Lord Slynn, at [15] and [19].

[19] The United Kingdom is not obliged to harbour a terrorist who is currently taking action against some other state (or even in relation to a contested area of land claimed by another state) if that other state could realistically be seen by the Secretary of State as likely to take action against the United Kingdom and its citizens.'

9.80 The broad interpretation to cater for prevention or detection of crime is supplemented by the which expressly included the prevention and detection of serious crime as being within the role of the Security Services. Section 2 provides that warrants that can be granted to the Intelligence Agencies by the Secretary of State:

2 Warrants

For subsection (3) of section 5 of the Intelligence Services Act 1994 (which excludes property in the British Islands from the ambit of warrants issued by the Secretary of State in support of the prevention or detection of serious crime) there shall be substituted –

'(3) A warrant issued on the application of the Intelligence Service or GCHQ for the purposes of the exercise of their functions by virtue of section 1(2)(c) or 3(2)(c) above may not relate to property in the British Islands.

(3A) A warrant issued on the application of the Security Service for the purposes of the exercise of their function under section 1(4) of the Security Service Act 1989 may not relate to property in the British Islands unless it authorises the taking of action in relation to conduct within subsection (3B) below.

(3B) Conduct is within this subsection if it constitutes (or, if it took place in the United Kingdom, would constitute) one or more offences, and either –

(a)　it involves the use of violence, results in substantial financial gain or is conduct by a large number of persons in pursuit of a common purpose; or

(b)　the offence or one of the offences is an offence for which a person who has attained the age of twenty-one and has no previous convictions could reasonably be expected to be sentenced to imprisonment for a term of three years or more.'

9.81 The ability to obtain warrants is one of the most significant and powerful means to investigate an incident. This power is available to an array of investigating authorities, and is certainly not limited to the intelligence services or the police. The Serious Fraud Office, Her Majesty's Revenue and Customs and even Trading Standards may utilise warrants in relation to an investigation.

OBTAINING OF WARRANTS

9.82 There will be circumstances when a warrant will be required for an investigating authority to lawfully conduct an action because it is otherwise outside his lawful authority. The actions that may require a warrant that might otherwise be beyond the investigator's powers are search (where this will include gaining entry to a vehicle or premises beyond the statutory powers), seizure, production of documents and interception of communications. This work is cyber specific and written from a corporate defence perspective so the following examples are thought to be apt rather than exhaustive. Drugs searches for example are not considered.

9.83 There are separate pre- and post-arrest powers.

Pre-arrest

9.84 Pursuant to the Police and Criminal Evidence Act 1984 (PACE 1984) investigators have limited pre-arrest entry and search powers. Section 17 permits a constable to enter and search a premises in order to execute a warrant of arrest; to arrest a person for an indictable offence; to conduct an arrest in relation to specified summary offences; or recapture a person unlawfully at large. There is also a general provision granting the right of entry to 'save life or limb or prevent serious damage to property'.[29]

9.85 With the exception of 'saving life or limb' the constable must have 'reasonable grounds for believing that the person whom he is seeking is on the premises' and are limited to a specified number of dwellings. Therefore this section would not permit entry into corporate premises.[30]

9.86 The power to search a location is limited to that necessary to complete the relevant task. Entry to search for documentation or material is prohibited within the scope of these provisions.[31]

Post-arrest

9.87 In terms of post-arrest powers s 18 applies. Except for the qualification at s 18(5) the post-arrest search powers require inspector authorisation. Again, the powers are limited; the requirement for the premises to be occupied or controlled by the arrested person mean corporate premises would be outside this ambit; the police can enter premises in search of items only if the suspect has been arrested for an indictable offence and there are items relating to the offence that will be useful as evidence. In this case an officer of the rank of inspector or above must give their authorisation in writing:

18 Entry and search after arrest

(1) Subject to the following provisions of this section, a constable may enter and search any premises occupied or controlled by a person who is under arrest for an [indictable] offence, if he has reasonable grounds for suspecting that there is on the premises evidence, other than items subject to legal privilege, that relates –

---

[29] See PACE 1984, s 17(1)(e).
[30] See PACE 1984, s 17(1)(2).
[31] See PACE 1984, s 17(4).

(a)   to that offence; or

(b)   to some other [indictable] offence which is connected with or similar to that offence.

(2) A constable may seize and retain anything for which he may search under subsection (1) above.

(3) The power to search conferred by subsection (1) above is only a power to search to the extent that is reasonably required for the purpose of discovering such evidence.

(4) Subject to subsection (5) below, the powers conferred by this section may not be exercised unless an officer of the rank of inspector or above has authorised them in writing.

(5) A constable may conduct a search under subsection (1) –

(a)   before the person is taken to a police station or released on bail under section 30A, and

(b)   without obtaining an authorisation under subsection (4),

if the condition in subsection (5A) is satisfied.

(5A) The condition is that the presence of the person at a place (other than a police station) is necessary for the effective investigation of the offence.]

(6) If a constable conducts a search by virtue of subsection (5) above, he shall inform an officer of the rank of inspector or above that he has made the search as soon as practicable after he has made it.

(7) An officer who –

(a)   authorises a search; or

(b)   is informed of a search under subsection (6) above, shall make a record in writing –
       (i)   of the grounds for the search; and
       (ii)   of the nature of the evidence that was sought.

(8) If the person who was in occupation or control of the premises at the time of the search is in police detention at the time the record is to be made, the officer shall make the record as part of his custody record.

9.88   The power to seize evidence from the search is found at s 19:

19 General power of seizure, etc

(1) The powers conferred by subsections (2), (3) and (4) below are exercisable by a constable who is lawfully on any premises.

(2) The constable may seize anything which is on the premises if he has reasonable grounds for believing –

(a)   that it has been obtained in consequence of the commission of an offence; and

(b)   that it is necessary to seize it in order to prevent it being concealed, lost, damaged, altered or destroyed.

(3) The constable may seize anything which is on the premises if he has reasonable grounds for believing –

(a) that it is evidence in relation to an offence which he is investigating or any other offence; and

(b)   that it is necessary to seize it in order to prevent the evidence being concealed, lost, altered or destroyed.

(4) The constable may require any information which is contained in a computer and is accessible from the premises to be produced in a form in which it can be taken away and in which it is visible and legible if he has reasonable grounds for believing-

(a)   that –
    (i)   it is evidence in relation to an offence which he is investigating or any other offence; or
    (ii)   it has been obtained in consequence of the commission of an offence; and

(b)   that it is necessary to do so in order to prevent it being concealed, lost, tampered with or destroyed.

(5) The powers conferred by this section are in addition to any power otherwise conferred.

(6) No power of seizure conferred on a constable under any enactment (including an enactment contained in an Act passed after this Act) is to be taken to authorise the seizure of an item which the constable exercising the power has reasonable grounds for believing to be subject to legal privilege.

9.89   The powers of seizure were notably enlarged by the Criminal Justice and Police Act 2001, Part 2, which better enables officers to seize material that is linked or intermingled with relevant retainable material and avoid the pitfalls of 'where there was found to be *no* entitlement to seize items outside the scope of the warrant with a view to sifting through and identifying the warrant material at a later stage. This is important where cyber evidence is concerned and the need or desire to seize computers or other devices that may contain evidence that is both within and without the terms of the warrant. Section 50, at Part 2 of the Criminal Justice and Police Act 2001 is pertinent:

50 Additional powers of seizure from premises

(1) Where –

(a)   a person who is lawfully on any premises finds anything on those premises that he has reasonable grounds for believing may be or may contain something for which he is authorised to search on those premises,

(b)   a power of seizure to which this section applies or the power conferred by subsection (2) would entitle him, if he found it, to seize whatever it is that he has grounds for believing that thing to be or to contain, and

(c)   in all the circumstances, it is not reasonably practicable for it to be determined, on those premises –

(i)   whether what he has found is something that he is entitled to seize, or

(ii)   the extent to which what he has found contains something that he is entitled to seize,

that person's powers of seizure shall include power under this section to seize so much of what he has found as it is necessary to remove from the premises to enable that to be determined.

(2) Where –

(a)   a person who is lawfully on any premises finds anything on those premises ('the seizable property') which he would be entitled to seize but for its being comprised in something else that he has (apart from this subsection) no power to seize,

(b)   the power under which that person would have power to seize the seizable property is a power to which this section applies, and

(c)   in all the circumstances it is not reasonably practicable for the seizable property to be separated, on those premises, from that in which it is comprised,

that person's powers of seizure shall include power under this section to seize both the seizable property and that from which it is not reasonably practicable to separate it.

(3) The factors to be taken into account in considering, for the purposes of this section, whether or not it is reasonably practicable on particular premises for something to be determined, or for something to be separated from something else, shall be confined to the following –

(a)   how long it would take to carry out the determination or separation on those premises;

(b)   the number of persons that would be required to carry out that determination or separation on those premises within a reasonable period;

(c)   whether the determination or separation would (or would if carried out on those premises) involve damage to property;

(d)   the apparatus or equipment that it would be necessary or appropriate to use for the carrying out of the determination or separation; and

(e)   in the case of separation, whether the separation –

(i)   would be likely, or

(ii)   if carried out by the only means that are reasonably practicable on those premises, would be likely,

to prejudice the use of some or all of the separated seizable property for a purpose for which something seized under the power in question is capable of being used.

9.90 Additional entry and search powers will arise in relation to certain specific serious crime, such as drugs offences or terrorism. Section 66 of the

Serious Organised Crime and Police Act 2005 enables an officer to enter and seize documents not produced pursuant to a disclosure notice (or where it is impractical or prejudicial to an investigation to serve such a notice). Section 42 of the Terrorism Act 2000 permits a search of premises for a person liable to arrest under s 41 of the Act ie that he is suspected of being a terrorist. Schedule 5, para 1 to the Terrorism Act 2000 enables a constable to search premises and anyone found there for the purposes of a terrorist investigation.

9.91 Schedule 5, para 2 to the Terrorism Act 2000 additionally permits entry search and seizure of material that may be relevant to terrorist investigations. Schedule 5, para 3 allows a search and seizure of evidence relevant to terrorist investigations within a specified area. An order under Sch 5, para 5 may require a specified person to provide to a constable any material he has in his possession for the purposes of seizure and retention; to give the constable access to the material and to state to the best of his knowledge the location of the material to which the application relates. Schedule 5, para 11 permits entry to seize relevant excluded or special procedure material required for investigation of terrorist cases.

9.92 Section 28 of the Terrorism Act 2006 enables a constable to enter and search any premises, and seize any terrorist publications.

9.93 Section 52 of the Anti-terrorism, Crime and Security Act 2001 enables a constable to enter and remove nuclear, chemical or biological weapons. Sections 65 and 66 of the Act allow entry to sites to inspect security applying to pathogens and toxins, and to search for and seize dangerous substances.

9.94 Schedule 5 to the Terrorism Prevention and Investigation Measures Act 2011 permits a constable to enter and search premises to locate an individual for the purpose of serving a terrorism prevention and investigation measures (TPIM) notice or to prevent any breach of a TPIM.

9.95 Sections 92 and 96 of the Police Act 1997 allow officers to enter premises to maintain or retrieve any equipment, apparatus or device, the placing or use of which has been authorised by the Police Act 1997 or by Part II of RIPA 2000 (or under an equivalent Act of Scottish Parliament). This action must have been for the purposes of preventing or detecting serious crime. This is a covert entry power. For RIPA see below and Chapter 10 (Litigating and Rules of Evidence).

9.96 Section 17 of the Crime (International Co-operation) Act 2003 enables a constable or an authorised person to enter and search any premises and to seize and retain any evidence for which he is authorised to search. This is pursuant to a request for assistance received from overseas authorities.

9.97 Further entry and some search/seizure powers, outside the scope of this work, arise under the Extradition Act 2003, Poisons Act 1972, Immigration Act 1971, UK Border Act 2007, Private Security Industry Act 2001, Scrap Metal Dealers Act 1964, International Criminal Courts Act 2001, Firearms

(Amendment) Act 1988, Criminal Justice and Public Order Act 1994, Drug Trafficking Act 1994 and Misuse of Drugs Act 1971. This is not an exhaustive list.

9.98 When a warrant is required due to the absence or inadequacy of statutory powers, an application will need to be made to the relevant court, and careful thought will need to be given as to the type of search warrant required. There are two types of warrant that may be issued for the search of premises; these are a specific premises warrant or an all premises warrant.

SPECIFIC PREMISES

9.99 The officer can only enter and search the premises specified in the application. This application is premises specific. Caution should be exercised to ensure the premises are correctly identified and accurately described. This warrant will only be issued if the court is satisfied that all the following criteria are fulfilled:

- an indictable offence has been committed;
- there are items on the premises that will be of significant value when investigating the offence;
- these items will be useful as evidence during a trial;
- they are not legally privileged, excluded material or special procedure material (see post);
- that an officer will otherwise be prevented from entering the premises; and
- the search may be seriously affected if the constable does not gain immediate access, if they do not possess a warrant.

9.100 The application is to a magistrates' court under s 8 of PACE 1984.

ALL PREMISES WARRANT

9.101 This is also pursuant to s 8 of PACE 1984.

9.102 The officer can only enter and search premises that the person specified in the application lives in or controls. This application is person specific (not premises specific). This warrant will only be issued if all the above premises specific criteria are satisfied and in addition that:

- it is not reasonable to name all the premises that may need to be searched in the warrant; and
- it is necessary, because of the details and nature of the offence, to search any premises owned or controlled by the person in question that are not included in the application.

9.103 It should be noted that search warrants may be subject to strict scrutiny and even once a warrant is obtained the correct procedures must be scrupulously followed. Exaggerating or falsely representing a potential defendant's criminality or failing to disclose the true factual matrix may result in the warrant being defective and quashed as it was obtained by, what might be termed, equitable fraud and the applicant has a duty of full disclosure. The test will generally be whether any relevant material omitted would have reasonably led the magistrate to refuse the application.

9.104 In *R v Chief Constable of Lancashire ex p Parker*[32] a failure to comply strictly with the relevant sections of the PACE 1984, in providing a search warrant to a householder, rendered the search unlawful. Material obtained from an unlawful search must be returned:[33]

> 'The consequence of the breaches of section 16(5)(b) and (c) is that by virtue of section 15(1) the entries, searches and seizures were unlawful, so depriving the Chief Constable of any authority under paragraph 13 to retain any of the material seized. Mr. Shorrock relies, however, upon the power of retention conferred by section 22(2)(a) which, he submits, is designed to authorise the retention by the police of material which has come into their hands by unlawful means.'

PROTECTED MATERIALS

9.105 These are offered some protection from police search and seizure. There are three categories:

Legally privileged material

9.106 Any material relating to legal advice or to legal proceedings and any items related to either of these. Section 10 of the PACE 1984 defines this material:

10 Meaning of 'items subject to legal privilege'

(1) Subject to subsection (2) below, in this Act 'items subject to legal privilege' means –

   (a)   communications between a professional legal adviser and his client or any person representing his client made in connection with the giving of legal advice to the client;

   (b)   communications between a professional legal adviser and his client or any person representing his client or between such an adviser or his client or any such representative and any other person made in connection with or in contemplation of legal proceedings and for the purposes of such proceedings; and

   (c)   items enclosed with or referred to in such communications and made –

---

[32]   [1993] QB 577.
[33]   See *R v Chief Constable of Lancashire ex p Parker* [1993] QB 577, at 587.

(i)   in connection with the giving of legal advice; or

(ii) in connection with or in contemplation of legal proceedings and for the purposes of such proceedings, when they are in the possession of a person who is entitled to possession of them.

(2) Items held with the intention of furthering a criminal purpose are not items subject to legal privilege.

9.107   In practice, given the risk of seizing legally privileged material where cyber evidence is to be collected, the approach should be to have an independent lawyer (not one employed by those conducting the search) present at the search. This was noted in *R (Tchenguiz) v Director of the Serious Fraud Office*[34] where it was said an independent lawyer should have been present when there was a potential issue as to legal professional privilege. The Association of Chief Police Officer (ACPO) published guidance is an invaluable route through the conduct of search and seizure where inaccessible legally privileged material or restricted material (see post) may be present.

Excluded material

9.108   Excluded material includes business, trade, medical and other record that are held in confidence. This material may be accessed but a special procedure warrant must first be obtained by a constable. Application to a circuit judge is required under Sch 1 to PACE 1984.

Special procedure material

9.109   Special procedure material includes any material that does not fall under the first two categories but that the person holding it has stated they will keep confidential or have been entrusted to do so. Again, in this situation the officer may gain access but he will need to first obtain a special procedure warrant under Sch 1. Schedule 1 can also be invoked to enable production of or access to the material.

SCHEDULE 1 Special Procedure

1 If on an application made by a constable a judge is satisfied that one or other of the sets of access conditions is fulfilled, he may make an order under paragraph 4 below.

2 The first set of access conditions is fulfilled if –

(a)   there are reasonable grounds for believing –
   (i)   that an [indictable offence] has been committed;
   (ii)   that there is material which consists of special procedure material or includes special procedure material and does not also include excluded material on premises specified in the application or on premises

---

[34]   [2013] 1 WLR 1634.

occupied or controlled by a person specified in the application (including all such premises on which there are reasonable grounds for believing that there is such material as it is reasonably practicable so to specify);

(iii)   that the material is likely to be of substantial value (whether by itself or together with other material) to the investigation in connection with which the application is made; and

(iv)   that the material is likely to be relevant evidence;

(b)   other methods of obtaining the material –

(i)   have been tried without success; or

(ii)   have not been tried because it appeared that they were bound to fail; and

(c)   it is in the public interest, having regard –

(i)   to the benefit likely to accrue to the investigation if the material is obtained; and

(ii)   to the circumstances under which the person in possession of the material holds it,

that the material should be produced or that access to it should be given.

3 The second set of access conditions is fulfilled if –

(a)   there are reasonable grounds for believing that there is material which consists of or includes excluded material or special procedure material on premises specified in the application or on premises occupied or controlled by a person specified in the application (including all such premises on which there are reasonable grounds for believing that there is such material as it is reasonably practicable so to specify);]

(b)   but for section 9(2) above a search of [such premises] for that material could have been authorised by the issue of a warrant to a constable under an enactment other than this Schedule; and

(c)   the issue of such a warrant would have been appropriate.

4 An order under this paragraph is an order that the person who appears to the judge to be in possession of the material to which the application relates shall –

(a)   produce it to a constable for him to take away; or

(b)   give a constable access to it,

not later than the end of the period of seven days from the date of the order or the end of such longer period as the order may specify.

5 Where the material consists of information stored in any electronic form] –

(a)   an order under paragraph 4(a) above shall have effect as an order to produce the material in a form in which it can be taken away and in which it is visible and legible or from which it can readily be produced in a visible and legible form]; and

(b)   an order under paragraph 4(b) above shall have effect as an order to give a constable access to the material in a form in which it is visible and legible.

6 For the purposes of sections 21 and 22 above material produced in pursuance of an order under paragraph 4(a) above shall be treated as if it were material seized by a constable.

Notices of applications for orders

7 An application for an order under paragraph 4 above shall be made inter partes.

8 Notice of an application for such an order may be served on a person either by delivering it to him or by leaving it at his proper address or by sending it by post to him in a registered letter or by the recorded delivery service.

9 Such a notice may be served –

(a)   on a body corporate, by serving it on the body's secretary or clerk or other similar officer; and
(b)   on a partnership, by serving in on one of the partners.

10 For the purposes of this Schedule, and of section 7 of the Interpretation Act 1978 in its application to this Schedule, the proper address of a person, in the case of secretary or clerk or other similar officer of a body corporate, shall be that of the registered or principal office of that body, in the case of a partner of a firm shall be that of the principal office of the firm, and in any other case shall be the last known address of the person to be served.

11 Where notice of an application for an order under paragraph 4 above has been served on a person, he shall not conceal, destroy, alter or dispose of the material to which the application relates except –

(a)   with the leave of a judge; or
(b)   with the written permission of a constable,
        until –
        (i)   the application is dismissed or abandoned; or
        (ii)   he has complied with an order under paragraph 4 above made on the application.

9.110   The application of Sch 1 in reconciling the tension between the parties was addressed in *R (on the application of British Sky Broadcasting Ltd) v Central Criminal Court*.[35] The Commissioner of Police applied for a production order under s 9 of and Sch 1 to PACE 1984 requiring the claimant broadcaster to produce copies of emails that had passed between one of its journalists and two named persons.

9.111   The notice of application stated that access to the emails was sought for the purposes of an investigation into offences under the Official Secrets Act 1911 and that some of the evidence that was to be provided to the judge in support of the application would not be provided to the claimant. The hearing of the application opened *inter partes*, but the judge then heard counsel for the

---

[35]   [2014] UKSC 17, [2014] AC 885.

commissioner *ex parte* with a view to deciding whether the secret evidence should be disclosed to the claimant. In the course of that *ex parte* hearing the judge heard evidence from a police officer in addition to the secret evidence that he had previously read. He concluded that none of the secret evidence should be disclosed, finding that it neither detracted from nor assisted the claimant's arguments. Having heard further argument *inter partes* the judge granted the production order sought. The claimant sought judicial review of the production order on the ground that the procedure by which it had been obtained had been fundamentally unfair and unlawful. The Divisional Court of the Queen's Bench Division allowed the claim and quashed the order.

9.112 The Supreme Court (Lady Hale DPSC, Lord Kerr JSC, Lord Reed JSC, Lord Hughes JSC, Lord Toulson JSC) held that the general common law principle of fairness, which required that a party to a civil or criminal trial should have access to the evidence on which the case against him was based, did not extend to ancillary applications to obtain evidence from a person who was not a party or intended party to the litigation where that did not involve the determination of any question of substantive legal rights as between applicant and respondent.

9.113 However, the proper procedure requires that applications are heard *inter partes*. As a result the application and the making of such an application gives rise to a *lis* between the applicant and the person against whom it was made, and equal treatment of the parties, which was inherent in the concept of an *inter partes* hearing, requires that each should know what material the other was asking the court to take into account in making its decision and be given a fair opportunity to respond to it. The Supreme Court held accordingly, that the judge ought not have taken account of the evidence that had not been disclosed to the claimant, and the production order had properly been quashed:[36]

> 'Parliament recognised the tension between the conflicting public interests in requiring that an application for a production order shall be made 'inter partes'. The Government had originally proposed that a production order might be made ex parte, but that proposal met opposition and was dropped. When an application for a production order is made, there is a lis between the person making the application and the person against whom it is made, which may later arise between the police and the suspected person through a criminal charge. Equal treatment of the parties requires that each should know what material the other is asking the court to take into account in making its decision and should have a fair opportunity to respond to it. That is inherent in the concept of an "inter partes" hearing.'

9.114 Section 53 of the Criminal Justice and Police Act 2001 imposes a duty on the person for the time being in possession of the seized property in consequence of the exercise of the (search) power to ensure arrangements are in

---

[36] See *R (on the application of British Sky Broadcasting Ltd)*, at [29]–[30].

place to initially examine the property to determine what falls within the search power and for which there is authority to retain and to separate out what does not.

9.115 Section 54 places an obligation to return legal privilege material and s 55 to return excluded and special procedure material where its retention is not authorised.

9.116 It is vital that where there is a reasonable belief that excluded material or special procedure material will be present the correct application is made applying the appropriate procedure.

9.117 Search warrants for excluded material and special procedure material at solicitors' premises would be quashed for failure to comply with the requirements of PACE 1984, s 9 and Sch 1. In *R (on the application of S) v Chief Constable of the British Transport Police*[37] the police applied to the Crown Court for a warrant under the PACE 1984, s 9 and Sch 1 to search a solicitor's home address for a mobile phone and a computer, after finding a suspect's mobile phone within his briefcase.

9.118 The warrant was issued and the police seized the items. The solicitor was arrested on suspicion of having been party to a conspiracy to pervert the course of justice. After the suspect engaged another solicitor to represent him, the police applied for warrants to search the premises of the new solicitor's firm and that of the previous solicitor for custody notebooks and documents relating to the client's alleged attempt to pervert the course of justice and conceal criminal property. An independent counsel would be present to review the material on the premises and ascertain that the police seized only that which they had sought. After the warrants were granted, the police attended the offices where the solicitor handed over papers regarding the suspect. The independent counsel examined the papers and returned those subject to legal professional privilege without the police seeing them.

9.119 The Administrative Court (Aikens LJ, Silber J) held that the information laid in support of the warrant in respect of S's premises showed a total disregard for statutory requirements that had to be adhered to strictly. There were no reasonable grounds for believing that there was material that consisted of special procedure material and did not include excluded material on the premises; and the warrant was too wide and should have been more tightly drafted:[38]

> 'Amongst that material would have been records in the form of Emails, documents, and text messages that would have been acquired in the course of S's occupation as a solicitor. Any such material would plainly have been held in confidence. Accordingly, such material would fall within the definition of "special procedure material" but could possibly comprise "excluded material". If so, the

---

[37] [2013] EWHC 2189 (Admin).
[38] See *R (on the application of S)*, at [57]–[58].

first set of access conditions set out in paragraph 2 of Schedule 1 to the 1984 Act could not be used to obtain a warrant to search and seize such material.

Further, it must be highly likely that the material stored on the mobile phone and laptop computer of a solicitor will include items which are within the definition of being "items subject to legal privilege" as set out in section 10 of the 1984 Act. Accordingly, all such items would fall outside the definition of "special procedure materials" set out in section 14(2) of the 1984 Act. Accordingly, the first access conditions set out in paragraph 2 of Schedule 1 to the 1984 Act could not be used to obtain a warrant to search for and gain access to such material, because "special procedure material" as defined excludes items subject to legal privilege.'

9.120 Furthermore, an application for a warrant required full and frank disclosure but it was clear that the purpose of the warrant to search the solicitor's office had been to go far beyond what was expressly stated. The warrant was seeking all the documents that the solicitor held relating to its client in all his activities. Accordingly, the issue of the warrant had been unlawful and it had to be quashed:[39]

'Another way of putting the same point is that the applicant must give full and complete and frank disclosure. That means doing the exercise identified by Hughes LJ in *In re Stanford International Bank Ltd* [2011] Ch 33.

In the light of what was stated in the written "details of request", the judge clearly was not told what was really being sought and there was an attempt to search beyond the extent required for which the warrant was issued. Accordingly, given the terms of section 15(1) of the 1984 Act, the issue of the warrant was unlawful and it must be quashed.'

---

[39] See *R (on the application of S)*, at [79]–[80].

Part 3

LITIGATION, EVIDENCE AND REMEDIES

CHAPTER 10

REMEDIAL STEPS AND MITIGATING THE LOSS

INTRODUCTION

10.01 The practical issues surrounding the reaction to a cyber-attack highlight the greatest difficulty that the law faces at any given time, how to cope with technological changes that develop at enormous speed and render many of the tried and tested remedies wholly ineffective in dealing with the harm likely to be caused.

10.02 For example, there is often limited benefit in seeking an old-fashioned injunction to stop dissemination of the latest confidential design by a company when the material has already hit the internet.

10.03 In the same way, a carefully calculated hack designed to cause loss or nuisance, or both, cannot be easily stopped by the invocation of traditional legal remedies or sanctions.

10.04   The problems are huge and have, so far, been more obvious in terms of criminal actions rather than civil but this is only the start of what we believe will be an avalanche of claims, actions and proceedings based on computer or other cyber-related misuse.

10.05   One of the principal reasons that remedies in the criminal sphere appear to have developed more quickly is the sheer size of alleged criminal activities associated with the cyber field. In 2011, the Cabinet Office estimated that the cost of cyber crime in the UK was in the region of £27 billion a year. That is a staggering figure and one can only assume that without taking tough measures that figure will only continue to grow.

10.06   In short, the harsh reality is that the remedies set by law in both civil and criminal spheres are behind the technology and consequently are of limited effect.

10.07   We will discuss later practical steps that can be taken to prevent and deal with cyber intrusions; but, in short, the most sage advice that can be offered is to ensure that data controllers and information system providers have robust security measures in place to prevent becoming the victim of cyber-attacks or, if attacked, to aid quick discovery and enable prompt remedial action.

10.08   Such systems are absolutely vital not least because, once unlawfully obtained, information can be disseminated, in the modern age of instant and widespread publication, and it is almost impossible to reinstate its confidentiality.

10.09   If that has been done, a remedy may not be available; but instead the victim ought to consider how to mitigate the situation and/or to be compensated.

REMEDIAL STEPS

10.10   Seemingly in an attempt to control the escalating cost of fighting cyber crime and seeking to render proponents less effective, City of London police has recently announced a new initiative. The scheme aims to hand suspects' details to external law firms who will then pursue civil recovery through the courts. The suggestion is that this will remove the costly, and often inefficient, route of taking alleged perpetrators through the criminal courts and then seeking confiscation or compensation.

10.11   It is not proposed that there will be any legislative changes to introduce this process, the existing law being deemed sufficient.

10.12   Concerns have been voiced about the compatibility of this proposed procedure in relation to the handling and use of private and/or confidential information but supporters of the scheme suggest that it will not be state driven and is likely to take the form of a class of 'victims' taking action against alleged perpetrators.

10.13 The operation of the scheme will require careful handling given the potential, and seemingly inevitable, challenges, to the obtaining and use of data apparently protected by statute.

10.14 Besides initiatives of this kind, how can the courts seek to deal with the fast-moving and, often innovative challenges placed by those involved in cyber-attacks?

INJUNCTIONS IN CASES OF COPYRIGHT INFRINGEMENT

10.15 Copyright infringement on the internet is rife. There are countless websites that advertise and trade in counterfeit items. The so-called 'dark web' does not only deal in items which attract criminal liability. The cost of this on business is huge. Paragraphs 12 and 13 of *Cartier International AG & Others v British Sky Broadcasting & Others*[1] gauged the scale of the problem:

> 'A study published in 2008 by the Organisation for Economic Co-operation and Development ("OECD") entitled The Economic Impact of Counterfeiting and Piracy estimated that the value of counterfeited and pirated goods moving through international trade alone in 2005 amounted to up to US$200 billion. In 2011 Frontier Economics Ltd published a report entitled Estimating the Global Economic and Social Impacts of Counterfeiting and Piracy which estimated that the value of internationally traded counterfeit and pirated goods would increase to US$960 billion by 2015. In 2014 the European Commission published its Report on EU Customs Enforcement of Intellectual Property Rights: Results at the EU Border which recorded that in 2012 customs authorities at the external borders of the EU seized a total of over 39.9 million articles, representing a market value of almost 900 million EURO. The corresponding figures for 2013 were 35.9 million articles and 768 million EURO. The UK seized more articles than any other Member State.
>
> The internet has become an increasingly important channel of trade in counterfeit goods. The OECD study noted that the online environment was attractive to counterfeiters for a number of reasons, including anonymity, flexibility, the size of the market, market reach and the ease of deceiving consumers. The European Commission report noted that the top six categories of goods seized (measured by number of cases) were the kind of goods often shipped by post or courier after an order via the internet.'

10.16 In light of the anonymity provided by the internet to the true vendors of counterfeit items, companies can instead look to s 97A of the Copyright, Designs and Patents Act 1998 (CDPA 1988):

---

[1]   [2014] EWHC 3354 (Ch).

(1) The High Court (in Scotland, the Court of Session) shall have power to grant an injunction against a service provider, where that service provider has actual knowledge of another person using their service to infringe copyright.

(2) In determining whether a service provider has actual knowledge for the purpose of this section, a court shall take into account all matters which appear to it in the particular circumstances to be relevant and, amongst other things, shall have regard to –

(a) whether a service provider has received a notice through a means of contact made available in accordance with regulation 6(1)(c) of the Electronic Commerce (EC Directive) Regulations 2002 (SI 2002/2013); and
(b) the extent to which any notice includes –
   (i) the full name and address of the sender of the notice;
   (ii) details of the infringement in question.

10.17 It is clear from both the statue and the authorities that the onus is on the rights holder to be proactive and accurate. As was said in *Cartier* at para 59:

'As I stated in *20C Fox v BT (No 2)*, it is the right-holders' responsibility accurately to identify IP addresses and URLs which are to be notified to ISPs in this way.'

10.18 This law gave the High Court the power to grant injunctions against service providers, forcing them to block or at least impede access to websites which are infringing copyright. This means that the rights-holder does not need to identify the individuals involved, but instead identify the websites that are selling the counterfeit items. These so-called 'blocking injunctions' are a new means of seeking to deal with this huge problem.

10.19 In order for this to be done effectively companies wary of counterfeit items damaging their business should be monitoring the internet and responding accordingly.

10.20 This is an example of where the law can assist in mitigating the problem or at best 'nipping something in the bud' but for practical purposes it provides companies with a mitigating tool rather than a preventative one because the power only kicks in after the website is up, running, and identified by the rights-holder. There are various injunctive powers available to stop or impede the operation of counterfeit operations using the internet as a channel.

10.21 The law has further developed in the decision of the Court of Appeal in *Cartier*,[2] where Kitchin LJ, in upholding the decision of Arnold J in the lower court, provided helpful analysis of the development of the law, and in particular the ambit of blocking injunctions.

---

2   *Cartier v BskyB and others* [2016] EWCA Civ 658.

10.22 At para 46 of the judgment, he stated that 'the courts have shown themselves ready to adapt to new circumstances by developing their practice in relation to the grant of injunctions where it is necessary and appropriate to do so to avoid injustice ...'.

10.23 At para 65 in citing Art 11 of the Enforcement Directive 2004/48 he concluded that the Article gave:

> 'a principled basis for extending the practice of the court in relation to the grant of injunctions to encompass, where appropriate, the services of an intermediary, such as one of the ISPs, which have been used by a third party to infringe a registered trade mark. There is no dispute that the ISPs are intermediaries within the meaning of Article 11 and accordingly, subject to the threshold conditions to which I shall shortly come, I believe that this court must now recognise pursuant to general equitable principles that this is one of those new categories of case in which the court may grant an injunction when it is satisfied that it is just and convenient to do so.'

10.24 At first instance, Arnold J stated, at [139], the threshold conditions necessary for an injunction against an intermediary on the basis that its services have been used to infringe copyright or related rights:

(1) The defendant is a service provider.

(2) The users and/or the operator of the website in question infringes the claimant's copyrights.

(3) The users and/or the operator of the website is using the defendant's services to do that.

(4) The defendant has actual knowledge of this.

10.25 It was postulated that in relation to the infringement of other intellectual property rights the High Court discretion was 'entirely unfettered'. However, Arnold J rejected this approach and held that 'similar threshold conditions must be satisfied in order for a website blocking injunction to be granted in a trade mark case'.[3]

10.26 The authors of this work recommend a careful reading of the Court of Appeal's lengthy summary of the principles relevant to the grant of blocking injunctions which are repeated and rehearsed both in the case at first instance and by a strong Court of Appeal. This new and developing area will be one to be watched with considerable interest in the near future.

10.27 We have seen above how blocking injunctions have begun to be deployed. There have been other statutory attempts to deal with issues arising from cyber-attacks.

---

[3] See *Cartier v BskyB and others* [2014] EWHC 3354 (Ch), at [141].

STOP AND DESIST NOTICES: DATA PROTECTION ACT 1998

10.28 An example of a statutory power that can be used proactively rather than reactively is s 10 of the Data Protection Act 1998 (DPA 1998). It means that a company or individual can apply to stop a 'data controller' from 'processing' personal data on certain grounds:

> (1) Subject to subsection (2), an individual is entitled at any time by notice in writing to a data controller to require the data controller at the end of such period as is reasonable in the circumstances to cease, or not to begin, processing, or processing for a specified purpose or in a specified manner, any personal data in respect of which he is the data subject, on the ground that, for specified reasons –

> (a)   the processing of those data or their processing for that purpose or in that manner is causing or is likely to cause substantial damage or substantial distress to him or to another, and
> (b)   that damage or distress is or would be unwarranted.

10.29 This therefore creates a number of hurdles to clear before submitting a cogent s 10 application – first the processing of the data must be *causing* or must be *likely* to cause *substantial damage* or substantial *distress to him or to another and* that the damage or distress is or would be *unwarranted*. And of course before the application gets off the starting blocks, the data has to be 'personal'.

10.30 'Personal data' is data which relates to a living individual who can be identified from those data or from those and other information in the possession or likely to come into the possession of the data controller.

10.31 In *Durant v Financial Services Authority*[4] the Court of Appeal expanded upon the term 'relate to' and found that in assessing whether data relates to the subject one should consider whether 'the information is biographical in a significant sense' or whether the person is the 'focus of the information'.

10.32 It should also be said that the term 'processing' is one that has been held to have a wide definition and can therefore cover all manner of different uses of data including, of course, publication into the print media.

WHERE THE S 10 NOTICES DO NOT APPLY

10.33 A s 10 notice cannot apply to the following situations:

> (1) The data subject has given his consent to the processing.

> (2) The processing is necessary –

---

[4]   [2003] EWCA Civ 1746.

(a)   for the performance of a contract to which the data subject is a party, or
(b)   for the taking of steps at the request of the data subject with a view to entering into a contract.

(3) The processing is necessary for compliance with any legal obligation to which the data controller is subject, other than an obligation imposed by contract.

(4) The processing is necessary in order to protect the vital interests of the data subject.

10.34   Part IV of the DPA 1998 also creates a number of what one may call 'common sense' exemptions such as the processing of personal data for the purposes of national security, crime detection, taxation, regulatory activity and public interest publication.

WHO OR WHAT IS A DATA CONTROLLER?

10.35   The requirements of the DPA 1998 are imposed on the 'data controller'. A data controller is 'a person who (either alone or jointly or in common with other persons) determines the purposes for which and the manner in which any personal data are, or are to be, processed'.

WHAT MUST THE DATA CONTROLLER DO UPON RECEIPT OF A S 10 NOTICE?

10.36   Subsection (3) of the DPA 1998 states that:

The data controller must within twenty-one days of receiving a notice under subsection (1) ('the data subject notice') give the individual who gave it a written notice –

(a)   stating that he has complied or intends to comply with the data subject notice, or
(b)   stating his reasons for regarding the data subject notice as to any extent unjustified and the extent (if any) to which he has complied or intends to comply with it.

10.37   The service of a properly made out s 10 application presents a data controller with two stark options – comply with the notice or argue why the notice is unjustified.

10.38   Subsection (4) gives the court the power to order the data controller to comply with a s 10 notice as the court thinks fit.

WHAT IF DAMAGE HAS ALREADY BEEN SUFFERED?

10.39 Under s 13 of the DPA 1998 an individual who suffers any damage by reason of any contravention of the DPA 1998 by a data controller can claim compensation.

10.40 Furthermore, by s 13(2), an individual who suffers distress by reason of any contravention is entitled to compensation for that distress if:

(a) the individual also suffers damage by reason of the contravention; or
(b) the contravention relates to the processing of personal data for 'special purposes'.

10.41 Overall therefore the DPA 1998 can be used as a powerful tool in either the prevention or eradication of material used or to be used unjustifiably. These powers can be used in the prevention of other forms of cyber-attack as well as the prevention of private information becoming public. For example, should an individual wish to publish personal information about an ex-partner as a means of harassment, the DPA 1998 could be used as a means of preventing such dissemination or for the deletion of the information and subsequent compensation.

WHO TO APPROACH?

10.42 The individual may choose to lodge a complaint with the Information Commissioner who has power to order a data controller to alter its processing, but the Commissioner has no power to order compensation. Therefore, those seeking compensation ought to seek such remedy through the courts.

10.43 An individual that has had private or unfair information broadcast about them in this jurisdiction may also wish to complain to the Office of Communications, although it can only adjudicate upon complaints post-transmission and cannot award compensation.

10.44 As regards the press, complaints can be made to the Independent Press Standards Organisation, so long as the publication is a member of it.

CRIMINAL PROSECUTIONS

10.45 Companies and individuals may also consider reporting a particular matter to the police for the contemplation of a criminal prosecution.

10.46 It can once again be said that the criminal code has not progressed at the same rate as technology or social behaviour in technology. However, prosecutions can and have been brought using existing legislation and common law. Here are a few examples of how existing provisions can be used to prosecute the unscrupulous users of the internet.

COMPUTER MISUSE ACT 1990

10.47 The Computer Misuse Act 1990 (CMA 1990), although originally enacted in 1990, has considerable relevance to the cyber crime of today. Furthermore, it has recently been amended to deal with the development of technology (see Chapter 1). It has created several offences that prohibit unauthorised access to computer material – in other words, hacking.

10.48 It not only prohibits the act of hacking *simpliciter*, but also the act of distorting data accessed unlawfully, such that it becomes 'unreliable'.

10.49 Section 3(1) and (2) of the CMA 1990 states:

(1) A person is guilty of an offence if –

(a) he does any unauthorised act in relation to a computer;
(b) at the time when he does the act he knows that it is unauthorised; and
(c) either subsection (2) of subsection (3) below applies.

(2) This subsection applies if the person intends by doing the act –

(a) to impair the operation of the computer;
(b) to prevent or hinder access to any program or data held in any computer;
(c) to impair the operation of any such program or the reliability of any such data; or
(d) to enable any of the things mentioned in paragraphs (a) to (c) above to be done.

10.50 This legislation was originally intended to deal with large-scale hacking operations that threaten the integrity of large digital platforms, such as a large bank or government. However, on reading the statute at its most basic in the context of social media today, one can envisage its use at a more day-to-day level.

10.51 If, for example, person X was able to access person Y's Facebook account without Y's consent and wrote untruths about that person online, would that constitute unauthorised access intending to impair the reliability of the data on the account?

10.52 What if what was written by person X on the account was true or reliable? Could that form a defence to a s 3 offence?

10.53 On conviction on indictment a person shall be liable to imprisonment for a term not exceeding 10 years or to a fine or to both.[5]

---

[5] Section 6(3) of the CMA 1990.

DATA PROTECTION ACT 1998: THE CRIMINAL OFFENCES

10.54 The Data Protection Act 1998 (DPA 1998) created a number of criminal offences that affect both individuals and organisations. It came into force in March 2000 and has had widespread repercussions on how individuals and organisations govern their information-processing procedures. There have been a number of criminal prosecutions in this area and whilst the offences created by the DPA 1998 are punishable by way of fine only, defendants have found themselves prosecuted under different charges, such as conspiracy to defraud or misconduct in public office, which can of course carry sentences of imprisonment.

Unlawful obtaining etc of personal data (s 55(1))

10.55 It is an offence to knowingly or recklessly obtain, disclose or procure the disclosure of personal information without the consent of the data controller.

10.56 This offence can of course be committed in many different ways, such as 'hacking' or 'blagging'. An employee of a data controller can access an information database and obtain an individual's name, address and telephone number, for example. There have been cases in which an employee has obtained such information and disclosed it to a third party for their own purposes.

10.57 The defences to such an allegation include a public interest defence, that such activity was done in order to prevent crime and reasonable belief of consent.

10.58 It should however be said that the enthusiasm of prosecuting defendants under the DPA 1998 has waned because of the limited sentencing powers the statute provides.

10.59 There are no custodial sentences in respect of DPA 1998 offences and no powers of arrest; all offences are punishable only by a fine (s 60(2)). Search warrants are available on application to the Information Commissioner by virtue of s 50 and the powers outline at Sch 9 of the DPA 1998.

10.60 This it seems represents a long-term source of frustration to the Commissioner. In *Summers (Daniel)* unreported 2012 (Crown Ct (Kingston)) the defendant 'blagged' companies to reveal personal data to him. Rather than charging the defendant with a s 55 offence, the defendant was charged with others in a conspiracy to defraud. This of course exposed the defendants to a custodial sentence, rather than restricting the court to a financial penalty as s 55 would have done. Summers received two 12-month sentences of imprisonment which ran concurrently.

10.61 In response to the sentences the Commissioner said:

'If SOCA had been restricted to pursuing this case solely using their powers under the Data Protection Act these individuals would have been faced with a small fine and would have been able to continue their activities the very next day. We must not delay in getting a custodial sentence in place for section 55 offences under the Data Protection Act.'

10.62 Indeed, because of the limited sentencing powers provided by the DPA 1998, prosecutors may prefer to charge defendants with other offences which still deal with the criminality involved. For example, in *Dickinson (Barry Saul)*[6] the defendant obtained and disclosed personal data of individuals whilst working for the DVLA. He did so without the consent of the data controller, contrary to s 55 of the DPA 1998. The information was disclosed to animal rights activists who used the data to harass certain individuals. The defendant pleaded guilty to one count of misconduct in public office.

10.63 In light of this established practice, clients ought to be advised that whilst on the face of the allegation the suitable charge is under s 55 of the DPA 1998, punishable only by way of a fine, they could also face different charges, such as misconduct in public office or fraud, which provide the court with much greater sentencing powers. The current inadequacies of the criminal law in this area have been examined by the Law Commission's Consultation Paper published on 2 February 2017.[7] That Consultation recognised the need for coherence in relation to the free standing DPA 1998, s 55 offence as well as other miscellaneous disclosure offences to ensure the entire range of offences was properly set out in Statute. It further recommends that the Official Secrets Act 1911, 1920 and 1989, all dated in approach (the 1911 Act being particularly archaic) and conceived in a pre-digital age, should be repealed and replaced with new legislation with extra-territorial reach that enables the prosecution of non-British nationals abroad and stiffer penalties; the maximum sentence for the most serious offences contained in the 1989 Act is a mere 2 years' imprisonment. The Commission noted that 'this does not reflect the relative ease with which individuals may, by digital means, disclose vast amounts of sensitive information'. The Commission's final report to Government is expected in Summer 2017. The criminal law and penalties relating to cyber disclosure will consequently be ratcheted up significantly and the current lacunae plugged.

PRACTICAL STEPS

10.64 Alternative dispute resolution (ADR) procedures for online material have developed to mitigate the cost of litigation through the courts. In relation to the unauthorised use of trade marks in domain names a system of registration and summary decision making has reduced the need for long and expensive court actions.

---

6 [2004] EWCA Crim 3525.
7 *Protection of Official Data*, Law Comm No 230.

10.65 A generic top-level domain (gTLD) such as .com or .net, which contains a recognised trade mark, can be registered with the Internet Assigned Numbers Authority (IANA), a department of the Internet Corporation for Assigned Names and Numbers (ICANN), a non-profit private American corporation that oversees global IP address allocation, autonomous system number allocation, root zone management in the Domain Name System (DNS), and other Internet Protocol-related symbols and numbers. Those who register with the IANA must submit to ADR procedure known as the Uniform Domain-Name Disputes-Resolution Policy (UDRP). The World Intellectual Property Organization (WIPO) is one of a number of dispute resolution services recommended by the IANA.

10.66 Under the UDPR, a trade mark owner can obtain the cancellation or transfer of a gTLD domain name that is identical or confusingly similar to his trade mark if the registrant: has no right or legitimate interest in the domain name; has registered the domain name in bad faith; and is using the domain name in bad faith. The UDPR is an appropriate ADR for the most clear-cut cases as UDPR panels have been keen to interpret 'right or legitimate interest' in the broadest sense.

10.67 In the most obvious cases of infringement, and if the domain name was registered after 1 January 2013, a Uniform Rapid Suspension Service (URS) is available. The URS is designed to be an even quicker alternative to UDPR and represents the swiftest summary determination in relation to domain name trade mark infringement available. As a result, there must be no issue of fact and the evidential requirement upon an applicant is 'clear and convincing evidence'.

10.68 An applicant must prove that the allegedly infringing domain name is at least confusingly similar, if not identical to a word or mark, over which the applicant holds a valid registration and that is in current use. The applicant's domain name must have been validated through a court proceedings or subject to specific protection under a statute or treaty. The applicant must then meet the requirements under the UDPR: that the owner of the infringing domain name has no legitimate right or interest to use the domain name and the domain name was both registered and used in bad faith.

10.69 Those seeking to register top-level domain names, such as .uk or .de must similarly submit to ADR procedures provided by the relevant country register. In the UK, Nominet is responsible for registration with EURid the relevant administrator for the .eu domain.

10.70 In the UK, a trade mark owner can obtain the cancellation or transfer of a .uk domain if it was an 'abusive registration'. The trade mark owner must demonstrate that the domain name was registered or has been used in a manner which has taken 'unfair advantage of or was unfairly detrimental' to the rights of the trademark owner. There is a rebuttable presumption of an abusive registration where a respondent has been found to have made an abusive registration on three or more occasions over the previous 2 years.

10.71 Where ADR procedures are deemed to be unsuitable, traditional paths of litigation through the courts remain available to a claimant.

CHAPTER 11

LITIGATING AND RULES OF EVIDENCE

CONTENTS *Para*

INTRODUCTION

11.01 This chapter seeks to deal with those litigious and evidential issues which specifically arise in computer and electronic storage device cases. Investigating and litigating cases that centre around computer and other electronic storage devices do not belong in a special category. Statutory and common law principles are not displaced and the good practice in evidence gathering and presentation remain paramount. Despite the relatively novel concept of claiming jurisdiction by territorial link (discussed below) there are no special rules in place for jurisdictional issues in respect of potential litigation relating to actions based on use and misuse of computers and other electronic storage devices.

11.02 There are, however, particular challenges for evidence gathering in cases involving computers and other electronic storage devices. Maintaining the integrity of material gathered will be at the forefront of the minds of investigators, those who are examining claims in civil matters, and those who have to respond to criminal allegations and civil claims.

11.03 The fraught nature of evidence gathering in cases of this type has resulted in a history of cases collapsing, evidence improperly obtained and well-intentioned people being subjected to criticism, due to a basic misunderstanding of the need for continuity in preserving material for the court room.

11.04 How are those involved in evidence gathering in these situations to approach this seemingly difficult task? Over the years, attempts have been made, by those investigating potential criminal breaches, to build in safeguards so as to avoid the pitfalls of attacks on the integrity of the material obtained.

Good Practice Guide for Computer Based Electronic Evidence

11.05 As previously stated, the regime which governs how investigators recover and collect evidence from computers and other electronic storage devices is clearly subject to the usual rules of evidence. However, in order to ensure best practice the Association of Chief Police Officers (ACPO) issued guidelines entitled *Good Practice Guide for Computer Based Electronic Evidence* in 2003. The guidelines were aimed at those attending crime scenes or making initial contact with the victim; investigators; evidence recovery staff and external consultant witnesses. The guidelines also dealt with procedures for obtaining evidence from mobile telephones and hand-held personal computers.

11.06 ACPO as an organisation no longer exists, closing in 2015 (now National Police Chief Council Digital Investigation and Intelligence); but in terms of practicality and best practice in collecting and presenting digital evidence, particularly by police officers and other investigators 'on the ground', the four principles set out in the guidelines are still followed. Those principles are:

- *Principle one*: no action taken by law-enforcement agencies or their agents should change data held on computer or electronic storage devices which may subsequently be relied upon in court.

- *Principle two*: in exceptional circumstances, where a person finds it necessary to access original data held on a computer or storage device, that person must be competent to do so and be able to give evidence explaining the relevance and justification for their actions.

- *Principle three*: an audit trail or other record of all processes applied to computer or storage device based electronic evidence should be created and preserved so that an independent third-party would be able to examine those processes and achieve the same result.

- *Principle four*: the person in charge of the investigation has the responsibility for ensuring that the law and these principles are adhered to.

11.07 The guidelines go on to make clear that in order to comply with the principles of computer-based litigation evidence, an image should be made of the entire target device where possible.

11.08 The guidelines set out which records should be kept and urge caution on what should or should not be seized. Best practice in terms of evidence recovery is set out showing the different processes involved in, and the examination of, material obtained from computers and other electronic storage devices. These processes include the recovery process; the collection phase; the examination process; the analysis phase, and the report or statement.

11.09 The overriding objective of these additional safeguards is to preserve the integrity of the evidence so that any findings from it cannot be challenged by recourse to arguments that the evidence has somehow not been preserved or cannot be accurately and properly tested by the other party or parties to the proceedings.

PRACTICAL ISSUES FACING LAW ENFORCEMENT AND OTHER OFFICIALS IN EVIDENCE GATHERING IN COMPUTER AND ELECTRONIC STORAGE DEVICES CASES

11.10 The process of obtaining evidence in the sense of gaining access to material based on computers or other electronic storage devices, is not straightforward. The ability to use the material so obtained, is subject to limitations which principally relate to the rights and principles of privacy and privilege.

11.11 Those engaged in law enforcement face challenges which recent legilsation has sought to alleviate. The balance between fundamental rights of individuals has to be set against the ability of law enforcement and other parties to the proceedings, to be able to do their jobs and not to attract arguments that the evidence has been obtained illegally or unlawfully.

11.12 The Computer Misuse Act 1990 (CMA 1990), s 10 contains provisions that relate to criminal investigations:

Computer Misuse Act 1990, s 10

Sections 1 to 3A have effect without prejudice to the operation –

(a)   in England and Wales of any enactment relating to powers of inspection, search or seizure or of any other enactment by virtue of which the conduct in question is authorised or required; and

(b)   in Scotland of any enactment or rule of law relating to powers of examination, search or seizure or of any other enactment or rule of law by virtue of which the conduct in question is authorised or required.

and nothing designed to indicate a withholding of consent to access to any program or data from persons as enforcement officers shall have effect to make access unauthorised for the purposes of any of those sections.

In this section –

'enactment' means any enactment, whenever passed or made, contained in –

(a)   an Act of Parliament;
(b)   an Act of the Scottish Parliament;
(c)   a Measure or Act of the National Assembly for Wales;
(d)   an instrument made under any such Act or Measure;
(e)   any other subordinate legislation (within the meaning of the Interpretation Act 1978);

'enforcement officer' means a constable or other person charged with the duty of investigating offences; and withholding consent from a person 'as' an enforcement officer of any description includes the operation, by the person entitled to control access, of rules whereby enforcement officers of that description are, as such, disqualified from membership of a class of persons who are authorised to have access.

11.13   The CMA 1990 was amended by the Serious Crime Act 2015 in order to assist investigators and other law enforcement officers by seeking to remove the burden of claims of illegality.

11.14   The Regulation of Investigatory Powers Act 2000 (RIPA 2000) does affect those involved in evidence gathering in this field and is dealt with extensively in Chapter 9. This chapter concentrates on those matters relevant to conducting investigation and litigation.

11.15   RIPA 2000 deals with, amongst other things, the regulation of interception of communications, acquisition and disclosure of data relating to communications, and the acquisition of accessing data protected by encryption or passwords.

11.16   Part I (ss 1–25) of RIPA 2000 deals with communications. Sections 1–5 regulate interception of communications, and the circumstances in which communications can be lawfully intercepted.

11.17   Part III (ss 49–56) of RIPA 2000 deals with investigation of data detected by encryption. Section 49 sets out the powers of law enforcement when protected information is obtained or otherwise seized or intercepted. This part of the Act allows a notice requesting disclosure to be served on someone reasonably suspected to be in possession of the key to the information. The grounds for service of such a notice are national security; prevention or detection of crime or the interests of the economic well-being of the United Kingdom. Section 50 sets out the effect of a notice imposing a disclosure requirement. Failure to comply with such a notice is a criminal offence. Section 54 creates an offence of tipping-off, which may be committed where the s 49 notice contains a provision requiring the person to whom the notice is given and every other person who becomes aware of it or of its contents to keep secret the giving of the notice, its contents and things done in pursuance of it.

11.18   Law enforcement officers engaged in obtaining evidence from computers or other electronic storage devices may need to seek authorisation under s 93 of the Police Act 1997 and under s 28 or s 2 of RIPA 2000. In this way what would otherwise be an unlawful interference is permitted provided the appropriate safeguards are in place to the satisfaction of the Commissioner. However, those engaged in this form of evidence gathering, or indeed those seeking to deploy RIPA 2000 to resist such applications, should be aware that courts have expressly indicated that RIPA 2000 does not affect all forms of what may be regarded as 'interference'.

11.19 In *R v Hardy* the Court of Appeal held that when one party made a tape recording of a conversation, it did not amount to interception of a communication in the course of its transmission within the meaning of s 2(2) of RIPA 2000. It is important to be remembered that 'party' here does not have to be an investigating authority, it means what it says, a party to the conversation. It could, for example, be an employer or a company.

11.20 Part III of the Police Act 1997 permits authorisation of covert entry into and interference with, property or 'wireless telegraphy' by the police or HMRC and other law enforcement agencies. This area is another which has been rich in litigation and again has a scope well beyond the ambit of this work.

SIGNIFICANT DISTINCTION BETWEEN 'DIRECTED' AND 'INTRUSIVE SURVEILLANCE'

11.21 It is important when examining the rights and obligations in this specific field to ensure that the appropriate regime is followed. There is a significant difference between 'directed surveillance' and 'intrusive surveillance' as these are governed by separate statutory regimes. Directed surveillance is defined as covert surveillance that is undertaken in relation to a specific investigation which is likely to result in the obtaining of private information about a person. 'Intrusive surveillance' is covert surveillance carried out on anything taking place on residential premises.

11.22 All methods of surveillance which do not involve covert entry upon or interference with property or wireless telegraphy are governed by ss 26–28 of RIPA 2000.

11.23 Any attempt by law enforcement to monitor traffic to and from a computer or similar device, is likely to breach Part 1 of RIPA 2000, ie ss 1–5. Authorisation will be required for any interception of a public telecommunication service. If the system is private, the consent of the owner of the system would be required.

11.24 By virtue of Telecommunications (Lawful Business Practice) (Interception of Communications) Regulations 2000,[1] an employer may carry out an interception at work in order to establish the existence of facts, in the interests

---

[1]   SI 2000/2699.

of national security, for the purposes of preventing or detecting crime, or for the purposes of investigating or detecting unauthorised use of that or any other telecommunication system.

11.25 By virtue of s 17 of RIPA 2000, intercept evidence is inadmissible:

17 Exclusion of matters from legal proceedings

(1) Subject to section 18, no evidence shall be adduced, question asked, assertion or disclosure made or other thing done in, for the purposes of or in connection with any legal proceedings or Inquiries Act proceedings which (in any manner) –

(a) discloses, in circumstances from which its origin in anything falling within subsection (2) may be inferred, any of the contents of an intercepted communication or any related communications data; or

(b) tends (apart from any such disclosure) to suggest that anything falling within subsection (2) has or may have occurred or be going to occur.

(2) The following fall within this subsection –

(a) conduct by a person falling within subsection (3) that was or would be an offence under section 1(1) or (2) of this Act or under section 1 of the Interception of Communications Act 1985;

(b) a breach by the Secretary of State of his duty under section 1(4) of this Act;

(ba) any person deemed to be the proper officer of Revenue and Customs by virtue of s 8(2) of the Customs and Excise Management Act 1979;

(c) the issue of an interception warrant or of a warrant under the Interception of Communications Act 1985;

(d) the making of an application by any person for an interception warrant, or for a warrant under that Act;

(e) the imposition of any requirement on any person to provide assistance with giving effect to an interception warrant.

(3) The persons referred to in subsection (2)(a) are –

(a) any person to whom a warrant under this Chapter may be addressed;

(b) any person holding office under the Crown;

(e) any person employed by or for the purposes of a police force;

(f) any person providing a postal service or employed for the purposes of any business of providing such a service; and

(g) any person providing a public telecommunications service or employed for the purposes of any business of providing such a service.

11.26 Section 17(1) does not cover questions asked or information obtained to ascertain whether the interception was lawfully authorised and/or whether the system was a public or private system.

JURISDICTIONAL ISSUES AND 'FORUM SHOPPING'

11.27 One of the issues which surrounds litigation in civil matters is who has jurisdiction when there are features of an action or actions which straddle different countries and jurisdictions. There has developed a practice of inserting a clause where the parties submit to the exclusive jurisdiction of a particular country. Once that has been freely selected, the courts, certainly in England and Wales, will be slow to interfere.

11.28 In *Donohue v Armco Inc*[2] the issue of the enforceability of exclusive jurisdiction clauses had to be decided along with several other matters not relevant for present purposes. The case concerned a group of companies incorporated in the United States and Singapore who appealed against the granting of an injunction restraining the prosecution of proceedings in the United States which arose from alleged fraudulent activity. The basis of the fraud was alleged to relate to a management buy-out which was governed by a sale and purchase agreement and two transfer agreements. Each of the agreements contained a clause giving exclusive jurisdiction to the English courts. Following the commencement of the proceedings in the United States, the defendant sought to invoke the clause and applied for an anti-suit injunction. The House of Lords allowed the appeal. At para 24 of the judgment Lord Bingham said:

> 'the general rule is clear: where parties have bound themselves by an exclusive jurisdiction clause effect should ordinarily be given to that obligation in the absence of strong reasons for departing from it. Whether a party can show strong reasons, sufficient to displace the other party's prima facie entitlement to enforce the contractual bargain, will depend on all the facts and circumstances of the particular case.'

11.29 It is submitted that in cases involving the flow of data which can transcend many jurisdictions, the advantage of inserting an exclusive jurisdiction clause will, if that jurisdiction is the law of England and Wales, provide clarity as to the appropriate forum to resolve disputes. It will need to be noted that, once selected, the clause is likely to be upheld unless there are very specific reasons to depart from it.

LOCUS OF THE PERPETRATOR

11.30 In many instances the perpetrator of a cyber breach may be remote. The locus (as well as the status) will need to be determined in order to pursue an appropriate and effective remedy. By way of example, whilst an injunction might in appropriate circumstances be obtained ex parte and served via email or other method, it will not have impact or jurisdiction where the perpetrator is, in fact, located outside England and Wales. There will also be questions as to

---

2   [2001] UKHL 64.

which jurisdiction is the proper forum both for any civil or criminal investigation or prosecution and has been outlined in **11.27** above.

11.31 For civil proceedings, the current position (but see Chapter 12 as to the impact of Brexit) is that the Recast Brussels Regulation (No 1215/2012) applies to all member states of the European Union. In relation to proceedings commenced on or after 10 January 2015, Art 4 provides that (subject to certain exceptions) for both natural and legal persons litigation should be in the member state where they are domiciled.

11.32 A natural person is domiciled in a jurisdiction if they are:

(i)   resident in the jurisdiction; and

(ii) the nature and circumstances of their residence indicate a substantial connection with the jurisdiction.

11.33 A natural person can be resident in a number of member jurisdictions. The test would be whether, in all the circumstances there is sufficient permanency for the person to be settled in the UK so that it is his or her usual place of abode. A court will compare the ties to the UK and time spent here in comparison to tie to and time spent at other jurisdictions.

11.34 A legal person, ie a UK corporate body, will be domiciled at the place where it has its registered office. Where the corporate is not a UK (or Irish) company one should examine where it has its principal place of business, centre of administration or seat of incorporation: see Chapter 6 (Commercial Espionage) for further discussion and cases on when there might be derogation from Art 4 but for present purposes, Art 7(2) provides (a derogation from Art 4) that a person domiciled in a Member State may be sued:

> 'in matters relating to tort, delict or quasi-delict [which includes claims for trade mark infringement and passing off], in the courts for the place where the harmful event occurred or may occur.'

Wintersteiger AG v Products 4U Sondermaschinenbau GmbH[3]

11.35 The case of *Wintersteiger* is of assistance in determining where a cause of action in tort arises. These will generally include tortious liability such as torts of conversion and trespass (see Chapter 6). Where the breach or other 'harmful event' was in the UK then the perpetrator might be sued in the UK regardless of his/her or its jurisdiction of domicile. However, in *Wintersteiger*, which concerned a national trade mark infringement dispute, it was held that the harmful event was too remote from the chosen jurisdiction (see **6.101**).

11.36 The courts of England and Wales will have jurisdiction over a perpetrator domiciled outside the European Union if the perpetrator can be

---

[3] *(C-523/10)* [2013] Bus LR 150.

served with the claim form while in this jurisdiction. This includes where papers are served on a perpetrator who is only visiting the jurisdiction. However, in these circumstances the perpetrator may argue that the UK court should not exercise its jurisdiction if there is a more appropriate forum applying *forum non conveniens*. If the service cannot be effected in England, then a claimant would need a court's permission to serve the claim form outside this jurisdiction. In summary, this will involve showing that:

(1) there is a serious issue to be tried in relation to the foreign defendant;

(2) there is a good arguable case that the claim falls within one or more of the 'jurisdictional gateways' set out in the Civil Procedure Rules; and

(3) England/Wales is evidently the appropriate forum for the case and the court ought to exercise its discretion to permit service of the proceedings out of the jurisdiction.

11.37 Where, following a cyber-attack, criminal proceedings are contemplated, the identified offences will be essential in determining whether the UK has criminal jurisdiction. Readers are referred to the offences set out in Chapter 1 (Cyber Crime). Those offences include the extra-territorial offences. The Serious Crime Act 2015, s 43, extended the territorial scope of the Computer Misuse Act 1990, at ss 4 and 5, by extending the offences to cover 'nationality' as a category with a 'significant link to the domestic jurisdiction'. The provisions and implications surrounding the new test of territorial link are extensively reviewed in Chapter 1.

EVIDENCE OBTAINED ABROAD – GENERAL PRINCIPLES INCLUDING LETTERS OF REQUEST

11.38 In cases involving evidence and material to be obtained from computers or other electronic storage devices, there are more likely to be issues of jurisdiction outside of those relating to any alleged perpetrator.

11.39 It is clearly not straightforward to be able to determine where particular events happened as information can be transmitted and received from different locations. The general common law rule is that jurisdiction attaches where 'the essence or the gist' of the offence occurred.

11.40 Of course those rules remain part of English law but to combat the difficulties, recent legislation, most notably the CMA 1990, has introduced the concept of the territorial link test (for a full treatment of this new enactment see Chapter 1).

Obtaining evidence from abroad

11.41 Obtaining evidence from abroad in criminal cases is governed by the Crime (International Co-operation) Act 2003. Section 7 sets out the procedure:

(1) If it appears to a judicial authority in the United Kingdom on an application made by a person mentioned in subsection (3) –

(a) that an offence has been committed or that there are reasonable grounds for suspecting that an offence has been committed, and
(b) that proceedings in respect of the offence have been instituted or that the offence is being investigated,

the judicial authority may request assistance under this section.

(2) The assistance that may be requested under this section is assistance in obtaining outside the United Kingdom any **evidence** specified in the request for use in the proceedings or investigation.

(3) The application may be made –

(a) in relation to England and Wales and Northern Ireland, by a prosecuting authority,
(b) in relation to Scotland, by the Lord Advocate or a procurator fiscal,
(c) where proceedings have been instituted, by the person charged in those proceedings

...

(7) If a request for assistance under this section is made in reliance on Article 2 of the 2001 Protocol (requests for information on banking transactions) in connection with the investigation of an offence, the request must state the grounds on which the person making the request considers the **evidence** specified in it to be relevant for the purposes of the investigation.

In terms of the use of this legislation to assist with requests from abroad, the courts have stressed the importance, such requests are lawfully made.

11.42 In *JP Morgan Chase Bank National Association v Director of the Serious Fraud Office*[4] a letter of request was issued by the public prosecutor of Milan which, on being found to be outside the scope of his authority, was unlawful under Italian law. The decision by the Secretary of State to refer the request to the Serious Fraud Office and their subsequent decision to issue notices under s 15 of the above act was judicially reviewed. The Administrative Court in granting the application stated that had the Secretary of State scrutinised the request it would have been seen to be 'obviously unlawful' and the decisions to issue notices could not stand.

11.43 The procedure to be followed in civil matters in respect evidence from abroad is to be found in Civil Procedure Rules, Pt 34 and PD34A.

---

4 [2012] EWHC 1674 (Admin).

EVIDENCE OBTAINED ILLEGALLY – GENERAL PRINCIPLES

11.44 In respect of the authorisations required when obtaining evidence from interception and other interference methods it is important to remember that failure to obtain the necessary authorisation is not a criminal offence under the RIPA 2000 or the Police Act but leaves any evidence so obtained liable to attack under s 78 of PACE 1984 and/or the Human Rights Act 1998. The test is whether the activity was both necessary and proportionate.

11.45 In other cases where it is suggested that evidence has been obtained unlawfully, the governing statute will be s 78 of PACE 1984.

11.46 In deciding whether to exclude evidence obtained during or in consequence of an unlawful search, or other alleged unlawful act, the judge has a discretion, as opposed to an obligation, to exclude the evidence under this section. The exercise of that discretion should take into account an assessment of the effect of the admission of the evidence, any bad faith and/or deliberate breach of the law. A detailed examination of the principles of s 78 of PACE 1984 is outside the scope of this work.

11.47 However, for a case which argued for a different remedy from exclusion see *R v Redmond*,[5] where the applicant had been convicted of drugs offences on evidence obtained by undercover police officers who had recorded conversations in person and on the telephone with him in Spain and Ireland. The applicant argued that there had been a deliberate course of conduct by the police which was designed to bypass Spanish and Irish law and procedure. He argued that this conduct ought to justify a stay of the proceedings as an abuse of process. The Court of Appeal held, dismissing the renewed application that, even if the judge had been in error in concluding that there had been no breach of Spanish and Irish law, his decision to permit the prosecution to proceed was within his lawful discretion. Evidence obtained illegally was not automatically inadmissible. The crucial factor was whether the crown had abused its powers and the officers had acted in bad faith.

11.48 The leading authority in civil matters is *Calcraft v Guest*[6] which has long settled the law on the ability to use privileged documents which come in to the possession of another party to the proceedings. In this case the Court of Appeal (Lindley MR, Rigby and Vaughan Williams LJJ) held that documents illegally obtained remained admissible within the civil jurisdiction:[7]

> 'Where an attorney intrusted confidentially with a document communicates the contents of it, or suffers another to take a copy, surely the secondary evidence so obtained may be produced. Suppose the instrument were even stolen, and a correct copy taken, would it not be reasonable to admit it?'

---

[5]   [2006] EWCA Crim 1744.
[6]   [1898] 1 QB 759.
[7]   See *Calcraft v Guest* [1898] 1 QB 759 at p 764.

11.49   It is submitted that this remains a correct statement of the law. In more recent times the two principal areas of evidence affected by claims of illegality in terms of how evidence is obtained, have concerned legal professional privilege and breach of confidentiality.

11.50   In *Dubai Aluminium v Al Alawi*,[8] the claimant sought damages against a former employee for breach of contract, and to recover an unquantified sum in secret commissions. The claimant was granted relief to preserve the defendant's assets. The defendant sought to discharge these orders on the basis that evidence used in support of the applications was illegally obtained and subject to legal professional privilege. Rix J held that legal professional privilege did not apply in relation to any relevant documents unlawfully obtained. As he said at p 1969 'it seems to me that criminal or fraudulent conduct for the purposes of acquiring evidence in or for litigation cannot properly escape the consequence that any documents generated by or reporting on such conduct and which are relevant to the issues in the case are discoverable, and fall outside the legitimate area of legal professional privilege'.

11.51   However, in *Imerman v Tchenguiz*[9] (Lord Neuberger MR, Moses, Munby LJJ) the Court of Appeal was required to determine whether an injunction, preventing the use of material obtained in breach of confidence, had been properly imposed. The material had been obtained from a work computer database by an employee, who was related to a party petitioning for divorce. At para 103 of the judgment, Neuberger MR, in dealing with the wrongful and potentially unlawful obtaining of confidential documents in family proceedings said:

> 'the fact that accessing the documents can be said to have been to protect Mrs Imerman's rights can scarcely be said to render it "in the public interest", even if it was done with a view to exposing, or preventing, Mr Imerman's anticipated wrongful concealment of assets.'

He continued at para 146 that:

> 'Mrs Imerman should not be entitled to benefit in any way from the wholesale, wrongful, and possibly criminal, accessing and copying of Mr Imerman's confidential documents, particularly as she could have been expected to apply for a peremptory order.'

11.52   It is important to note that in *Calcraft v Guest* and in the *Dubai Aluminium* case, the judgments were concentrated on the effects of whether privileged documents could become admissible in the hands of another party to the proceedings. In *Imerman*, Neuberger MR's comments appear to anticipate the availability of a lawful course of action open to Mrs Imerman as opposed to the course pursued.

---

8   [1999] 1 WLR 1964.
9   [2010] EWCA Civ 908.

Part 4

THE FUTURE

CHAPTER 12

THE LEGAL ENVIRONMENT POST-BREXIT

THE EFFECT OF BREXIT

12.01　On 23 June 2016 the United Kingdom voted to leave the European Union. The effect of 'Brexit', as it has become known, is dependent upon the activation of Art 50 of the Treaty of Lisbon.

12.02　The legal provisions relating to data management, storage and cyber issues are inextricably linked with European legislation. This book has a context in which a large part of the regulations facing corporates and individuals have emanated from the European jurisdiction. Against that background, it is appropriate that we deal briefly with the immediate future and potential effects of Brexit in relation to the ongoing rights and obligations of UK corporate bodies; and we feel it is appropriate to deal extensively with the single most important pronouncement of the European Union in respect of data management, the General Data Protection Regulation (GDPR). Further, although less wide ranging in its application, the Directive on Security of Network and Information Systems (NIS Directive) is also worthy of mention.

The immediate future

12.03　The effect of activation of Art 50 will be to commence a withdrawal period from the European Union. The process is likely to take at least 2 years and may take longer as the UK unravels itself from regulation from Brussels. During the currency of the withdrawal period, save for any direct involvement on the EU side during negotiations for withdrawal, the UK retains all rights and obligations to the European Union. This means that any existing laws and/or

Directives are still binding on corporates and individuals, and any laws or Directives introduced during the currency of the withdrawal period are of a similar binding effect. It is therefore important to bear in mind that for at least the next 2 years all laws and Directives emanating from Europe outlined in this book will need to be adhered to.

The medium term

12.04 What happens at the end of the withdrawal period is currently the subject of much debate but very little certainty. If, for example, United Kingdom remains in the European Economic Area (EEA), it is very likely that little will change in terms of the effect and influence of European legislation. If, for example, freedom of movement is retained as part of the single market obligation, much of the existing regulations will remain to govern those employment relationships and the protection, dissemination and management of data. Even if the United Kingdom is able to argue for some reduction in the amount of obligations which follow membership of the single market, it is still extremely likely that the UK government will insist upon continuing compliance with previous European-based rules as marking, at the very least, best practice.

PRACTICAL STEPS

12.05 The biggest challenges faced by corporates and individuals in the immediate future is how best to position themselves during the undoubted uncertainty over the future shape of trading relationships with Europe and others with European connections.

12.06 In the opinion of the authors of this work, greater rather than less scrutiny of practices and contractual arrangements will be required during this transitional period. The type of issues which will need to be considered relevant to the protection and organisation of data are set out below. These are simply meant to be indicators and are not an exhaustive list of features which will have relevance during this period.

12.07 There is a strong likelihood that regulators, both in the United Kingdom and in EU countries, if trade is conducted with companies or individuals in those nations, or it is contemplated that it might be, will seek additional information from companies in the United Kingdom who may in the long term not be bound by basic European rules and Directives. In our opinion it is likely that the United Kingdom, trading outside of the EU, will need a regime for data protection and management which will inspire confidence in any trading partner, particularly European, such that the level of protection will be at least equivalent to the basic principles laid down under European legislation. As discussed below, it is our firm opinion that 'adequacy' must be achieved to retain the possibility of meaningful future trading relationships with our erstwhile European partners.

12.08   The terms and conditions of contracts with parties in Europe will also need to have been scrutinised so that they are able to be performed with recourse to a common information management regime and clearly defined territorial provisions in the event of dispute.

12.09   It is an obvious point to make, but a valid one all the same, that information flows will need governance both during the withdrawal period and after such withdrawal. The reaction of the Information Commissioner is unlikely to sanction any form of relaxation of compliance which may lead to insecurity of information or systems for the management or storage of information. Any such relaxation would leave the UK open to attack as an easy target, and ensure that those contemplating trade with any UK-based company would have severe reservations about committing its future.

12.10   It is obviously early days in respect of Brexit, but in our opinion it will be impossible to conduct any business cross-border without a regime which is at least equivalent to the current and prospective minimum safeguards outlined by European laws and Directives. The future, in our opinion, of conducting business in the post-Brexit era will tend to greater as opposed to lesser regulation. Accordingly, the rights and obligations set out in this work will continue to remain valid and relevant, and are likely to be the basic level of compliance as opposed to the gold standard of practice.

12.11   The best example, in our view, of this is the implementation of the flagship regulation of data by the European Union. On 25 May 2018, the European General Data Protection Regulation (GDPR) will become law across the remaining European Union states. Does that mean that in the light of Brexit, it will have no relevance to the UK? The answer is an emphatic no.

DIFFERENT INTERCONNECTIVITY MODELS

12.12   As discussed above, there appears, post-Brexit, to be three broad choices as to the path the UK could follow.

12.13   There is joining the European Economic Area (EEA). This is the route adopted by Norway. Membership of the EEA will require the UK to implement rules and procedures that are equivalent to those of the European Union.

12.14   Then there is the option where UK signs bilateral trade deals with the EU. This is likely to result in the UK having to agree to a duty to apply laws which are at least as demanding as European Union legislation. This is an option which has been adopted by Switzerland.

12.15   The other possibility is that the UK signs an, or a series of, independent trade deals without taking on the burden of accepting equivalent EU obligations.

12.16   As we shall see later, the difficulty with this approach, which is particularly relevant in the context of data protection, is that unless the UK can show that it has 'adequate' protections in place, the EU is likely to disallow its members to pass information to the UK, thus rendering the possibility of unfettered access to the EU for UK companies unlikely, to say the least.

12.17   It would seem that whichever of these three broad models is followed, there is little choice but for UK to adopt a regime in relation to data protection which is broadly the same as GDPR.

12.18   In that light, it is important to consider what general approach the UK will follow in respect of the short term in untangling itself from EU regulation.

12.19   It is impossible, in our view, to seek to debate and pass legislation to cover all of, indeed most of, the areas which EU-based legislation currently covers, in the days, weeks and years leading up to, and immediately post, Brexit. The most likely scenario is that UK will approach matters from the opposite direction and pass legislation broadly keeping the status quo until more detailed changes can be made.

WHERE DOES THAT LEAVE GDPR?

12.20   Bearing in mind it is due to become directly enforceable in other EU member states in May 2018, it is almost certain that the UK Parliament, faced with a heavy workload at this time, will admit the Regulations into law in an unvarnished form.

12.21   On the face of it, that seems a sensible and realistic option. The difficulty, however, is that GDPR as a body of regulations does not just impose substantive changes. Chapter VI of the Regulations provides for the establishment of independent supervisory authorities.

12.22   Article 51 makes provision for each member state to have in place one or more independent public authorities responsible for the monitoring of the Regulation. Article 52 imbues each authority with complete independence in performing tasks. Article 57 provides that each supervisory authority shall monitor and enforce the application of the Regulation, promote public awareness and understanding of the risks in relation to processing, and handle complaints by a data subject. Article 58 gives each supervisory authority powers over controllers and processors to provide any information required to carry out investigations and obtain access to premises; and empowers the authorities to issue warnings, reprimands, clients' rectification and withdrawal of certification. Article 59 states that each supervisory authority shall draw up an annual report on its activities.

12.23 At the core of the enforcement provisions is cooperation between advisory authorities and, by virtue of Art 68, a European Data Protection Board.

12.24 The article provides for the composition of the Board and by virtue of Arts 69 and 70, sets out the independence and tasks of the Board. Amongst its principal tasks is to set out and issue guidelines, recommendations and best practice.

12.25 Chapter VIII of the Regulation deals with remedies, liability and penalties. Article 77 gives the data subject the right to lodge a complaint with a supervisory authority. Article 79 gives the data subject the right to an effective judicial remedy where he or she considers that his or her rights under this Regulation have been infringed as a result of the processing of his or her personal data in non-compliance with this Regulation. Article 82 gives a right to compensation to any person who has suffered material or nonmaterial damage as a result of an infringement of this Regulation.

12.26 Article 83 lays down the general conditions for the imposition or administrative fines in respect of infringements of the Regulation, and states that in each individual case they should be effective, proportionate and persuasive. The article also deals with the criteria which govern the imposition of these fines and sets out that due regard should be given to the nature, gravity and duration of the infringement; the intention or the negligent character of the infringement; any action taken by the controller or processor to mitigate the damage suffered by data subjects and a degree of responsibility of the controller or processor taking into account technical and organisational measures implemented by them pursuant to Arts 25 and 32.

12.27 Article 84 provides that member states shall lay down the rules on other penalties applicable to infringements of this Regulation which envisages that member states should introduce domestic legislation, in particular, for infringements which are not subject to administrative fines as specified in Art 83 and shall take all measures necessary to ensure that they are implemented. It restates the principle that the penalties shall be effective, proportionate and dissuasive.

12.28 These articles encapsulate the difficulty that the UK legislature faces. The conundrum it has to solve is that it cannot simply adopt the GDPR outside of the European Union because there simply will not be the legislative bodies to police it. There will be no automatic supervisory body. The European Data Protection Board will have no sanction. So do they hastily form equivalent bodies? Do they adopt the sanctions? Do they continue to seek to achieve consistency in the enforcement of the Regulation in line with the articles? If they do not, then the price is a high one. If the UK does not achieve adequacy status, then it will mean that no European Union country can exchange information with the UK. In practical terms, the effect on United Kingdom is potentially devastating.

12.29 What of those parts of the Regulation which envisage initiatives by member states to introduce domestic legislation, for example Arts 10 and 19? What about those areas directed at personal liability, for example criminal sanctions in appropriate cases? How does the UK, in striving to have adequate regulations in place, balance its domestic version of the Regulation with other rights such as freedom of expression?

12.30 The United Kingdom legislature has to act, and soon, to avoid United Kingdom being starved of the most precious commodity in the digital age, data.

Jurisdiction

12.31 By virtue of Art 3, the territorial scope of the Regulation is set out. It is wide ranging. The Regulation applies to the processing of personal data in the context of the activities of an establishment of a controller or processor in the Union, regardless of whether the processing takes place in the Union or not.

12.32 Further, the Regulation applies to the processing of personal data of data subjects who are in the Union by a controller or processor not established in the Union whether processing activities are related either to the offering of goods or services to such data subjects in the union; or the monitoring of their behaviour as far as their behaviour takes place within the union.

12.33 Article 4 sets out the definitions of the significant terms in the regulations:

> *'Personal data'* means any information relating to an identified or identifiable natural person ('data subject'); an identifiable natural person is one who can be identified directly or indirectly by reference to an identifier such as a name, identification number, location data, online identifier or to one or more factors specific to the physical, physiological, genetic, mental, economic, cultural or social identity of that natural person.

> *'Processing'* means the operation or set of operations which is performed on personal data or sets of personal data, whether or not by automated means, such as collection, recording, organisation, structuring, storage adaptation, or alteration, retrieval consultation, use disclosure by transmission, dissemination alignment or combination, restriction erasure or destruction.

> *'Profiling'* means any form of automated processing of personal data consisting of the use of personal data to evaluate certain personal aspects relating to a natural person, in particular to analyse or predict aspects concerning that natural person's performance at work, economic situation, health, personal preferences, interests, reliability, behaviour, location or movements.

> *'Pseudonymisation'* means the processing of personal data in such a manner that personal data can no longer be attributed to a specific data subject without the use of additional information, provided that such additional information is kept separately and subject to technical and organisational measures ensure that the personal data are not attributed to an identified or identifiable natural person.

'*Controller*' means a natural or legal person, public authority, agency or other body which, alone or jointly with others, determines the purposes and means of the processing of personal data.

'*Processor*' means a natural or legal person, public authority, agency or other body which processes personal data on behalf of the controller.

'*Recipient*' means a natural or legal person, public authority, agency or other body to which the personal data are disclosed, with a third party or not.

'*Consent*' of the data subject means any freely given, specific, informed and unambiguous indication of the data subject's wishes by which he or she, by a statement or by a clear affirmative action, signifies agreement the processing of personal data relating to him or her.

'*Personal breach data*' means a breach of security leading to the accidental or unlawful destruction, loss, alteration, or unauthorised disclosure of, or access to, personal data transmitted, stored or otherwise processed.

'*Biometric data*' means personal data resulting from specific technical processing relating to physical, physiological, or behavioural characteristics of a natural person, which allow or confirm the unique identification of that natural person.

How extensive are the new proposals?

12.34 Article 5 contains six principles. Personal data must be:

(1) processed fairly, lawfully and in a transparent manner in relation to the data subject ('lawfulness, fairness and transparency');

(2) collected for specified, explicit and legitimate purposes and not processed in a manner which is incompatible with those purposes ('purpose limitation');

(3) adequate, relevant and limited to what is necessary in relation to the purposes for which they are processed ('data minimisation');

(4) adequate and where necessary kept up to date ('accuracy');

(5) kept in a form which permits identification of data subjects for no longer than is necessary for the purposes for which the personal data are processed ('storage limitation'); and

(6) processed in a manner that ensures appropriate security of the personal data, including protection against unauthorised or unlawful processing and against accidental loss, destruction or damage using appropriate technical or organisational measures ('integrity and confidentiality').

12.35 It is, put simply, a game changer. Regulation (EU) 2016/679 is the first attempt at providing a Europe-wide standard.

12.36 Further, Art 6 sets out the parameters of the lawfulness of processing. It provides processing shall be lawful only if:

(a)   the data subject has given consent for one or more specific purposes;

(b)   processing is necessary for the performance of the contract to which the data subject is party or in order to take steps at the request of the data subject prior to entering into a contract;

(c)   processing is necessary for compliance with a legal obligation to which the controller is subject;

(d)   processing is necessary in order to protect the vital interests of the data subject or of another natural person;

(e)   processing is necessary for the performance of the task carried out in the public interest when the exercise of official authority is vested in the controller;

(f)   processing is necessary for the purposes of the legitimate interests pursued by the controller or by a third party except where such interests are overridden by the interests or fundamental rights and freedoms of the data subject which require the protection of personal data, in particular, where the data subject is a child.

12.37   Article 7 sets out the conditions for consent. It states where processing is based on consent, the controller shall be able to demonstrate that the data subject has consented to the processing of his or her personal data. The data subject shall have the right to withdraw his or her consent at any time.

12.38   Article 9 outlines special rules relating to the processing of special categories of personal data.

12.39   Article 13 sets out the information to be provided where personal data are collected from the data subject. The controller must provide identity and contact details for himself and his representative; contact details of the data protection officer where applicable; the purposes of the processing for which personal data are intended; the legitimate interests pursued by the controller or third party; the recipients or categories of recipients of the data and, if applicable, the fact the controller intends to transfer personal data to a third country and whether that country is covered by an adequacy decision of the Commission. The article also deals with periods for which data can be stored, rights of access, rectification or erasure and complaints.

12.40   Articles 15, 16 and 17 deal with the right of access by the data subject, the right of rectification and the right to erasure ('the right to be forgotten').

12.41   Article 20 lays down conditions governing the right to data portability.

12.42   Chapter IV sets out the obligations of the controller and, in a novel departure, those of the processor.

12.43   By virtue of Art 24, the controller is obliged to implement appropriate technical and organisational measures to ensure and to be able to demonstrate that processing is performed in accordance with the Regulation. Article 25 provides that the controller shall implement appropriate technical and organisational measures for ensuring that, by default, only personal data which are necessary for each specific purpose of the processing are processed. This is data protection by design and default.

12.44 Article 28, for the first time, places obligations on the processor. The article states that the controller shall use only processors providing sufficient guarantees to implement appropriate technical and organisational measures in such a manner that processing will meet the requirements bought by this Regulation and ensure the protection of the rights of the data subject. Further, the processor shall not engage another processor without prior specific or general written authorisation of the controller. The processor will have binding legal obligations and shall act in accordance with the regulation. By virtue of Art 30, the controller shall keep records of processing activities and, in accordance with Art 32, shall have obligations regarding security of processing.

12.45 Article 33 sets out what has to be done in the event of a personal data breach. The controller shall without undue delay and where feasible, not later than 72 hours after having become aware, notify the personal data breach to the supervisory authority. The processor shall also have a duty to notify the controller without undue delay after becoming aware of the personal data breach. The article sets out what must be included in the notification and Art 34 places a gloss on Art 33 where the personal data breach is likely to result in a high risk to the rights and freedoms of the data subject.

12.46 Section 3 of Chapter IV of the Regulation introduces a new feature called a data protection impact assessment.

12.47 Article 35 states that where a type of processing is likely to result in a high risk to the rights and freedoms of natural persons, the controller, prior to the processing, shall carry out an assessment of the impact of the envisaged processing operations on the protection of personal data. The assessment is required to include a description of the processing operations and the purposes of it; an assessment of proportionality in relation to the processes; an assessment of the risks to the rights and freedoms of the data subjects affected; and the measures envisaged to address the risks.

12.48 Article 37 introduces the concept of the data protection officer. It requires the appointment of a data protection officer where the processing is carried out by public authority; where the core activities of the controller or processor require regular and systematic monitoring of data subjects on a large-scale; or where the core activities of the controller or processor consist of processing on a large scale of special categories of data.

12.49 The data protection officer shall be designated on the basis of professional qualities and, in particular, expert knowledge of data protection law and practices. He/she should be involved in all issues which relate to the protection of personal data. He/she should not be impeded in any way in the task. Those tasks are to inform and advise the controller or processor and the employees of their obligations under the Regulation; to monitor compliance with the Regulation; to provide advice in respect of data protection impact assessments; to cooperate with the supervisory authority and to act as the contact point for that authority.

12.50 As referred to above, the Regulation imposes a new fines regime which is a departure from anything previously known.

12.51 Article 83 restates the proposition that fines should be effective, proportionate and dissuasive. Fines can be imposed in addition to, or instead of, other measures contemplated by the Regulation and the article sets out the criteria which should be followed when determining whether and how much to fine.

12.52 The article states that in each individual case, due regard should be taken of:

(a) the nature, gravity and duration of the infringement taking into account the nature, scope or purpose of the processing concerned as well as the number of data subjects affected and the level of damage suffered by them;

(b) the intentional or negligent character of the infringement;

(c) any action taken by the data controller or processor to mitigate the damage; and

(d) the degree of responsibility of the controller or processor taking in to account technical and organisational measures implemented by them pursuant to the Regulation.

12.53 The track record of the controller or processor will be taken into account and any other aggravating or mitigating feature applicable to the circumstances of the case.

12.54 Infringements of Arts 8, 11, 25–39, 42, 43 shall be subject to fines of up to 10 million euros or, in the case of an undertaking, up to 2% of worldwide annual turnover for the preceding year, whichever is higher.

12.55 Infringements of Arts 5, 6, 7, 10–22, 44–49 shall be subject to fines of up to 20 million euros or, in the case of an undertaking, up to 4% of worldwide annual turnover for the preceding year, whichever is higher.

12.56 As can be clearly seen, this Regulation is a complete departure from anything that has gone before. Due to its wide-ranging jurisdiction, UK corporates are duty bound to gear up for its inception.

WHAT CAN BE DONE NOW TO ENSURE THAT THE TRANSITION TO COMPLIANCE WITH THE GDPR OR UK EQUIVALENT IS AS SMOOTH AS POSSIBLE?

12.57 The following should be done now to ensure that the transition to compliance with the GDPR or UK equivalent is as smooth as possible:

(1) Undertake a regular review of the data that the organisation is processing, including the type of data and any changes to the type of data processed:
    (a) Can any data be psuedonymised?
    (b) Where is the data going?
(2) Review your processes for data breach notification; security; answering data subject requests and risk assessment.
(3) Carefully review the contents of contracts; do you need a data protection impact assessment?
(4) Carefully review your relationships with processors if you are a controller.
(5) Train your workforce:
    (a) Do you need a data protection officer?
    (b) Do you have adequate processes in place for employees to handle a serious data breach?
    (c) Are your contracts of employment and/or contracts with sub-contractors compliant with GDPR?
    (d) Are you giving employees the correct information?

The GDPR, or whatever UK equivalent eventually comes onto the statute book, will change the face of the processing of personal data. It is beyond doubt that, bearing in mind the novel obligations it imposes and the potential draconian sanctions in the event of non-compliance, it would be a bold move for corporates and others affected not to begin the process of compliance as soon as possible.

DIRECTIVE ON SECURITY OF NETWORK AND INFORMATION SYSTEMS (NIS DIRECTIVE)

12.58 The Directive on Security of Network and Information Systems (NIS Directive) was introduced on 6 July 2016. It entered in to force in August 2016. At the time of introduction it set down a timetable of 21 months for transposition into national law, the same month as GDPR binds. By virtue of Art 25, compliance is expected by 9 May 2018. It is said to represent 'the first EU wide rules on cyber-security'.[1]

12.59 Before going on to deal with its provisions, it is important to draw a distinction with GDPR which is of significance to all EU member states but particularly important to the UK post-Brexit. The Directive is just that. It has to

---

[1] European Commission Fact Sheet, 6 July 2016.

be 'transposed' in to the domestic law of the member state. It is likely to have achieved the status of being required to be transposed prior to UK leaving the EU but unlike GDPR it does not have the status of a Regulation. Therefore there is a lot less certainty as to whether all, some or none will ever make it on to the UK statute books. That is not to suggest any perceived lack of appetite, it is simply to point out the legal and practical difference between the Directive and GDPR.

12.60 The objective of the Directive is 'to achieve a high common level of security of network and information systems within the Union' (Art 1).

12.61 That objective is to be met by means of improved national levels of cyber-security, increased cooperation between member states and risk management and reporting obligations for operators of specified essential services and digital service providers.

12.62 Member states will be required to adopt a 'national strategy on the security of network and information systems' (Art 7) and to designate a national competent authority to monitor national application of the Directive (Art 8).

12.63 Compliance will involve the designation of one or more Computer Security Incident Response Teams (CSIRTs) (Art 9).

12.64 The Directive has at its heart, increased cooperation amongst members states in relation to cyber-security both at national level (Art 10) and amongst member states (Art 11) and reporting and risk management obligations for operators of what are deemed to be 'essential services' (Art 14). Those are operators in the energy, transport, banking, financial markets, health, water and digital infrastructure. The Directive states that member states identify these by 9 November 2018 (Art 5).

12.65 Significantly, cloud computing services will be deemed to be digital service providers under the Directive. The obligations and sanctions relating to digital service providers are set out in Arts 16 and 17.

12.66 The Directive, of course, does not set down sanctions for breach or non-compliance, but the provisions of Art 15 leave the member states to set up 'a competent authority' to police compliance. However, Art 21 provides that by 9 May 2018, member states shall publish penalties for non- compliance. In a strong echo of GDPR those penalties shall be 'effective, proportionate and dissuasive'. This would suggest that the message of severe punishment for non-compliance with GDPR will apply equally for non-compliance with this Directive.

12.67 There are various timelines set down for review of the functioning of the Directive but, it is submitted, for those who are preparing for implementation of the major changes occasioned by GDPR, those directly affected by the provisions of this Directive would be well advised to become compliant with the NIS Directive as soon as possible, not least to ensure attainment of best practice.

the parties to the dispute have outlined all their resources to resolve complaints and the alternative arbitration as possible, instead to reach a resolution of both parties.

INDEX

References are to paragraph numbers.